The Perfect Summer

The Perfect Summer

England 1911,
Just Before the Storm

JULIET NICOLSON

Grove Press
New York

First published in Great Britain in 2006 by John Murray (Publishers), a division of Hodder Headline

Quotation from *A Shropshire Lad* by A. E. Housman is reproduced by kind permission of the Society of Authors (as the Literary Representative of the Estate of A. E. Housman). Quotation from *The Way Through the Woods* by Rudyard Kipling is reproduced by kind permission of A. P. Watt Ltd. (on behalf of The National Trust for Places of Historic Interest or Natural Beauty).
Quotations from Royal Archives material: p. 19 RA/GV/CC/25/100 7 May "I am dressed in grey"; p. 19 RA/GV/CC/25/100 7 May "tiresome trousseau"; p. 20 RA/GV/CC/25/100 7 May "the fashions of the season . . . so hideous"; p. 34 RA/GV/QMD/1911 15 May "Most amusing"; p. 38 RA/GV/QMD/1911 19 May "It began at 10 and was over at 1"; p. 38 RA/GV/QMD/1911 20 May "a great success"; p. 188 RA/GV/QMD/1911 9 August "heat perfectly awful"; p. 190 RA/GV/QMD/1911 10 August "At 11:00 a.m. we heard."

Printed in the United States of America

Library of Congress Cataloging-in-Publication Data

Nicolson, Juliet.
    The perfect summer : England 1911, just before the storm / Juliet Nicolson.
        p. cm.
    Originally published: London : John Murray, 2006.
    Includes bibliographical references and index.
    ISBN-10: 0-8021-1846-1
    ISBN-13: 978-0-8021-1846-2
    1. Great Britain—Social life and customs—20th century. 2. Great Britain—History—George V, 1910–1936. 3. Social classes—Great Britain—History—20th century. 4. Great Britain—Social conditions—20th century. 5. Social structure—Great Britain—20th Century. I. Title.
    DA566.4.N54 2007
    942.083—dc22   2006048854

Grove Press
an imprint of Grove/Atlantic, Inc.
841 Broadway
New York, NY 10003

Distributed by Publishers Group West

www.groveatlantic.com

07 08 09 10 11 12   10 9 8 7 6 5 4 3

For Clemmie and Flora

Contents

Illustrations

The author and publishers would like to thank the following for permission to reproduce illustrations: Plates 1, 5, 8, 16 and 23, Getty Images; 2, 3, 4, 10, 22 and 28, The Illustrated London News Picture Library; 6, Topfoto/Public Record Office/HIP; 17, Topfoto; 7, The Savoy; 9, 33 and 34, Artemis Cooper; 11 and 13, V&A Images/ Victoria and Albert Museum; 12 and 19, Bettmann/CORBIS; 14 and 15, Calkin Family; 18, E. O. Hoppé/CORBIS; 20 and 21, Adam Nicolson; 24, 26 and 32, Hulton-Deutsch Collection/ CORBIS; 25, TUC Library Collections; 27, The Royal Institution of Cornwall; 29, The National Archives (ref.: COPY 1/559); 35: The National Archives (ref.: COPY 1/560); 30, NRM/Science & Society Picture Library; 31, The de László Foundation.

Acknowledgements

I am extremely grateful to Her Majesty The Queen for permission to quote from HM Queen Mary's Diaries of 1911 and from HM Queen Mary's letters to her Aunt Augusta, Princess Augusta Caroline, Grand Duchess of Mecklenburg-Strelitz.

Miss Pamela Clark, the Registrar at the Royal Archives, has been most helpful.

I owe a huge thank-you to the Dowager Duchess of Devonshire, who has allowed me unlimited access to the Chatsworth Archive, and also to Charles Noble, Keeper of the Collection, and to Helen Marchant and Andrew Peppitt, who have willingly answered my many questions.

I am indebted to Artemis Cooper for her memories of her grandmother, Lady Diana Manners, and for the loan of the photographs from her private family albums. I am most grateful to Richard Shone for allowing me to quote from his private letters from Duncan Grant, and also to Kevin Brownlow, who illuminated 1911 for me through his marvellous archive of film.

I would like to thank Paul Calkin, and particularly Ian Calkin, for their generosity in sharing their heroic relation Brian Calkin's papers and photographs with me, and also for permission to quote in full the last letter Brian wrote.

The staff of the London Library have, as always, been extremely helpful, as have the staff at the British Newspaper Library at Colindale and the staff at the Churchill Library in Cambridge, who gave me the opportunity to read the Churchill papers concerning the summer of 1911.

ACKNOWLEDGEMENTS

I am grateful for the picture research of Clemency Humphries in the V&A Images Department, and also for the research of Heather Vickers. I thank Luci Gosling and Marcelle Adamson at the Illustrated London News Picture Library for their enthusiastic assistance.

I would like to thank Christine Coates, the Trades Union Congress Library Collections librarian, for all her help, and Susan Scott at the Savoy Hotel archives for her interest and support. I would also like to thank the staff at the Royal Opera House Archives for the chance to see the Marchioness of Ripon's albums and the Royal Opera House's collection of ballet and opera programmes from 1911.

During the writing of this book, I have been given an amazing amount of advice, encouragement, clarification of facts, and guidance on fashion, and have been told some fascinating contemporary stories. Among those to whom I owe so many thanks are Patricia Anker, Lady Anunziata Asquith, Antony Beevor, Georgie Boothby, Susan Boyd, William Boyd, Charlie Boxer, Piers Brendon, Aly Brown, Adam Chadwick (Curator MCC at Lord's Cricket Ground), Catrine Clay, Caroline Clifton Mogg, Pedro Da Costa, Sophie Dundas, Susannah Fiennes, Lady Antonia Fraser (for telling me about the distant rumble), Lord Glenconner, Lady Annabel Goldsmith, John Graham at *Tatler*, Christopher Hawtree, Alexandra Hayward, Lucy Johnston (Curator in the Fashion and Textile department of the V&A Museum), Sandra de László, Katie Law, the late Patrick Lichfield, James Macmillan-Scott, Philip Marsden, Brian Masters, Rebecca Nicolson, John Julius Norwich, Mollie Norwich, Harold Pinter, Paul Raben, Sarah Raven, Hon. Lady Roberts, Julia Samuel, the staff at John Sandoe, Rebecca Servito, Jane Shilling, Foni Shann, Suzanne Sullivan, Kathleen Tessaro, Henry Wyndham, Rachel Wyndham, Philip Ziegler, and especially my late, much-loved, father Nigel Nicolson.

I consider myself most fortunate in my agent Ed Victor, who understood the point from the very beginning and has shepherded me through the process of writing my first book with such care. I would also like to thank Philippa Harrison for her invaluable comments and Maggie Phillips, Hitesh Shah and Linda Van at Ed Victor's office.

At John Murray I would like to thank Roland Philipps, my editor Gordon Wise, and Cathy Benwell for their wonderful enthusiasm and commitment, and also Nikki Barrow, James Spackman and Caroline Westmore for their energetic support. Thanks are due to Douglas Matthews too, for his superb work on the index.

I would like to thank Charles Anson for his loving patience and sustaining encouragement even when absorption in the book threatened to remove me entirely from everyday life.

Clementine Macmillan-Scott and her assistant Flora Macmillan-Scott have been model researchers and have never complained once how the demands of the book have consumed the attentions of their mother. The book is for them with my deep love.

Above all I would like to thank my brother Adam, whose unflagging wisdom, generous sharing of his time, and belief in the book and in me have been more precious than I can begin to quantify.

Introduction

This is a biography of a summer, a particularly lovely English summer, for some the most perfect of the twentieth century.

THE SEASON FROM May to September 1911 was one of the high sunlit meadows of English history. It was a time when England – rich, happy, self-indulgent and at least slightly decadent – felt most contentedly itself. And yet the exuberance and self-congratulatory spirit of those few months was in many ways illusory. Osbert Sitwell, friend of the Prime Minister's wife Margot Asquith, and one of Society's most glamorous escorts, observed some time later that 'an air of gaiety, unusual in northern climates, prevailed. Music flowed with the lightness and flash of water under the striped awnings and from the balconies; while beyond the open illuminated windows in the rooms, the young men about to be slaughtered, feasted, unconscious of all but the moment.'

During the long hot summer of 2003 I had been reading, for the first time in many years, L. P. Hartley's wonderful novel of class conflict and heated adolescence, *The Go-Between*, and I began to wonder whether there was a real English summer like that – and whether I could write about it in a way that would bring the reality of that half-forgotten time to life. I wanted to evoke the full vivid richness of how it smelt, looked, sounded, tasted and felt to be alive in England during the months of such a summer.

I began with the weather itself. The almost uninterrupted sunshine of 1911 classified the year as one of the hottest of the twentieth century and all previous records were broken when in the middle of August the temperature hit 100 degrees Fahrenheit. The summer itself suggested my title, but the closer I looked, the more I realised the title could be misleading: 'perfect' maybe, but for whom?

The English are famously bad at dealing with high temperatures, and for those alive in the summer of 1911, even the rich, conditions became intolerable. Just as the petals of an English rose in June prepare to fall at the very moment when the flower is at its loveliest, so the apparently flawless beauty of the summer weather wilted in its own heat. A succession of cloudless days had given people confidence in an unbroken pattern of continuing sunshine. Yet there were unmistakable signs of perfection overreaching itself, as the rumble of thunder and several dramatic storms interrupted the sunny constancy of those months.

And as the unpredictability of the summer weather unfolded, so the country was brought to a near-standstill by industrial strikes and the breadth of the chasm between the privileged and the disadvantaged became ever more obvious. It was a summer when, as the Countess of Fingall put it, 'We danced on the edge of an abyss.' There was a sense of urgency about that summer. Socialites crammed in their gaiety as intensively as the poor made their grievances apparent. It was as if time was running out.

The country had not known war at first hand for many years, and people were growing both restless and complacent. Artistic, sexual and political boundaries were being breached. The underprivileged were no longer willing to accept their lot. Imaginative, emotional, practical and human needs were being expressed, and sometimes with violence. Political questions such as the vast gulf between the rich and the poor and the needs of women and of the British work-force to fight for their rights all added to the tensions of 1911. The lives of the disadvantaged as well as the materially blessed, their hardship, and their glamour, were clasped together in a single drama.

In choosing a single season, I gave myself the luxury of space to focus on the minutiae of day-to-day routines, and in the tight lens of these months appear queens and politicians, debutantes and women trade unionists, poets and jam-makers, ballet dancers and painters, shop keepers and landowners, butlers and schoolboys. They *are* England in 1911, but governing the whole story is another character, the one that links them all: the almost un-broken, constant, sometimes wonderful and sometimes debilitating heat of the summer itself.

I

The Summer of 1911

The only drawback of an English summer is that it lasts so
short a time.

Country Life, 1 May 1911

ON THE FIRST day of May 1911 temperatures throughout
England began to rise, and everyone agreed that the world
was becoming exceedingly beautiful. The cold weather of April
had held back the flowering of many of the spring bulbs, and with
the warmth of the first week of summer there had been a sudden
burst of growth. The verges of the country lanes were frothing
with cow parsley while late primroses still dotted the roadside
banks. Top-hatted men strolling in the London parks had decided
it was warm enough to abandon their scarves. Straw-bonneted
women had gathered up country bluebells to sell in wilting
bunches on street corners in the smarter parts of London, and
window boxes were already spilling over with scarlet geraniums
and marguerites. Tiny pink flowers covered the branches that
would later produce crab apples, while the ocean of white blos-
soms produced by other fruit trees had prompted *Country Life* to
declare that 'few people can remember any parallel to its profusion.' England was plump with promise.

The unaccustomed warmth coincided with the lifting of official Court mourning, a relief after the constraints of the preceding black-edged year: Edward VII had died in the spring of 1910.
A few months before his death the poet Wilfrid Blunt had

watched him take his seat in the Royal Box at Covent Garden. The King reached for 'his opera glasses to survey the glittering women', and Blunt saw 'a man who looked, I thought, extremely genial and satisfied with his position in the scheme of the world.' But on 6 May Edward fell suddenly and severely ill with bronchitis and 'smoker's throat'. He managed, between puffs on a final cigar, to take in the news that his horse Witch of Air had won the 4.15 p.m. at Kempton Park, and died later the same day, moments before midnight, at the age of 68.

London went into a temporary but immediate state of gloom. A Jermyn Street grocer filled his window with the famous black Bradenham hams. A society hostess sewed black ribbons onto her daughter's underwear. Crowds outside the gates of Buckingham Palace were delirious with shock. There was a Lying-in-State at Westminster Hall, and on 20 May Margot Asquith, the wife of the Prime Minister, stood on a red carpet outside the door of the medieval Hall waiting for the funeral procession of eight visiting kings and an emperor, on its way from the Palace. At the door of the Hall the Archbishop of Canterbury received the dead King's widow first, followed by her son George. Soon afterwards the King's brother the Duke of Connaught arrived with Kaiser Wilhelm of Germany. Margot Asquith observed the Kaiser with his 'observant eyes and immobile carriage', and could not help thinking 'what a terrifying result a bomb thrown from Big Ben would have had upon that assemblage.'

Society had breathed a sigh of relief when, days after Edward's funeral, the new King and Queen announced that Royal Ascot would not, as had been expected, be cancelled. The race meeting of 1910 had been a surprisingly beautiful if sombre occasion. Gazing down from the stands above the racecourse, the Countess of Fingall thought that all the large black feathered hats made it look at first glance as if 'an immense flight of crows had just settled', but as she continued to watch the crowd move in monochrome synchronicity she concluded that 'when you came close to them, never in their lives had the beautiful women looked more lovely.'

In certain circles, those that had formed the inner court of Edward VII, some anxiety persisted about whether the new King was quite up to the job. This man now ruled over the four hundred million subjects of the British Empire. Short and red-faced, he seemed a distant and nervous figure, and was accompanied in his new role by an unsmiling, aloof and – let it be acknowledged only in a whisper – less beautiful woman than his glittering mother, the Dowager Queen, Alexandra. That day there was much hushed talk on the racecourse and in the packed stands that had witnessed some of Edward VII's most spectacular sporting triumphs. Conversations about change predominated. Lillie Langtry, one of the dead King's first mistresses, was ruined by debt; Alice Keppel, one of his most recent mistresses, had fled to China. The grieving widowed Queen refused to move out of Buckingham Palace to make way for her son. For some it seemed as if a world had come to an end. People 'anticipate a good deal of change', George Cornwallis-West, step-father of Winston Churchill, wrote to his daughter, and some alarmed race-goers even questioned whether the unshakeable confidence of upper-class Edwardian England had disappeared forever. With withering sarcasm they spoke of 'a sweeter simpler reign'.

Although the Age of Edward was over, among the privileged, with their servants, their houses, their money and the convenient rigidity of the class system, there was an unspoken determination that a supremely enjoyable way of life should not alter, as the crown shifted from one head to another. Hopeful that the momentum generated by Edward would remain powerful enough to ensure their untroubled existence, by May of 1911 the aristocracy was looking forward to a glorious summer dominated by the Coronation of George V and filled with an unprecedented number of parties.

Mrs Hwfa (pronounced Hoofa) Williams, wife of the manager of Sandown racecourse (Sandown had been Hwfa's brother's estate, the racecourse Hwfa's idea), a committed socialite and an impressively dedicated social climber, was keeping notes for a book for which she had already chosen the title: *It Was Such Fun*. Mrs Hwfa (she was always referred to by her husband's Christian name rather than her own) seldom ran short of material. 'The London Season was always strenuous,' she wrote, with no reason to expect that 1911's would be any different. And though she was well into her sixties, her sense of fun guaranteed her an invitation to every smart party of the season. Her engagement diary confirmed her popularity: 'Throughout the week practically every night people were at a dinner party, or a ball or the theatre or opera,' she wrote. 'I do not say we were busy in the daytime but there was always something to do and combined with a succession of late nights, the end of the week inevitably found me exhausted.'

Osbert Sitwell had a particular affection for Mrs Hwfa, observing that 'at every dance to which she went, she was surrounded by a crowd of young men, waiting for her arrival, and they always addressed her as Madam.' Sitwell knew how much effort she had to put into these parties: Mrs Hwfa was extremely deaf. 'It is not easy', he sympathised, 'for someone afflicted with deafness to be amusing; it calls for unceasing alertness which must be a great tax on energy.' Sometimes, he noticed, she lost her way, and with only the odd word to guide her did not always guess correctly when trying to assume an expression suitable for the moment. She would hazard 'a smile for the whimsical, a laugh for the witty, a striking look of interest for the dealer in the dramatic, a tear for those who wore their heart on their sleeve.' One small comfort was the knowledge that the Dowager Queen herself, Alexandra, suffered from a similar disability.

In line with Mrs Williams's expectations, *The Times* Court Circular on 1 May 1911 overflowed with announcements for the coming months, including balls and weddings, race meetings and Royal investitures. Mrs Cornwallis-West was planning a spectacular Shakespeare Costume Ball. Under the patronage of Lady Ripon, Diaghilev was to bring his Russian dancers to Covent

Garden to make their English debut in June. Over the last few years militant suffragettes, led by Mrs Pankhurst, had been campaigning for the vote for women and lobbying the Government with varying degrees of aggressive persuasion. But the Prime Minister, Mr Asquith, had pledged to address their demands immediately after the summer recess, so they had promised to lay down their window-smashing bricks and hold a truce for the Coronation summer. And members of the House of Lords were hoping that they would defeat the Liberal Government's proposed bill for a Parliament Act that would if passed place significant restrictions on their voting powers.

To avoid being crushed by boredom the privileged classes who made up one per cent of the population and owned sixty per cent of the country would go to impressive lengths. According to Lucy Masterman, the observant wife of a Liberal minister, the upper class consisted of 'an aggregation of clever, agreeable, often loveable people trying with desperate seriousness to make something of a life spared the effort of wage earning.' Men sat about for much of the day in their clubs; ladies spent the early part of the morning in consultation with the cook over the dinner menu, followed by a shopping expedition to the new 'department stores' Selfridges and Whiteley's (which boasted a staff of 6,000) or a dress fitting at Lady Duff Gordon's fashionable Mayfair salon which traded under the name 'Madame Lucille'. A meeting on a Tuesday with a friend involved in the same charitable cause and an amusing diversion to the gallery of Sir Francis Jeune's divorce court on a Thursday helped to while away the hours. In spare moments they wrote anonymous letters to *The Lady*, a magazine which offered them detailed advice on servant management, home decoration, wigs, superfluous nasal hair, and flatulence control.

And yet the upper classes were still bored. Osbert Sitwell's sister Edith, aged 23, watched her parents' friends at play and saw them with the contempt of youth as 'semi animate persons like an unpleasant form of vegetation or like dolls confected out of cheap satin, with here and there buttons fastened on their faces in imitation of eyes.' Semi-animate they might be, but most of these dolls mustered the energy to fill the empty spaces in their lives. Bridge was a passion, played not just at home but in the new women's clubs, including the Army and Navy in Cork Street and The Empress in Dover Street. Carriages came to the house in the afternoon, the driver having earlier in the day dropped off small white cards (stiff for gentlemen, flimsy for ladies) at selected addresses to give advance notice of their employer's intended visits. Since the house telephone was often positioned in a frustratingly public hallway, a call in person was imperative if any urgent society scandal were to be passed on discreetly. Other people's love lives were endlessly fascinating (that May Lady Cunard was caught *in flagrante* with a man not her husband). *Cinq-à-sept* appointments – the late afternoon and early evening hours allocated for sex – thrived under the complicit though theoretically unseeing gaze of the servants. The servants' hall, it was said, was privy to more secrets than Asquith's Cabinet. The actress Mrs Patrick Campbell was reassuring. 'Does it really matter what these affectionate people do in the bedroom,' she asked, 'as long as they don't do it in the street and frighten the horses?'

The fashions of the time positively invited flirtation and dalliance. For grander evening occasions married women displayed erotically low-cut décolletage, and the innovative French couturier Paul Poiret had recently brought his sheer evening gown 'La Vague' across the Channel. The dress fell straight from the bosom to swirl seductively and wave-like round the body, allowing a tantalising glimpse of the natural feminine curves beneath. A new form of underwear, the brassière, permitted the full form of the body to be defined more clearly.

Dinner parties, eight-course affairs with handwritten menus that might be inscribed on the shiny surface of a water-lily leaf or on the sail of a miniature boat, were so elaborate that they became a triumph of presentation and slick teamwork between the cook and the butler. People still spoke of the summer when Mr Hector

Baltazzi was so overcome by winning the Derby that he instructed his chef to float a pearl in every plate of watercress soup served at dinner that night. At 10 p.m. carriages would arrive to carry their bejewelled occupants to one of the great Mayfair residences – Devonshire House, perhaps, or Londonderry House or Spencer House – where the grand staircase leading to the ballroom would be wound around with thick garlands of lilies, the musky-sweet scent filling the candlelit space. Dance music was usually provided by a band, but the rich, golden voice of Enrico Caruso had started to resound from crimson enamel horns, the huge metal tropical flowers of a thousand gramophones. New dances accompanied the new music, and couples took to the floor in the turkey trot, the bunny-hug and the chicken scramble.

No one referred to 'weekends'. The term was considered 'common' or, in the current vogue term, '*canaille*'. The rich would leave London not on a Friday but for a 'Saturday-to-Monday'. On Saturday 'The Noah's Ark', a huge domed trunk containing enough clothes for six changes a day, would be loaded into the car or, for more distant destinations, a train and transported to country houses belonging to families whose names would have been familiar to Shakespeare. The Northumberlands welcomed their guests to Alnwick, the Salisburys to Hatfield, and the Warwicks to Warwick Castle. Between arrival on Saturday and departure on Monday morning, a sequence of pleasures would unfold. There were tennis parties and croquet matches, bicycle rides followed by picnic lunches, their charm enhanced by white lacy parasols and juicy strawberries and flutes of champagne packed in wicker baskets. During long lazy afternoons in hammocks that summer of 1911 the pampered guests looked forward to reading aloud from the caricaturist and wit Max Beerbohm's just-published romance *Zuleika Dobson,* a love story about a group of young men fated to die as a consequence of misplaced idealism. E. M. Forster, whose own novel *Howards End* had been a bestseller only the year before, found in Beerbohm's story 'a beauty unattainable by serious literature'. Maurice Baring, another young novelist, described how in the afternoons the gilded youth 'moved in muslin and straw hats and yellow roses on the lawns of gardens designed by Le Nôtre, delicious with ripe peaches on old brick walls, with the smell of verbena and sweet geranium; and stately with large avenues, artificial lakes and white temples.'

At dinner the *placement* in the dining room upstairs would be mirrored in the servants' hall below, the resident butler taking the head of the table with the highest-ranking visiting lady's maid on his right. After dinner, in the upstairs drawing rooms, small tables lit with lamps in shades of tightly wrapped dark red silk would be laid for bridge or the whist-drives at which Lady Diana Manners, who was making her debut at Court that summer, excelled. Turkish and Egyptian cigarettes would be set out in little boxes. Maurice Baring remembered how they sometimes 'bicycled in the warm night past ghostly cornfields by the light of a large full moon' before retiring upstairs, where much silent and furtive corridor-creeping between one double bedroom and another took place. In the morning, a convenient hour before the required appearance, fully dressed, at breakfast, a bell would be rung and the creeping went on again, in reverse.

Some of the rich and privileged were *not* enjoying themselves at the beginning of that summer. Lady Ida Sitwell could not rouse herself to join in at all. Her life was one of total indolence, as she tried to fill 'the blank stretch between hour and hour'. Staying in bed all day was convenient because, as her daughter observed, 'there was nothing to do if she got up.' Edith was full of contempt for her mother, a woman so wildly extravagant that her husband had to limit the cash available to her. She claimed Lady Ida was kept so short of money that she would be sent out to pawn her mother's false teeth in exchange for a bottle of whisky that would make the hours in bed pass a little more quickly.

The eighth Earl of Sandwich had enough time on his hands to become inordinately distressed by his female guests' habit of lunching with their hats on. At one of his lunch parties the ladies had scarcely begun to enjoy their sole *meunière* when the opera star Dame Nellie Melba, the guest of honour that day, was taken aback to see the butler, sporting a smart bowler above his black suit, approach Lord Sandwich carrying a tweed cap on his silver tray. In vengeful silence Lord Sandwich lifted the cap to his head and pulled it down over his eyebrows, glowering fiercely round the room.

Sir Herbert Tree found himself challenged by boredom. Visiting his local post office to buy a stamp, he waited while the clerk behind the counter produced a sheet containing a gross of identical sticky squares featuring the King's head. There was a long period in which no word was spoken: Sir Herbert could not make up his mind which stamp to buy. Finally he arrived at a decision, and the clerk's face remained impassive as with some dexterity he retrieved Sir Herbert's choice. He had plumped for the one in the very centre of the sheet.

The odd dissenter was heard, but in general there were good reasons for those outside the life of unchanging aristocratic privilege to feel equally joyful at being alive in 1911. Recently returned to England after six and a half years in the civil service in Ceylon, Leonard Woolf detected 'a sweeping away of formalities and barriers' which he found 'new and exhilarating'. There was a mood of energy and innovation. The motor car had become a more familiar sight at least in the big cities, although the spectacle of a daring young woman, Vita Sackville-West, at the wheel of her elegant De Dion Bouton (known as 'Green Archie') with its electric ignition and water-cooled engine, speeding down her local High Street in Sevenoaks, was enough to bring people running to their doorways to stare.

The car gave its driver a position of power, raising, as Osbert Sitwell noticed, 'the rich and even the humble lorry driver to a new and god-like level.' That spring, Rolls-Royce had commissioned Charles Robinson Sykes to design a new mascot for the bonnet of the car, and his elegant winged figure leaning bravely into the facing wind in her body-clinging gown was named, 'The

Spirit of Ecstasy'. Sykes's inspiration was the lovely Miss Eleanor Velasco Thornton, whose liaison with Lord Montagu, a leading enthusiast among the collectors of Rolls-Royce cars, had remained a secret for a decade.

Men who until recently had only been able to take their sweethearts on a bicycle made for two were now flying down country lanes in a state of speed-induced sensuality. Osbert Sitwell described 'their hair blown back from their temples, features sculptured by the wind, bodies and limbs shaped and carved by it continually under their clothes so that they enjoyed a new physical sensation, comparable to swimming except here the element was speed not water.' Young people had never been so unchaperoned, and 'no other generation had been able to speed into the sunset'.

In Vita Sackville-West's novel *The Edwardians,* set during the first eleven years of the twentieth century, the mistress of the Duke of Chevron returns exhilarated from a drive. 'What I like better than anything is driving in that racing motor of yours,' she says to her lover, 'then I feel we may be dashed to death at any moment.' Just as speed had never been so invigorating, so the lack of responsibility had never provided such intoxication.

And yet there were dangers involved on the roads. Not all cars had windscreens; their engines blew up, their tyres exploded; and inexperienced drivers took to the wheel with gusto. Pedestrians were still unused to this mechanical hazard. The Metropolitan Police Statistics for accidents caused by vehicles in London in 1909 were published in 1911. There had been 3,488 accidents recorded involving motor-cars and motor cycles, 2,220 for trams, 1,343 for motor omnibuses, 304 for horse-drawn omnibuses and 6,033 for other horse-drawn vehicles. Of these accidents, 303 were fatal. In the middle of June F. E. Smith, MP, lawyer, and close friend of the Home Secretary Winston Churchill, found himself late for dinner. As he drove along beside the banks of the Thames, on the approach to the House of Commons, his car hit a man who was crossing Westminster Bridge. The man had not, according to *The Times*, been paying full attention to the road, but looking up at the clock on the tower that housed the Westminster bell, Big Ben. He was killed instantly. Later in the summer the Prime Minister, Henry Asquith, was being driven in his official car to London from Berkshire when his car collided with a young woman riding her bicycle; she was critically injured.

Change for this generation was rapid. The novelist H. G. Wells thought Queen Victoria had 'like a great paperweight sat on men's minds and when she was removed their ideas began to blow about all over the place haphazardly.' The Edwardians were the beneficiaries of this exciting and ever-shifting wind. In London new lines were being opened on the underground train system every few years. In 1906, to prove its safety and reliability, a man with a wooden leg had been invited as the inaugural passenger on the first moving underground staircase, on the Bakerloo line. The 'escalator' had proved such a success that a larger version was ready for use at Earl's Court by May of 1911, for the Festival of Empire. An immense ship, said to be as tall as the highest skyscraper in New York and 'practically unsinkable', was nearing completion in the Belfast shipyard of Harland and Wolfe. The first journey by air over the Channel had taken place two years earlier. Moving films, after the first blurry jerky days, were becoming both an increasingly sophisticated art form and, screened in conjunction with the topical news films, a hugely popular form of entertainment. A visit to the cinema became a valuable source of information about current affairs. Over-busy theatre lovers, including the Queen, enjoyed the new service offered by the post office: special headphones that provided a live link from private homes to many of the shows and operas on the West End stage. Cornflakes and tea bags had arrived on breakfast tables.

The fixity of the nineteenth century had vanished, yet change brought with it a mixture of excitement and anxiety. The rapidly increasing military and naval power of Germany and the continuing debate between the Unionists and those who supported Home Rule in Ireland were England's predominant off-shore concerns that summer, and the strength of the internal unrest that began to find expression took many by surprise. The vast labour force of industrial England was flexing its muscles, on the verge of reaching full political maturity. The profound despair felt among the poor of the country remained unvoiced no longer, and strike action marked the whole summer of 1911. Even domestic servants were beginning to question their long-accepted role.

Many of the very poor sent their children abroad, after replying to daily newspaper advertisements that seemed to offer the next generation better opportunities. The sum required to separate child from parent, perhaps forever, was a quarter of the average annual wage of a farm labourer. Dr Barnado's advised that '£10 a head for the outfit and for travelling' would be a good investment for a 'guaranteed good home in Canada, for the benefit of the Empire'. Children were evacuated as if to escape a war that had not been declared.

However, many people in England were united in their national preoccupation with the weather. They hoped that the beautiful early summer days would last at least until the Coronation. One woman, however, was doubtful whether even the sunshine could dispel her mood of anxiety. From her bedroom window at the top of the Mall she could hear the hammering of wooden stands being knocked into place in preparation for the unveiling of the memorial to Queen Victoria in two weeks' time. Queen Mary was not looking forward to the months ahead.

2

Early May

The position is no bed of roses.

HM Queen Mary

MARY HAD NEVER felt so lonely. She had been shy all her life, a self-conscious woman who now found herself at the pinnacle of a society that alarmed her. On 22 June she would be crowned Queen. She had been flattered when many years earlier her godmother Queen Victoria, recognising in her the potential to make a good Queen, had singled her out as a suitable bride for her grandson George. But Mary had not expected the position of joint head of state to come vacant so suddenly.

Mary lived in a palace lit by two hundred thousand electric light bulbs, with a faithful husband, six loving children, dozens of servants, twelve personal postmen doing their rounds inside the palace, a private police force, and six florists. It felt like a trap. Both her parents were dead, her favourite relation, her Aunt Augusta, lived abroad and was too old to travel to England, and her husband's mother and sisters were jealous of her. Even Mabell Airlie, her Lady-in-Waiting and closest friend, was unavailable for advice and support: she had returned for the summer to her home, Cortachy Castle in Scotland, to spend time with her young children.

Mary had been formally christened 'Victoria Mary' but May, the month of her birthday, had given her the childhood nickname by which she had been known all her life. 'May' was not considered a weighty enough name for a Queen, however, and a second 'Victoria' would have been thought disrespectful to her husband's grandmother (even though she had been dead for a full decade) so there was really no choice in the matter, and 'Queen Mary' she was to be. The change brought with it an erosion of her old identity. Unable to conceal her regret at the loss, she wrote two letters, the first to Aunt Augusta: 'I hope you like my new name, Mary. George dislikes double names and I could not be Victoria but it strikes me as curious to be re-christened at the age of forty-three.' Filled with nostalgia for her lost private life, and only half-joking, she also wrote to Lady Airlie to confide that 'there is one thing I never did and wish I had done: climb over a fence.'

Preparations for the Coronation of George V were already evident in London. Tottering, tiered, wooden viewing platforms under construction were disfiguring many of the most famous streets and the huge stands that dwarfed the buildings along the route seemed top-heavy and ugly. St Clement Dane's church in the Strand had almost disappeared beneath scaffolding. Advertisements for seats that promised good views of the procession crammed the popular newspapers. The quantity of public engagements that packed the Queen's diary for the month of May filled her with gloom. Four 'Royal Courts' were planned – the official receptions to each of which more than a thousand worthies would be invited and at which the season's debutantes would be presented. In anticipation, *The Times* had carried a 'semi official intimation', released on the instruction of the Lord Chamberlain's Office and directed at the leading Court dressmakers, to discourage the making and wearing of the hobble skirt. This highly fashionable close-fitting garment, another design by the trend-setting Frenchman Paul Poiret, forced women to totter like geishas and made the deep curtsey required in the presence of the Sovereign impossible. The word of warning in *The Times* was a triumph for the Rational Dress League in its long campaign for the abolition of restrictive female clothes, sparked after their President, Viscountess

Harberton, in the middle of a bicycle tour of the Home Counties, arrived in the salon of the Hautboy Hotel in Ockham, Surrey wearing 'bifurcated garments'. The management had asked her to leave, arousing in her and her loyal allies a lifelong outrage.

May was weary of the draining black and purple she had been obliged to wear for so long, and very ready to celebrate the ending of the official mourning period for Edward VII. On 7 May, in her weekly Sunday letter to her Aunt Augusta in Austria, she wrote: 'I am dressed in grey, and feel quite odd.' But this was her view of herself. She did not look odd at all. She looked elegant if vulnerable, a little unconfident or uncomfortable under the gaze of strangers, her shyness mistaken for severity. That afternoon, glad to feel the warmth of the sunshine of early summer, she set out for the park wearing a buttery-yellow hat with a large blue feather pinned on her poodle-fringed, wheat-coloured hair, her famously prominent bosom draped in the palest grey silk. May had good reason to hate mourning dress. Her mother had died fourteen years before, her father three years after that; two British monarchs had died within nine years of each other; and only six weeks after Edward VII was buried her adored younger brother Frank was struck down by pleurisy after a minor operation on his nose: for years May had been enveloped in black dresses trimmed with crepe, with black shoes, black gloves, black fans, and black feathers sewn onto black hats. The sight of a whip with black crepe ribbon tied to the tip wielded by a horse-drawn taxi driver became enough to sink her into total despondency. And though the mourning was over, the subject of clothes had been making her feel anxious for months. Again and again, as she had complained, she had endured a hard day's work at her 'tiresome trousseau'. She had never enjoyed shopping, even though her mother-in-law Queen Alexandra teased that she was always 'looking in her glass'. There had been dozens of tedious fittings for the impending balls and parties and she had spent £2,000 on velvet and silk dresses, equivalent to the turnover of a small factory. As she confided to Aunt Augusta, she considered 'the fashions of the season . . . so hideous that it has been a great trouble to evolve pretty toilettes out of them, however I hope some of the gowns will be a success.'

That sunny morning of 7 May 1911, May's chauffeur drove her car through the new iron gates at the front of Buckingham Palace and turned left up Constitution Hill. The streets were already packed with motorised taxis edging their way past the horse-drawn hansom cabs, pretty in their gay summer tasselled trappings, made by the drivers' wives. Horse-drawn buses were becoming an increasingly rare sight, and some of the traditions of Victorian London were disappearing with them. Every retired driver missed the customary gift of a brace of pheasant or partridge shot on his estate that they had received on Lord Rothschild's birthday. In gratitude, they had worn the Rothschild colours tied to their whips. With the phasing out of the hansom cabs people were no longer reminded that it was the Oxford and Cambridge Boat Race day by the sight of the contrasting light and dark blue colours flying from the whips. Nor was St Patrick's Day still commemorated with fluttering emerald green ribbons.

Notice had been given that year of the withdrawal of horse-drawn fire engines, for it had become obvious that the straining animals could not match the speed of machine-driven equivalents. Taxi drivers earned their licences to criss-cross the eight square miles of London by taking an exam that was said to require more study time than a degree from Oxford or Cambridge. Chauffeurs rounded Hyde Park Corner in gleaming Rolls-Royces as their passengers, failing to make themselves heard above the din of the engine, jabbed them in the neck with the tip of an umbrella to attract their attention. An over-talkative driver would be asked to 'shut his trap' by closing the sliding panel that allowed conversation between a chauffeur and his passenger. Bicyclists and pedestrians had to keep their wits about them to avoid the frequent crashes at unmonitored junctions. The pure scent of the early May air clashed with the stink of horse dung and thick diesel exhaust.

★

As the Royal car edged through the streets of south London, its passenger allowed herself the smallest of smiles. She enjoyed these outings to Richmond, the park which as children she and her brothers had grown to know well from their home in White Lodge and where they had been able to run about freely with their spinning hoops. To her delight she had found that she was greeted with warmth by fellow strollers. The press noted that she was given a friendly reception from all classes and that she appeared pleased when people would crowd round her as she walked under the splendid oak trees that were just beginning to unfurl their buds of brilliant green. May's back was as straight as a ceremonial sword, and her rounded face gave the curious impression that she had a small greengage wedged high in each cheek. E.M. Forster was reported to have bowed to a wedding cake, having mistaken it for the new stiffly-structured silhouette of the Queen. However, her solemn-looking outward confidence disguised a deep discomfort in her public role. She had begun the year of 1911 with her profound sense of duty in conflict with feelings of apprehension, inadequacy and fear. She knew she was more capable and intelligent than she had the self-assurance to reveal.

As well as all the elaborate official commitments scheduled to take place inside the dark walls of Buckingham Palace, there were to be many public appearances up and down the country. In May alone she faced the prospect of The Trooping the Colour, the opening of the Festival of Empire, and a visit from her husband's first cousin, Kaiser Wilhelm of Germany and his family. This last would be particularly demanding, involving five days of official lunches, dinners and balls as well as a visit to Windsor culminating with the main event of the trip, the unveiling of the statue of Queen Victoria at the top of the Mall outside Buckingham Palace. The summer programme of celebration was so packed that May wondered if she would get through it. A tour of England had been planned, and visits to Wales, Ireland and Scotland were also part of the agenda, all of it a source of dread. A different woman, perhaps the dead King's mistress Alice

Keppel, or the beautiful aristocratic Marchioness of Ripon, subject of one of the great portrait painter John Singer Sargent's most seductive paintings, or even her own mother, the late Duchess of Teck, might have taken to the role of Queen with relish. May did not. 'The position is no bed of roses', she had written to her aunt the summer before. Ceremonial occasions, even those in her own home, filled her with alarm. She hated the sound of a gun salute, having been terrified by thunder as a child, and had a self-confessed antipathy to 'a surfeit of gold plate and orchids'. She had abhorred long meals from childhood, when lunch had lasted up to three hours, during which she was obliged to listen to her greedy overweight mother rolling her Rs in relish over the words 'rich cream', her favourite brand of biscuit. At Buckingham Palace, under the direction of the new King, a five-course dinner could now be dispatched within the hour, but even so the Prime Minister Henry Asquith was known to find dining there more exhausting than an entire evening's debate in the House of Commons. The Queen had no gift for small-talk, and politics bored her. An observant royal aide was aware of an unfortunate abruptness in the Queen's habit of 'a shy nod, which offends so much'. Her self-consciousness and lack of ease among the sophisticated beau monde of Edward VII's Court had increased her feelings of inadequacy, and Lady Airlie noticed a shell of self-preservation beginning to form over the natural gaiety that had once so captivated Queen Victoria. 'The hard crust of inhibition which gradually closed over her' was, her Lady-in-Waiting observed, 'hiding the warmth and tenderness of her personality.'

The scrutiny of the press did not diminish May's discomfort during the first year of the reign. Although at five foot six inches the Royal couple were the same height as each other, journalists ignored this equality and, perhaps as a comment on May's evident deference to the King, referred to them as 'King George the Fifth and Mary the Four Fifths'. Furthermore, two scandalous old rumours had resurfaced to blight the preceding year. There was much behind-the-hand whispering that George, whose voice was naturally strident and his complexion blotchy because of poor digestion, had an alcohol problem. Only by demonstrating a consistently steady hand when holding a shotgun and equally consistently refusing a second glass of port did he manage to quash the rumour. A malicious report that he had secretly married the daughter of a naval captain in Malta the week before proposing to May caused much hilarity at Court until that story too was proved libellous. May had found both episodes upsetting.

Her anxieties were exacerbated by her mother-in-law. Lacking Alexandra's glamour and style, May inevitably suffered unfavourable comparisons with her predecessor. 'Dazzlingly beautiful, whether in gold and silver by night or in violet velvet by day,' swooned Margot Asquith of Edward VII's widow, 'she succeeded in making every other woman look common beside her.' Margot's step-daughter Violet Asquith, aged 24, was charitable in noting her first impression of May after a Downing Street dinner. 'Much less plain than I thought,' she wrote in her diary, adding, however: 'quite a tidy dreary face, with regular Royal hair in exact imitation of the old one without any of her beauty and grace.'

Alexandra's response to her own new position as Dowager Queen did not help. After 47 years of marriage she was not coping well with change, although Edward's death had at least presented her with an opportunity for self-pity, the admissible indulgence of a grieving Queen. Having been reluctant to move into Buckingham Palace on her husband's accession, she was now unwilling to move out to make way for May and George and their family. When she finally agreed to go, she wrote to May in poorly disguised criticism. '*OUR* dear old rooms,' she sighed. 'I shall indeed be very curious and anxious to see them and how you have arranged it all. Yes the sitting room with its nice and pretty bow window is certainly very cold and draughty in the winter – particularly where my writing table stood – I wonder where you have put yours – and the lovely bedroom with its pretty arches which I hear you have *removed*. How is that arranged?'

But May was sensitive enough to see beyond Alexandra's difficult behaviour. Her capriciousness and vulnerability reminded May of her own mother, and endeared Alexandra to her. Like Mary of Teck, Alexandra was infuriatingly unpunctual, sweeping into a room where everyone had been waiting for ages, crying 'Oh, am I late?' and disarming everyone with her beautiful smile. There was something else about Alexandra that aroused May's compassionate nature: she had become very deaf. She had tried to learn lip-reading but had failed to master it, and May would observe her brave attempts to follow a conversation over dinner, watching for someone else to laugh so she could give a little wave of her hand to indicate she too had enjoyed the joke. May's sweetness over her disability was not unappreciated by Alexandra, who wrote to her daughter-in-law: 'You are always so dear and nice to me, and whenever I am not quite *au fait* because of my beastly ears you always, by a word or even a turn towards me, make me understand. I am most grateful, as nobody knows what I have to go through to understand.' May understood: Alexandra was lonely too.

May's sisters-in-law made her no such overtures of affection. Having grown up with three brothers she had been starved of feminine companionship of her own age for much of her life, and had longed to get on with Louise, Victoria and Maud, but Queen Victoria's demonstrative favouritism had aroused a deep jealousy in George's sisters and their dislike of her never faded. Under the pretence of persuading a dinner guest to put her new sister-in-law at her ease, George's unmarried younger sister Toria implored: 'Now do try to talk to May at dinner, though one knows she is deadly dull.' Looking for companionship within her own family, May had been urging her adored Aunt Augusta, the Grand Duchess of Mecklenburg, her late mother's only surviving sister, to come from Austria for the Coronation to give her some support. There had even been a wild suggestion of arranging a flying-machine to bring her across to England, but by early summer May had realised that the visit would not be possible. At 85, Aunt Augusta was too old.

Loneliness was best countered, May found, by spending time with her family and by indulging the private passions that had sustained her over many years – arranging pictures and furniture and cataloguing her precious collections of china and porcelain. Occasionally she was alone for the evening with her husband, and while he wrote up his game book or sorted out stamps for his collection she would knit and smoke a cigarette. When George was away on extended visits to the grouse moors, she would invite her growing children to join her in her small sitting room, where she would tell them stories of royal history. May had not enjoyed the babyhood and infancy of her six children – Edward (known as David), Albert George, Mary, Henry, George, and the sickly John. As was the convention of the day they had all been entrusted to the care of nannies, but their abusive treatment by one in particular had gone unnoticed by May, even in the imposed intimacy of York Cottage, their small country residence at Sandringham, until a lady-in-waiting drew her attention to it. However, as the children grew up she spent more time with them, doing her best to protect them from their father's often over-strict reactions. The children loved these rare weeks spent with her in their father's absence. 'We used to have the most lovely time with her alone, always laughing and joking,' her eldest child David remembered. 'She was a different human being away from him.' His mother's experiences of her years in Italy before her marriage and her cultivated and well-read mind made a great impression on him. He treasured the hours before bedtime with her as 'the happiness associated with this last hour of a child's day.'

When her children were in the schoolroom, May was most content when she could spend hours by herself organising the porcelain, hanging and rehanging her huge collection of miniatures, or pasting and labelling her photographs into albums. She always went to bed early, noting in her diary with a few exclamation marks the rare times she stayed up beyond midnight. Unexpansive in her speech, she was just as sparing in her diary, and only relaxed in the long weekly letters to her adored aunt.

For all her lack of small talk and dislike of politics, May was probably more responsive to Asquith's conversation and jokes than he realised. She often checked herself, as she told Mabell Airlie: 'I always have to be so careful not to laugh because you see I have such a vulgar laugh!' Her family, however, recognised a twitching of the mouth as a sign that a laugh was on the brink of emerging. A small elongating of her lips, never quite dramatic enough to reveal her teeth, indicated a smile. When May did speak it was quietly, her voice clipped, precise and deliberate in enunciation, with a hint of a German accent.

May's public shyness and lack of confidence was due in part to the overwhelming personality of her mother and in part to the early difficulties of her life, including her troubled search for a husband. She was the only daughter of the shockingly greedy Princess Mary of Cambridge, at 250 pounds 'a personage of unusual girth', in the words of one observer, and her considerably less substantial husband Francis, first Duke of Teck. Tiny Queen Victoria found the size of her first cousin Mary 'fearful. It is *really* a misfortune', and a courtier described her as a 'a mountain of a girl'. In her youth Mary of Cambridge was a liability in the ball-room, notorious for executing the polka with such vigour that an accidental collision with other dancers would send them flying. Her chest was winched so high that it almost grazed her chin, and she looked rather like a plumped-up, feather-filled sofa, with an extra cushion in the wrong place. To everyone's surprise, at the age of 33 – until then, by polite universal agreement, a confirmed spinster – she found a man 'prepared to countenance so vast an undertaking'. Francis was the younger by four years, but Queen Victoria judged him to be 'very nice and aimiable'. There was only one obvious drawback to the match for Mary, a woman excessively fond of life's pleasures: Francis had no money. However, the couple seemed happy enough together and further confounded their families' expectations by producing four children, following their eldest child May with three brothers, Adolphus (Dolly), Francis (Frank), and Alexander.

At first Queen Victoria looked after the impoverished Tecks by providing them with a large apartment in Kensington Palace and a more rural home, White Lodge, in the heart of Richmond Park. Fat Mary of Teck, as she was publicly and affectionately known, was devoted to her children, and used to visit the local Richmond studio to watch her daughter's dancing lessons. With embarrassment May saw the other girls sniggering behind their hands as her mother was given *two* gilt chairs on which to spread her bulk. This experience was one cause of the shyness from which May was to suffer for decades.

Queen Victoria enjoyed Fat Mary's company for the sheer ebullience of her spirits and for a long time was patient with her extravagances, but eventually she wearied of shouldering her cousin's debts and the Tecks were discreetly packed off to live in Italy. Her exile in such a vital and cosmopolitan city as Florence became for 16-year-old May one of the happiest and most stimulating times of her life. Able to live, if not anonymously, at least away from the attentions her family received in England, she discovered a passion for art, language, architecture, furniture and literature, and a life of the mind.

The Tecks spent eighteen months abroad, but in 1885 May and her family returned to England in preparation for her debut. After six years back at White Lodge, and five years after officially 'coming out', there was no sign of a suitable husband for May. Intelligent, educated and pretty enough, she was in danger of being left on the shelf. Mabell Airlie knew that 'anyone who failed to secure a proposal within six months of coming out could only wait for her next season with diminishing expectations. After a third attempt there remained nothing but India as a last resort before the spectre of old maid became a reality.'

But Queen Victoria had been studying May closely and began to have an idea that she would make an ideal bride and eventually an ideal queen for her eldest grandson, the Duke of Clarence and Avondale. The Queen and the Duke's parents, the Prince and Princess of Wales, had experienced great difficulty in finding a suitable wife for the heir presumptive. Eddy, as he was known to his family, with his overlong neck, listless eyes and succession of moustaches each more preposterous than the last, was said to 'lack manliness' and rumoured to be homosexual, though he had pursued several romantic attachments with women, in particular with Princess Hélène d'Orléans and Princess Alix of Hesse. Neither had agreed to marry him.

May and Eddy had barely met since they played together as children, but to her 'great surprise' he proposed to her at a ball at beautiful eighteenth-century Luton Hoo in Bedfordshire. May accepted immediately 'of course', and Fat Mary could hardly contain her excitement at this turnaround of fortunes, and even more at the treats that went with life in the glow of renewed Royal favour. 'A capital HOT lunch of chicken and rice and beef-steaks and fried potatoes!' she wrote, smacking her lips in delight, at the end of one train-ride to Sandringham. But Fat Mary's contentment was not to last.

Six weeks after his engagement Eddy caught the influenza that had reached epidemic proportions in the country and had been infecting other members of the Sandringham house party, and May was amazed by the speed with which the illness felled him. On his birthday on 8 January 1892 he was struggling with nothing more than a bad cold; the following morning the breathlessness settled on his weak lungs and turned to pneumonia. The doctor looking after the dying Prince during those dreadful few days, chancing to look out of his patient's sickroom window, had seen May walking in the garden below, being comforted by her fiancé's younger brother George. Within three days Prince Eddy was dead and May was left shocked, confused, and back once more on that shelf. Queen Victoria was horrified at the unexpected outcome of her apparently successful match-making. 'It is one of the most fearful tragedies one can imagine,' she said, 'it would sound unnatural and overdrawn if it was put into a novel.' May's mother could not bring herself to watch as her daughter, instead of carrying the flowers at her imminent wedding, laid the redundant bridal bouquet of orange blossom on Eddy's coffin.

Not long afterwards, with his indefatigable grandmother's encouragement, Eddy's brother George began a cautious courtship of May, and five months after Eddy's death was persuaded by his sister Louise to take the plunge. They were having tea at Louise's house at Sheen in Surrey when he invited May into the garden to look at some frogs in the pond and, against a background of loud croaks, asked if she would become his wife. She agreed immediately to marry a man she knew only a little better than she had his brother. An observer, Lady Geraldine Somerset, noted shortly after the engagement that George appeared 'nonchalant and indifferent' while May seemed 'placid and cold'. Mary of Teck felt no such reserve when she heard the delightful news and, unable to wait until the announcement was official, splashed out on sending telegrams to everyone she knew.

George was not a demonstrative man, the stifling adoration of his mother having made him hesitant in any display of warmth, even to those he really loved. May craved affection, but she too was inhibited when it came to showing her feelings. Writing to him during their engagement, she apologised for her reserve when left alone with him. 'I am very sorry that I am still so shy with you,' she wrote. 'I tried not to be so the other day, but alas, failed. I was angry with myself! It is so stupid to be so stiff together.' He replied immediately: 'I think it really unnecessary for me to tell you how deep my love for you, my darling, is and I feel it growing stronger and stronger every time I see you; although I may appear shy and cold.' May hoped that with George's encouragement her virginal reserve would dissipate after their marriage.

The wedding took place on 6 July 1893 at the Chapel Royal in St James's Palace, then May and George spent their honeymoon at York Cottage on the Sandringham estate. Cramped and vicarage-like, it was their wedding gift from the Prince of Wales. Princess Alexandra, 'Mother dear' to her son, showed no sensitivity to whatever desire for privacy the honeymooners may have felt, and could not resist walking the mere five minutes that separated York Cottage from 'The Big House' to drop in unannounced for tea with the newlyweds. She wanted to see how her 'Georgie' was coping with married life. Thinking back on those early weeks, May observed quietly: 'I sometimes think we were not left alone enough.' On her engagement she had received a letter from her future mother-in-law expressing the hope that 'My sweet May will come straight to me for everything', an invitation that held little appeal for someone so self-contained. Georgie, although exasperated by his mother, remained unable to resist her powerful influence.

By the summer of 1911, and after seventeen years of marriage, May had accepted that her husband would not entertain any other style of dress than that established by his mother, a woman 22 years her senior. Not from weakness of character but more out of her unwavering, almost oriental reverence for the monarchy, as personified by her husband, May deferred to his wishes. Although she longed to wear a scarlet dress, she dared not, because George hated red. She asked her friend Lady Airlie to try on one of the new shorter skirts one day, just to test the water. But when May enquired whether George had liked her friend's new dress, he had told her 'No, I did not. It was too short.' Lady Airlie was not surprised by this reaction, and, let her hem down 'with all speed'. She was well aware that the Queen had been 'gifted with perfect legs', but observed that they continued to remain fully concealed. May did allow herself one small act of defiance: to George's consternation, she often appeared wearing huge dangling earrings.

Beauty, wit, wealth, sophistication and affectation had been the qualifications for an invitation to his father's Court; George's tastes were severe by contrast, more reflective of the regime his grandmother had adopted after the death of her husband Prince Albert. He was passionate about shooting and stamp collecting and shunned parties whenever he could. The middle classes admired the reassuring air of a respectable family man that he had about him. He suffered from insomnia and toothache as well as poor digestion, and had spent much of his childhood in splints to correct his knock knees. He favoured simplicity and disdained pretension. At Buckingham Palace dinners wine bottles had their labels steamed off, lest the Royal family be thought to be showing off the superiority of their cellars. George considered the French language effeminate, and would deliberately employ an exaggerated English accent when ordering his favourite dish of '*Erf On Cock Ott*'. To his son's dismay, he took against the rather more relaxed, informal way of dressing the younger men were adopting. In the poem T.S. Eliot was writing that summer, Prufrock intended to wear the bottoms of his trousers rolled: George loathed 'turn ups', thinking they looked as if a man had rolled up his trousers to keep the hems out of a puddle. If his son appeared wearing them, he would ask, with raised eyebrow, 'Is it raining in here?'

George loathed change. He was a man of routine. Habits were set firm after fifteen years of naval training. He continued to consult his barometer twice a day, and to his satisfaction the summer weather of his Coronation, as the air pressure rose ever higher, was providing him with some particularly interesting readings. First thing in the morning and last thing before going to bed, according to a watchful courtier, the King would 'peer at the glass, tap the case sharply to make sure the needle was not stuck, and set it again.'

During the years of marriage largely spent out of the public gaze, May and George had settled into a loving relationship in which George relied heavily on his wife. In his diary on the day after his father's death he wrote confidently that 'Darling May will be my comfort as she has always been.' Later that summer he wrote to her: 'My love grows stronger for you every day mixed with admiration and I thank God every day that he has given me such a darling devoted wife as you are.'

In 1911 George found himself ill at ease in his new role. He was a second son, not brought up to succeed. Life in the Royal Navy had distanced him from politics as well as from the gay society and easy interaction with people that had been such a mark of his father's personality, and during the summer of 1911 a

Constitutional crisis forced him to become involved, despite his reluctance, in controversial legislation at the heart of the political life of the country. Upper-class men had controlled the governmental process for centuries; now the gradual extension of the right to vote had begun to threaten the pattern for the first time since the Civil War more than 250 years earlier. The Liberal Government under the Prime Minister Herbert Henry Asquith and his Chancellor Lloyd George found itself opposed by the huge Conservative majority in the House of Lords in the passage of the Bill for a National Insurance Act, designed as 'a measure to provide insurance against loss of health and unemployment and prevention and cure of sickness'. The Act was to be funded largely by a compulsory deduction levied on all wage-earners and employers, but also in part by a tax on rich landowners. This was a hit at the very core of the House of Lords, which counted among its members some of the wealthiest landowners in the country. Not surprisingly, they resisted, despite the fact that traditionally their power of veto was never implemented against a 'Money Bill'. Asquith needed help. In secret talks he sought the King's intervention, asking him to threaten to use his Royal Prerogative to create four hundred new Liberal peers, to swamp the Conservatives and force the Bill through the second chamber. He proposed that this should be followed by a Parliament Act that would severely restrict the powers of the House of Lords, and prevent the recurrence of such an impasse. Despite the new King's inexperience, Asquith told his daughter that he found himself 'deeply moved by his first audience with [him] and impressed by his modesty and common sense.'

But George's new preoccupation with affairs of State put a strain on his marriage. When Parliamentary business first began to absorb his attention in the early months of 1911, May became concerned that they seemed to be 'drifting' away from the intimacy of the early years. She might feel veneration for her husband's position, and George might still write her occasional letters of reassurance, but May was human enough to mind that the duties which now absorbed much of his attention did not leave him a great deal of time for her.

George had always lived on the edge of rage. His children began to notice the strain their father was under, and hated him taking it out on their mother. David, the eldest, confessed: 'I've often seen her leave the table because he was so rude to her and we children would follow her out. He was a repressive influence.' May genuinely loved her husband, and her acceptance of the effect on him of the tensions of the office thrust on him through birth was tinged with reverence but, as Lady Airlie realised, 'Her devotion to the Monarchy demanded the sacrifice of much of her personal happiness.'

A few days after her visit to Richmond Queen Mary, making the most of the sunny weather, arrived in Hyde Park, swaying in her horse-drawn carriage as it trotted along the red earth of Rotten Row past uniformed nannies pushing their huge prams. There were many other carriages in the Park that day, victorias and landaus and family coaches with coachmen in livery on their way to teatime appointments, their lady passengers dressed to impress in their new diaphanous tea gowns (known as 'teagies'), a small square mesh bag over one wrist containing a gold pencil, a handkerchief and a flat gold wallet for calling cards. The news-papers wrote enthusiastically about the unseasonal but welcome 'August blue' of the skies. Only a week earlier the Duchess of Roxburgh had been photographed at the Horticultural Hall, paying special attention to the prize-winning carnations grown by green-fingered Mr Cutbush. Queen Mary had announced with pleasure that she had chosen the pink carnation 'Lady Hermione' as her official Coronation flower.

The scaffolding that had covered the colossal marble edifice at the top of The Mall for many months was still in place. Visible at the top, poking through the metal work and glinting in the sun-shine, was the gilt figure of Peace – which, May confided in a letter to her Aunt Augusta, did not appeal to her at all. Edward VII had planned the tribute to his mother as a celebration of

England's greatness at the heart of the British Empire and a memorial to an age of internal peace, delighting in the thought that he would be reminded of the Empire every time he looked out of his window. But his reign had come and gone and still the work was not finished. In ten days' time George's first cousin Wilhelm of Germany would arrive in England for the unveiling of the monument built in memory of the grandmother they had shared, the final public ceremony associated with a queen who had died ten years earlier.

By 16 May the scaffolding had been removed. It was a warm day as Sir Walter Parrott, Master of the Royal Musick, climbed onto a specially-built elevated platform at the side of the monument and raised his baton for silence. The choirboys of Westminster Abbey, St Paul's Cathedral, The Chapel Royal, St George's Chapel, Windsor and St James's Palace had gathered an hour earlier and were waiting for the ceremony to begin.

The German Royal party had arrived the day before in the Royal Yacht *Hohenzollern*, the Kaiser bringing with him his wife the Kaiserin and their daughter Princess Victoria Louise. They had taken the train to Victoria Station, where May and George had been waiting to meet and escort them to Buckingham Palace. There they were shown to rooms for which May had personally overseen the preparations. After a family dinner there was an impromptu dance which, May noted in her green leather, red-cornered diary had been 'most amusing'. The Kaiser issued a statement to the press: 'always delighted to visit England and to see his relations and . . . is especially gratified on this occasion at the cordiality of the reception accorded to the Empress and himself by the people of London.' Showing no signs of tiredness from the gaieties of the night before, the Royal party walked out of the new gates at the top of The Mall into the sunshine, their parasols furled, and took their places at 'Grandmama's monument'. George had recorded 68 degrees Fahrenheit on his thermometer that morning. The ceremony organisers had been a little nervous about the weather prospects, for only a couple of days earlier during severe thunderstorms a collier in Swansea and a farmer on horseback in Cardiganshire had both been killed. But on 16 May the storm clouds stayed away from London and there was not a raised umbrella in sight.

Huge crowds had come out that morning to watch the unveiling ceremony, to enjoy the balmy weather and to listen to the brass bands. Funerals and weddings, coronations and unveilings, tragedies and triumphs always brought people onto the streets. Although the daily papers, particularly the half-penny tabloids the *Daily Mail* and the *Daily Sketch*, were guaranteed to carry photographs of the events the next day and there would be an opportunity to see the Pathé newsreels in one of the new picture palaces, there was a hunger to witness the physical reality of the event itself. The street vendors and hawkers had packed away last year's mourning handkerchiefs imprinted with a portrait of the dead King and were doing a pleasing trade in flags and in pictures of the new statue pasted on to card. Buckingham Palace servants who had climbed up to the roof to watch the ceremony lined the parapet, decorating the skyline in their crimson uniforms. Grandfathers who remembered the old Queen with affection carried their grandchildren high on their shoulders for a good view. Women who had put on their weekend hats, piled high with enough flowers for an exhibit at the forthcoming Chelsea Flower Show, were accused of obscuring the scene from those standing behind them. Every green sixpenny deckchair in St James's Park was taken, the scent of lilac drifted across from the park to The Mall, and the little rowing-boats on the lake bobbed and swayed with the weight of onlookers. Soldiers had taken up positions on the roof of the Wellington Barracks on the other side of the Park, and three wobbling workmen were spotted balancing themselves on top of a single telegraph pole. Now that the scaffolding had been removed, the pale shroud that engulfed the memorial stood out against the dirty blackness of the Palace behind (the stonework had not been cleaned for decades: Edward VII had always referred to his London home as The Mausoleum).

Brian Calkin, a thirteen-year-old member of the St Paul's Cathedral Choir School, was having the time of his life. St Paul's was one of the five choirs chosen to sing not only at the unveiling of the statue of the old Queen but at the Coronation itself the following month. As the band began to play and the choir launched into what *The Times* called 'that grand old hymn', 'Oh God, our help in Ages Past', the fresh cream roses and delicate feathers on Queen Mary's hat trembled in the early summer breeze. She was wearing a richly embroidered biscuit-coloured dress with the blue ribbon of the Order of the Garter draped over her lace bodice. She looked elegant, particularly as compared with the German Empress who, apparently unaware that mourning was over, or indifferent to the fact, had encased her substantial figure in, as the *Daily Mail* reporter observed, 'a dull black fabric dress, embroidered with dull gold, with a long coat of black net and a black hat.'

Lord Esher, chairman of the executive committee in charge of the monument, opened the ceremony by describing the symbolism of the statue. Then the King spoke a few words in memory of Victoria's son, his father, Edward VII. Winston Churchill, the Home Secretary, had drafted the speech for him, but George had raised the emotional content with notes added the night before in his own hand. 'King Edward VII is more than ever in our loving thoughts today,' he said in a firm voice full of filial pride, before turning to face the shrouded statue to read the dedication: 'No woman was ever held in higher honour,' he declared loudly. 'No Queen was ever loved so well.'

Then, watched by his family and by leading members of his Government, the King pressed a small electric button built into a wooden panel beside him. With a little help from two officials who gave the edges of the sheeting an encouraging yank, the white veil parted and fluttered to the ground. The Royal children, both German and English, gawped as if at an apparition. 'There was something', the *Daily Mail* said, 'in the attitude of the effigy seated enthroned, with the orb and the sceptre of power and authority which recalled the beautiful motherliness of her character', but in truth the statue, with its grandeur and size and its 2,000 tons of marble, did not much resemble the tiny, gentle, 'Granny' figure George remembered. The Kaiser, a neat, tight figure, his thick, clipped moustache twirled upwards and outwards at the ends, moved briskly forward to lay an evergreen wreath at his grandmother's feet. A salute from the Royal Horse Artillery was followed by the playing of the National Anthem, then the King beckoned Mr Thomas Brock, the architect of the monument, to approach. Mr Brock stepped forward, then knelt, the King touched him gently on the shoulder of his morning coat with his sword, and the newly-honoured Sir Thomas rose to his feet to more enthusiastic cheering. With that, the ceremony was over; May felt that the whole morning had been 'very well arranged'.

There was a celebratory lunch for the family, and that evening a dinner attended by the cream of English political and aristocratic society including the Prime Minister, the Foreign Secretary, the Home Secretary, the War Minister Viscount Haldane, Lord Kitchener, the Opposition leader Arthur Balfour, and several Dukes and their Duchesses. An expedition to attend a gala performance of *Money*, a popular comedy about the effects of wealth by the Victorian playwright and close friend of Charles Dickens, Edward Bulwer-Lytton, rounded off the evening. The theatre had been swagged in ivory- and gold-embroidered velvet and the boxes banked with tulips. The people in the waiting crowd were gratified to see how splendid the new Queen looked in her beautiful frock and diamonds. It was clear that May's generous bosom enabled her to carry off a lot of jewellery without appearing overladen. In a largely well-meaning joke, the French press were delighted to discover that a play on the French word for the supportive brassière, the *soutien-gorge*, described perfectly 'La Reine Anglaise'. Oh how they laughed whenever they found a way to refer to the Queen of England as the 'Soutien Georges'.

Over the next three days the Royal cousins were engulfed in a demanding social whirl that included a day's outing to Windsor, a

Naval and Military tournament at Olympia, and a Court Ball ('It began at 10 and was over at 1' gasped the exhausted May in her diary). They were guests of honour at the Coronation Exhibition at The White City that had opened earlier that week. Visitors enjoyed the illusion of travelling through the British Empire as they wandered through a succession of artfully decorated pavilions and installations, crossing from the steps of the Taj Mahal to a field in full harvest in Australia, past the Niagara Falls and towards the multi-turreted roofline of Balmoral Castle. The manuscripts of famous authors such as Rudyard Kipling and Marie Corelli proved a particular curiosity, having become 'a rare sight these days with the advent of the typewriter'.

After five exhausting days the German visit was over ('a great success', May noted) and Wilhelm and his Kaiserin went home to their castle at Potsdam outside Berlin in the expectation of returning only three weeks later for the Coronation. May knew she would have to brace herself for many more parties and functions before that date. What was more, she had been warned that the City of Norwich Alliance Caged Bird Association would be presenting her with a caged yellow canary for her birthday in two weeks' time. The bird was a particularly special example of its breed, having been raised by a shoemaker, George Camping, who had been 'in the fancy' for over forty years and had won a national competition to find the canary with the sweetest singing voice. But May had a sympathetic horror of caged birds.

Winston Churchill had been standing with the King and Queen and the Kaiser at the top of The Mall, his impassive face concealing his misgivings about the durability of the peace the statue personified. The day before the unveiling he had spoken in the House at the end of the Commons' debate on the controversial Parliament Bill, which had passed through the House with a majority of 121 votes and was now in the hands of a very divided House of Lords. Not that constitutional reform was the only challenge that faced the Government that summer. Churchill was grateful that for propriety's sake the suffragettes had agreed to a summer truce in their increasingly violent crusade. Relieved, policemen smoothed out their rolled-up mackintoshes (a thwack landing on a recalcitrant woman demonstrator was reported to be extremely painful) in preparation for a peaceful Coronation. But outside the small perimeter of Westminster the trade unions, especially those who represented the dock workers, were becoming increasingly dissatisfied with the way they were treated by their employers. Poor wages and a lack of guaranteed employment were inspiring the militant spirit of thousands of men up and down the country, and the union leaders were determined that their discontent be heard.

The threat to peace extended beyond the English coastline. Just yards from where Churchill stood on that sunny May day was a man whose lust for territorial power was unmistakable. He spoke fine words of family loyalty that morning, but the Kaiser was not as trustworthy as his cousin the King would have liked to believe. On his return to Potsdam he became immediately preoccupied with plans for deploying his new warship, *Panther*.

In his personal life Churchill was idyllically happy as he and his wife Clementine awaited the birth of their second child later in the month. His public life was not so serene, however. As he had written in his diary earlier in the year, 'All the world is changing at once.'

3

Late May

Nothing in the rules or intercourse of the Club shall interfere with the rancour or asperity of party politics.
                                    Rule 12 of The Other Club

THE SOUND OF whirring saws was never far away in central
London during those weeks. The scent of recently sawn
timber still hung in the air over the crowds that had attended the
unveiling of the Memorial, drifting across St James's Park from
Westminster Abbey, and was so strong that it almost succeeded in
swamping the fumes generated by traffic and horses. As the construction of Coronation viewing stands continued, passersby
were entertained by the sight of bowler-hatted officials jumping
up and down as if on a child's trampoline, to test the fragile platforms with their combined weight. The popular milk stall at the
Spring Gardens end of St James's Park was crowded with thirsty
customers and two cows – identical to the pair that had provided
Charles I with his last glass of fresh milk on his way to the exe-
cutioner's block – were working hard to fulfil the demand that
warm fine morning.

The settled May weather was fulfilling all the promise of the first
two sunny weeks of the month, and England had begun to dance
its way into high summer to the background sounds of Ragtime
and Stravinsky, humming bees and the fizz of champagne. The
cuckoo had been most effective in announcing its arrival in the
woods, where the oak and beech were, as *Country Life* magazine

had noticed, 'in all the glamour of their first fresh green wave.' A canopy of cream-coloured horse-chestnut blossom was visible high on the trees in London's Kensington Gardens and a scattering of buttercups and dandelions had begun to pattern the country meadows. In the cottage gardens the petals of tulips glowed and flashed in the first strong sunlight of the year. A summer breeze barely discernible except in the gentle lifting of a feather on a lady's hat suddenly faded entirely, leaving the air quite still.

With the gleaming new memorial behind him, Winston Churchill crossed The Mall and walked the short distance towards the Palace. Already famous enough for his likeness to have qualified for Madame Tussaud's waxworks, Winston with his 'slightly hunched shoulders from which his head jutted forward like the muzzle of a gun about to fire' – as his friend Violet Asquith put it – was instantly recognisable to the watching crowds, and a favourite subject of the daily cartoons in the popular half-pennies. He had admitted that to be given 'a nose on your face like a wart when really your nose is quite a serviceable and presentable member' could be distressing, but was 'resigned to and secretly pleased' by the notoriety that accompanied the humorous drawings. 'Just as eels get used to skinning,' he shrugged, 'so politicians get used to being caricatured.'

At 36 Winston Churchill was the youngest Home Secretary since Robert Peel nearly a hundred years earlier. Eloquent, inexhaustible and a radical risk-taker, Winston was a man both personally and professionally in full flight. He had accepted an invitation to dine that evening with Royal courtiers Lord Knollys and Lord Esher at the Café Royal in Piccadilly, promising to arrive at 8.30 sharp in order to allow time for dinner and, just as importantly, conversation before dashing to the House of Commons to hear reactions to that afternoon's presentation of the Budget by the Chancellor of the Exchequer, Lloyd George.

Meeting Winston at a party for the first time in 1906, Violet Asquith had found him striking not only in his 'magnificent and effortless use of language' but for his impressive and ambitious arrogance. 'We are all worms,' he told her, 'but I do believe I am a glow worm.' Winston had struggled with a lisp since his school-days and had not yet succeeded in eradicating it entirely: the 'S' sound continued to emerge like a 'sh'. But speech transformed his youthful face and Winston became by turns orator, pugilist, states-man; at times his expression was reminiscent of a puckish school-boy's. His face was incapable of concealing a secret and he was not afraid of using language that others considered over the top and grandiloquent. 'Winston thinks with his mouth,' remarked the Prime Minister.

Another young parliamentarian, who habitually sat opposite the House of Commons' green leather benches occupied by Winston and his Liberal colleagues, was almost as notorious as the young Home Secretary. Frederick Edwin Smith, generally known to everyone as 'F.E.', was a brilliantly successful lawyer and a Conservative back-bencher, just two years older than Winston and a man of electrifying oratory. Although he did not hold a job in the Shadow Cabinet, he was arguably the most famous member of the party after the former Prime Minister and present Opposition leader, Arthur Balfour. His opinions were so out-spoken that occupants of the Government benches often left the debating chamber reeling from his attacks, and with Balfour's position in the Tory party hierarchy seemingly precarious that summer, F.E. was assumed by many to be at the forefront of those in line for the leadership of his party. He and Winston held differ-ing views on almost all the fundamental issues of the current political term – on the power of the trade unions, on the pro-posed curbing of the powers of the House of Lords, on the enfranchisement of women. In fact, Winston's politics differed so violently from F.E's that he had even crossed the floor of the House to leave them behind. Yet despite their thrilling exchanges of political vitriol, F.E. Smith was Winston's greatest friend.

From the moment of their first meeting, shortly after F.E. gave his maiden speech, Winston was enchanted, dazzled and en-snared. He was reminded of the swagger, the confidence and the daring charisma of his own father, Lord Randolph Churchill. Though Lord Randolph had often behaved towards his son with detachment and indifference, Winston had grown to idolise his father. After his death in 1895 Winston's passionate allegiance intensified with time, rather than diminishing. Liberated from the disapproval and anxiety that had crushed him as a child, in adult-hood he was free to revere unchallenged a now-silent tormenter. In F.E. Smith he found not only someone to admire, but a soul-mate. The friendship became, in Winston's words, 'one of my most precious possessions. It was never disturbed by the fiercest party fighting.' Although F.E. was capable of breathtaking per-sonal insults in public, cautioning the Labour party that 'the socialists had better not cheer the name of Mr Churchill for he will most likely steal their clothes when they go bathing – if they do bathe, which I doubt', the friendship remained unassailable. 'It was never marred by the slightest personal differences or mis-understanding,' Winston explained; 'it grew stronger . . . never did I separate from him without having learnt something and enjoyed myself besides.'

Falling jubilantly upon an irresistible opportunity for political lampooning, the preceding year the *Punch* cartoonist had summed up their intriguing cross-party friendship. The two young men were depicted sitting on a sofa in such affectionate intimacy that their leaning heads were actually touching; they are reading a biography of Benjamin Disraeli and beneath the caption 'Students on the Make' they conduct the following exchange:

Mr F.E. Smith: 'Master of Epigram – like me!'
Mr Winston Churchill: 'Wrote a novel in his youth – like me!'
Together: 'Travelled in the east – like us. How does it end?'

The supporters of the 'Balfour Must Go' campaign had found themselves a strong candidate. There were also rumours that if F.E. did not become leader of his own party he might join the Liberals, and the two friends would thus merge their considerable strengths. In May of 1911 this controversial friendship of several years came to the attention of the wider public outside the chamber of the House of Commons. Dining with Knollys and Esher, Winston not only reviewed with them the success of the day's ceremonies in the Mall but also discussed the proposed name of the grand joint venture he and F.E. planned for the summer, the political club they were to found.

The members of London's clubs had been particularly suspicious of F.E. after he was discovered using the 'Gentlemen's Facilities' of the Liberal Club – of which he was, for obvious reasons, *not* a member. The Club was, however, conveniently situated on the corner of Whitehall Place and the Victoria Embankment, equidistant, in case of a pressing need, between his home in Pimlico and the House of Commons. When challenged as he emerged from the 'Facilities', F.E. had further damned himself by asking the affronted doorman, in a tone of surprise, 'Oh, is it a club as well?'

In December 1910 the distinguished literary institution founded in 1764 by Dr Samuel Johnson and the painter Sir Joshua Reynolds, known simply as 'The Club', had blackballed both Winston and F.E. Later, over a weekend at Winston's ancestral home, Blenheim, they devised their revenge. In consultation with Knollys and Esher, it was agreed to call the new venture 'The Other Club'.

On Thursday 18 May The Other Club was launched at the Savoy Hotel in the Strand. F.E. Smith kept a room in the Savoy, and staff there were accustomed to the brilliant young lawyer announcing that he would be preparing for a case the following day by working through the night. Having ordered two dozen oysters and a bottle of Bollinger champagne for sustenance he would remain locked in his room with his favourite pet dog and emerge the following morning, a carnation in his button-hole, dressed and prepared for the law courts. On that Thursday evening F.E. made his way to the grand mirrored and chandeliered Pinafore Room (so named by Richard D'Oyly Carte, under whose patronage the popular Gilbert and Sullivan operettas –

among them *HMS Pinafore* – had always been performed). There, at the invitation of F. E. and Winston, an extraordinary gathering had begun to assemble.

Many found the brilliant company of these two young men stimulating, but that reaction was by no means unanimous. Winston was viewed with profound scepticism by some members not only of the parliamentary Opposition, particularly those with roots in the aristocracy, but also by some in his own party. The grandson of a duke of Marlborough, born at Blenheim, one of the grandest houses in the land, Winston seemed to some to have betrayed his birthright when he crossed the floor to join the Liberals a few years earlier. He was opportunistic. He was flagrantly ambitious. He lacked modesty. He was unpredictable, verging on reckless. He was a man to be watched, with caution. F. E. Smith, a character of equal arrogance and a Conservative with no acknowledged 'background', inspired similar distrust. In a few of the grand social circles in which senior parliamentarians were accustomed to move, Winston and F. E. headed the list of untouchables. With considerable self-knowledge Winston admitted, 'I have a tendency, against which I should perhaps be on my guard, to swim against the stream.' Violet Asquith wondered whether Winston was 'inebriated by his own words', adding 'I did not care. I only knew that I was.'

Violet's pleasure in finding herself next to Winston at dinner was not a feeling universally shared. He was capable of remaining silent even in the company of the most scintillating conversationalist. So irritated was Lady Westmorland by his speechless self-absorption one day that she rose from the table, snatching up her knife and fork, and finished her lunch standing at the sideboard. Eventually Winston noticed the empty seat next to him and leaning across to Violet asked, in genuine puzzlement, 'what happened to that jolly little trout?' The society hostess Lady Desborough had observed with some irritation how at country house parties he 'leads general conversation on the hearthrug solely addressing himself in the looking glass.' The ill-judged

'Sidney Street Siege' earlier in the year had not been forgotten. A nine-day blockade at a house in Stepney in which a group of Latvian anarchists had barricaded themselves ended when a building caught fire and three policemen were killed. Winston was in the bath when he was told of the shoot-out and after ordering a detachment of Scots Guards and 750 more policemen to the scene, he dressed and hurried there himself. Directors of moving-picture palaces licked their lips over crowd-pulling footage of the Rt Hon. Winston Churchill, wearing an expensive astrakhan-collared coat and a silk top hat, personally directing the fire brigade while crouched in a doorway. He looked like a trigger-happy boy scout or, as a gleeful press put it, 'Marlborough facing the army of Louis XIV'. Such behaviour was viewed as unwise, interfering, and neither dignified, nor appropriate for a Home Secretary. Even Margot Asquith was unsure of her husband's cabinet colleague, writing in her diary: 'While Winston is love-able and sincere there is not much judgement behind his genius.' Others kept their reservations to themselves, and the inaugural dinner of The Other Club began with a reading of the Rules in a mood of optimistic fellowship.

The House of Commons was sometimes said to be the most elite club in the land, but this new venture was more select still. Its members were to number no more than 40, including a maximum of 24 MPs, these to come from the Conservative and Liberal parties. Representing either side of the political divide, the Liberal Chancellor of the Exchequer Lloyd George and the heavyweight Conservative Andrew Bonar Law were the most impressive recruits. No member of the Labour Party was considered eligible for an invitation to join, but the Club Register included distin-guished gentlemen from the Services and the worlds of business and the arts, and a few editors of national newspapers. T. E. Lawrence, a bright 23-year-old Oxford graduate working at the British Museum on plans for a dig in Mesopotamia was among those asked to become a regular, as were the actor and producer Herbert Beerbohm Tree, Lord Kitchener and Lord Northcliffe.

Sir George Riddell, owner of the *News of the World* though not as yet an actual 'newspaper baron', was another who attended that first dinner. The presence of the King's joint private secretaries, convivial Lord Esher and austere Lord Stamfordham, lent an irrefutable respectability. Representatives of the Church were barred. So were bores. And women. The membership was essentially made up of those who were young, witty and unconventional, several of them only hovering on the decorous fringes of the Establishment.

The chairmanship of The Club was to be rotated between the members of the two political parties. It was said that a waiter was co-opted to make up the number in the event that only 13 guests turned up to dine – until it was realised that he could not be trusted to keep his mouth shut, and a large wooden black cat was imported to fill the extra seat in his stead. 'To Dine' was the ostensible object of The Other Club, but at £2 a head, the equivalent of a week's wage for the average working man, and despite the inclusion of a delightful pudding of 'poires rafraichies au citron avec la Bombe glacée pralinée' and some extremely fine wine, it was an expensive evening. Churchill always ordered 'off the menu' when it came to the dessert course. His choice of Roquefort cheese, a peeled pear and mixed ice cream never varied.

The unspoken purpose behind the Club was the lessening of deeply divided political hostilities over a delicious dinner. The founding members hoped that the animosity expressed daily between the two parties on opposite benches of the two Houses would be tempered, at least for the course of the Thursday gatherings. Though it was intended that the proceedings be 'wrapped in impenetrable mystery', news of the appointment of the Chancellor of the Exchequer as Chairman of the Wine and Cigars Committee had somehow already been leaked to the press.

Rule number twelve laid down that a gathering of The Other Club was never to become a forum for the plotting of coalition plans. Written, as were all the rules, by F. E. Smith himself, it also dictated that 'Nothing in the rules or intercourse of the Club shall interfere with the rancour or asperity of party politics.' The Club offered a refuge, a place where conviviality thrived and a tolerant exchange of views was encouraged, during a summer in which party politics were already threatening to become more vicious than most members could recall. The Club was a symbolic manifestation of the friendship between Winston Churchill and F.E. Smith. The first evening was considered a triumph by everyone who attended, and all agreed to gather again at the Savoy the next Thursday, and thereafter on alternate weeks.

When F.E. and Winston had first met in the Commons in 1906, although an MP of only a few months' standing, F.E. Smith was even then a considerable political figure. His maiden speech, a triumph of sheer audacity, had brought him overnight fame, his reputation made as soon as he came to the end of his oration from the back of the Tory benches. He was tall and slim, with slick black hair, distinctively clean-shaven among the rows of moustachioed men; his pale high cheekbones contrasted dramatically with the crimson carnation he wore in his button-hole. In a beautifully cut tail-coat, his hands thrust deep into his pockets, he resembled a young blade who had sauntered in after a particularly successful day at the races. Violet Asquith was in the Speaker's Gallery that day, and realised when F.E. was invited by the Speaker to begin that some members of his own party were unaware of his identity. 'Who is this boy?' they grumbled. 'Haven't we got anyone better?' Maiden speeches are by convention short and uncontroversial, even deferential to all sides of the House; for *his* debut, F.E. dared to challenge the Government over their questionable tactics in winning the last election. 'Light badinage and cutting sarcasm came with equal dexterity in that even magnetic voice which never faltered, never failed,' wrote G.D. Faber admiringly in *The Times*; he went on to describe the speech as 'a long sustained tour-de-force which captivated and held friend and foe alike. His logic was inexorable; his denunciations were wonderful, his satire played like forked lightening.' Another MP marvelled how, during F.E's 'brilliant cluster of impertinences', he never once allowed an expression of utter contempt for the Liberals to leave his face. Violet Asquith watched from the gallery above as the Conservative rank and file 'shouted and roared in ecstasy, their leaders rolled about on the Front Bench in convulsions of amusement and delight.' As he sat down on the green leather bench at the end of an hour to the sound of a great ovation, she noticed 'a flutter of excitement in the Ladies' gallery', and a very important hostess leaned across to ask her if she knew how F.E. could be secured for a Saturday-to-Monday party. Invitations to dinner arrived from two of the most powerful figures in society, Lady Londonderry and Lady Desborough. A day after the speech, a hand-delivered envelope arrived at F.E's chambers: Lady Savile was having a very, very small party and would be pleased if Mr Smith could attend because the King had expressed a desire to meet him. *Everyone* wanted to know him. 'Who is this Effie Smith?' asked one distinguished old lady. 'She can't be a modest girl to be so talked about.'

Ambition had driven F.E. Smith all his life. 'The world continues to offer glittering prizes to those who have stout hearts and sharp swords,' he declared, determined to prove the truth of his words to himself. He was ambitious both materially and politically. In Winston's phrase, he wanted to make 'a great stock or scrip of securities'. The grandson of a Yorkshire miner, like Winston he had lost his father very young. He liked to talk about the poverty in which he had grown up after his father's death, and his story became elaborated in the telling: his elder daughter Elinor, with the insight, unforgivingness and brutality of youth, later revealed that her father came from a middle-class family in Birkenhead. 'He loved afterwards to exaggerate the miseries of his life, which was actually by no means wretched,' she explained. 'His father died when he was sixteen but as far as I can make out he lived until ten in complete comfort. If one reminded him of this he flew into a rage.'

After an impressive career in the Oxford Union while a scholar of Wadham College, F.E. altered his raw northern accent and practised the art of high living so effectively that no one on first meeting him dreamt that this sophisticated and arrogant young man had not been born into a life of privilege and breeding. There was an air of glamour about his arrest in a student demonstration during a visit to Oxford by Edward VII, while the story of how he had insulted Oscar Wilde by suggesting that that iconic figure was too narcissistically obsessed by his own life had become the stuff of undergraduate legend. After leaving Oxford F.E. read for the bar, to which he was called in 1899. In early 1906 he was elected Honourable Member for the constituency of Walton in Liverpool.

F.E. had been happily married to his accommodating wife Margaret since 1901. Margaret was neither disturbed by her husband's notoriety nor jealous of the time he spent in the Commons and on his legal commitments. The couple shared a love of their children and of sport, in particular tennis and riding. They had a country cottage near Oxford. Margaret was artistic and musical and had her own interests to absorb her. F.E. might enjoy discreet friendships with women, among them a chaste flirtation with a pretty girl named Frieda Dudley Ward, but for him it was the open doors to ambition-furthering salons to which these friendships often led that were important, rather than the liaisons themselves.

Winston's wife Clemmie did not share her husband's admiration. She liked Margaret Smith, but thought F.E. a most terrible influence on Winston, particularly in their joint passion for gambling. On the day Winston asked Clementine Hozier to marry him, F.E. and his wife Margaret were staying at Blenheim. As Winston and Clemmie left the little Greek temple in the park where she had accepted his proposal, Winston agreed to tell no one the news until Clemmie had found a chance to speak to her mother. But as they walked back to the house, they spotted F.E. Smith coming across the lawn towards them. Winston broke into a run and, to Clemmie's irritation, threw his arms around his friend and blurted out their secret.

In 1909 the Churchills had moved to 33 Eccleston Square, a cream terraced house on the Cubitt estate in the slightly scruffy, not-quite-Belgravia-smart area of Pimlico, just round the corner from Victoria Station. By 1911 they employed a manservant, a cook, two maids, and a nanny for the nearly-two-year-old Diana, who had been born in the house – this fairly modest household for such a senior minister, having recently been depleted: in April the butler Thomas Reynolds had left to make his fortune in New York (when a Mr Wild of 34th Street wrote to follow up Reynold's references, Winston, ever a man reluctant to forego personal involvement, found the time to write back himself to confirm that Reynolds did indeed have a certain style, though he 'was a little inclined to take advantage of easy going methods'). At about the same time the Churchills' cook Mrs Scrivens had given in her notice to apply for a post with Margarita Warwick of Hyde Park Square. But despite staffing problems, Number 33 was a happy place. The decoration of the house reflected Clemmie's gentle but elegant taste, though while briefly under the influence of Art Nouveau she had had her own room painted green, brown and orange, with a large orange tree laden with oranges appliquéd all over the walls. The French Ambassador, visiting one weekend, winced at the sight.

The most agreeable room in the house was the large first-floor library where Winston spent much time with their new lodger, the Foreign Secretary Sir Edward Grey. Clemmie had been delighted when the widowed Foreign Secretary, wanting a London base, accepted her husband's invitation to become a paying lodger at Eccleston Square, providing a welcome contribution to expenses to balance Winston's worrying extravagance. Winston was secretly pleased to have the daily company of a man whose calm balanced the ebullience of F.E. He liked to describe Edward Grey in Wordsworth's phrase, as 'a central peace at the heart of endless agitation'. During late-night talks in the library over glasses of fine cognac (at £27 a bottle) and Romeo and Julietta cigars, the two ministers became close friends, and to

Clemmie's pleasure Grey accepted an invitation to become a godfather to the baby she was expecting any day.

There was no coincidence in Winston's decision to live in that
pretty creamy terraced square. It was conveniently close to the
Houses of Parliament, yet not much of a taxi ride from the clubs
of Pall Mall and the dining room of the Ritz. And it was only a
few doors away from F.E., who had moved into number 70 in
1907. F.E.'s own son had been born there, and Winston was
Frederick Winston Furneaux's godfather. F.E. was delighted
when the compliment was returned and he was chosen – by
perhaps only one of the new parents – as the new Churchill baby's
second godfather.

Clemmie was not unjustified in her reservations about the
Smith household, for the goings-on inside Number 70 were definitely strange. F.E.'s daughter Elinor, though only nine years old,
had something of a reputation in the neighbourhood. One day
during a visit to her grandmother in adjoining Warwick Square
she had been sent out to play in the garden, and when hiding
behind a tree was pulled from her hiding-place by a gardener with
such force that in retaliation she kicked him. From that time she
was regarded as a child with delinquent tendencies, forbidden to
play in the garden again and confined to Eccleston Square, where
everyone stared at her and no other children would have anything
to do with her. And Elinor was not the only outlandish inhabi-
tant. In 1908 her parents had taken a cruise to Jamaica with a few
friends, among them the distinguished publisher John Murray.
While they were staying at the Constant Springs Hotel in
Kingston F.E. struck up an enthusiastic friendship with a Mr
Simpson, a West Indian he considered to be of 'ravishing appearance, a sable Apollo'. Persuading him to return with them to
England proved difficult until F.E. agreed that Mr Simpson might
bring with him the two gentle ponies he had adopted from the
Blue Mountains. But something about the London air sent them
mad: one attacked and destroyed a delivery cart in the street while
the other fell into a deep depression and lay down in a heap to die

under the dull English skies. No such loss of energy affected
Simpson himself. Whispers that on arrival he had eaten several
housemaids for dinner were never confirmed, but the cook swore
it was true that one afternoon Simpson approached her insisting
she provide him with a white cock for a ritualistic slaughter
demanded by his religion. Ransacking the larder of Eccleston
Square and finding no such bird, Simpson made a lunge for the
throat of the cook's green parrot Joey. Some residents were
appalled at the 'pagan behaviour' that lurked behind the placid
façade of number 70, but others felt Joey deserved his end, as he
had an unpleasant habit of chuckling to lure the curious over to
his cage, where he would snap at their noses through the bars.

On 24 May, six days after The Other Club had demonstrated
that it was possible for cross-party conversation to take place in
private without damaging consequences, F. E. Smith decided to
throw a cross-party party – a costume ball, in fact – partly for fun
and partly to show the press that parliamentary harmony was
achievable outside Westminster. His co-host was to be Lord
Winterton, who as an Irish peer was only eligible to sit in the
House of Commons. He owned seven hundred houses in the
London borough of St George's in the East, bringing him an
enviable annual income of £15,000, and at 28 was not only the
youngest Member of Parliament but one of the most outspoken
and also the tallest, towering over Winston – a mere five foot eight
– as he attacked him relentlessly for his policies. He exasperated
Winston, who wrote to Clemmie that 'Lord Winterton's
behaviour is detestable – he contributes nothing to any debate but
his offensive insolence.' Predictably, Winterton was a founder-
member of The Other Club.

By the third week of May, Clemmie Churchill's baby was
already two weeks overdue. An evening spent with F. E. Smith and
Lord Winterton was not a welcome prospect at any time, but she
was determined to make an appearance on this important symbolic occasion. The ball was to take place at Claridge's Hotel in
Mayfair, on the same evening as the second 'Court' of the summer

season. Those not attending the Court dined at one of several large parties given before the ball, including one by Lady Cunard at Claridge's itself; Lord Winterton and the F.E. Smiths were among the guests at another given by the Duchess of Marl-borough at Sunderland House. Afterwards guests made their way to Claridge's, where the beautiful salon was decorated with blue hydrangeas and Madonna lilies, while the adjoining dancing room was 'gay with rambler roses'.

The joint hosts had chosen their outfits with care. Lord Winterton was splendidly dressed as a *sergent de ville* with a cocked hat and aiguillettes and greeted everyone in colloquial French, while F.E. was in a white satin suit and powdered wig, the distin-guished and stylish costume of an eighteenth-century courtier. His wife was also in unrelieved white, her gown contrasting beau-tifully in its simplicity with the vibrancy of that worn by Lady Marjorie Manners, who had come as a rainbow. Lady Ripon, patron of the Royal Opera House at Covent Garden and busy as sponsor with preparations for the arrival in June of the Ballets Russes, wore a flamboyantly embroidered Russian dress, and a Russian diadem encircled her head. The Duchess of Westminster was a gorgeous sight in yellow and red, the colours of the Spanish flag, her white mantilla fastened with crimson roses.

Winston did not, however, appear comfortable with such an unashamed demonstration of parliamentary unity at an occasion as frivolous as a ball, and even Clemmie's serene presence as a demure nun in a full white robe did not serve to lighten his mood that evening. He had arrived in a dashing cape of scarlet – 'Has he come as a fireman?' the guffaw went round, in less than subtle reference to the events at Sidney Street. The *Tatler* professed itself disappointed: 'One expected so much and obtained so little, with only a red cloak flung hastily over his bowed shoulders,' sighed the society magazine. The other senior politicians had confined themselves to standard evening dress, but mocking Winston was an amusing pursuit. He always provided excellent copy, and the papers were only just getting over his latest escapade, the case of a Dartmoor shepherd who had been sent to jail countless times for robbing the village church collection box. As ever, Winston could not resist becoming personally involved in the detail, awarding the shepherd a compassionate release and finding him work and a home on a Welsh farm. The gesture backfired: the shepherd missed the companionship of prison life, stole some Welsh shillings and, smiling beatifically, was returned to his familiar cell. Once again Winston had provided the House and the press with an excuse to poke fun at their favourite target.

Winston and Clemmie stayed long enough at the Claridge's party to mingle with the other guests, among them the captivating debutante Lady Diana Manners (whose face, easily as beautiful as Helen's, his private secretary Eddie Marsh and Winston had both agreed, a 'thousand ships would be worth launching for'; Clemmie Churchill was the only other woman on whom they had bestowed such an accolade). Other personalities gliding along to the music in the ballroom included a couple of princesses, several duchesses, the Prime Minister, the leader of the Conservative party, and Lord Curzon. At midnight the MP Waldorf Astor made a flamboyant entrance wearing a peer's robes but with a workman's trousers and boots. A card with the number 499 was attached to one side of his coronet and the words 'one more vacancy' were scrawled on a card pinned to the other side, advertising the votes required to pass the Parliament Bill.

This allusion to the delicate negotiations for the Parliament Bill was a provocation too far for one member of the Second Chamber. Two days after the ball, *The Times* published a letter signed simply 'A Peer' in which the writer denounced the ball for 'being out of place in view of the alleged seriousness' of the inter party and inter house tension dominating the day to day life of both Houses at Westminster. 'It was', stormed the peer in angry condemnation, 'a painful surprise to read of smart ladies in every variety of costume from Cleopatra to a pink tulle ballet girl and among them elderly peers masquerading as Tudor kings.' It was also reported, spluttered the un-named Lord (who had *not* received an invitation) that even the Prime Minister had been seen laughing at all the high jinks. Amused by the letter, Winston recovered his mood and telephoned through an order to his wine merchants Payne and Sons for a dozen half-bottles of Moselle, for he seemed to be running short, and the baby still had not arrived. Small wonder that Clemmie worried endlessly about the household expenses. The proposed salary of £400 a year for Members of Parliament was not scheduled to come into effect until August: traditionally, MPs had funded themselves, from a private income or earnings outside the House of Commons. When F. E. was facing a large bill, he simply took on a new legal case; Winston made some money from his books and articles, but had no such lucrative resource, his father having died leaving many debts.

Life without champagne was inconceivable for Winston. He described the wine as imparting 'a feeling of exhilaration, the nerves are braced, the imagination is agreeably stirred, the wits become more nimble.' Nor was life imaginable without a regular supply of Havana cigars. Winston had been committed to them since a visit to Cuba in his twenties, and a new consignment, large and small, wrapped and naked, had just arrived from the Haymarket shop of Fribourg & Treyer. There was a romance about a cigar. 'Smoking cigars is like falling in love,' he wrote: 'first you are attracted to its shape and then you must always remember never, never to let the flame go out.' There were further drains on the Churchills' precarious income. In early May Winston had ordered a jaunty red Napier car from the newly established workshop in the Lower Richmond Road. It would cost him £610, about three times the annual rent of Eccleston Square. His finely woven pink silk underwear from the Army and Navy Stores cost £80 a year. 'I have a very delicate and sensitive cuticle which demands the finest covering,' he once told Violet Asquith, rolling up his sleeve to show her.

And yet for all his expensive and exclusive tastes, Winston had an exceptional grasp of what made up the social complexities of England which set him apart from the conventions and hedonism associated with a privileged birth. 'All the glitter of the world appeals to me,' he wrote, 'but not thank god in comparison to serious things.' During those long light summer evenings, Grey and Winston found Germany's increasing desire to demonstrate her naval superiority in Europe becoming a dominant subject in their conversation. A couple of years earlier Winston had spent part of one Parliamentary recess in Germany at the personal invitation of the Kaiser, who was happy to show off his increasing military resources. Churchill had been impressed by and envious of the army's size, and of its ability to march 35 miles a day. Grey realised during their talks that Winston was 'exhilarated by the air of crisis and high events', and was fascinated and concerned by the developing aggression across the Channel. Especially worrying was a conversation between King George and the Kaiser touching on German intentions in Morocco that Churchill had overheard during the Kaiser's visit to London for the Memorial unveiling. George had given his cousin his approval for the *Panther* to be sent to monitor the French occupation of disputed territory in Agadir, although Grey had given the French Ambassador *his* word that Britain would support France if Germany attacked French soil. Two years earlier, while Edward VII was still on the throne, a popular song had been familiar on the streets of London's East End:

> There'll be no wo'ar
> As long as there's a King like good King Edward.
> There'll be no wo'ar
> For 'e hates that sort of thing!
> Mothers needn't worry
> As long as we've a King like good King Edward.
> Peace with 'Onner
> Is his motter
> So God Save the King!

And despite 'Good King Edward's' death a bright optimism persisted, a belief that England, with its history of peace and its pre-eminence in the world, was almost divinely protected from foreign aggression. Some people considered the 'German Peril' laughable. Lord Charles Beresford would follow a cheery 'Good morning' with a jocular 'One day nearer the German War!' A new best-selling book, *The Great Illusion* by Norman Angell, argued that a war with Germany would be impossible because of financial deterrents on both sides. Viscount Esher, Edward VII's closest advisor and friend who remained an influential presence at Court, had been particularly convinced by Angell's thesis. The current King's ministers felt differently.

As a senior Cabinet minister Winston could not avoid the Royal Courts, and chose to attend on Friday 19 May, the day after the inaugural meeting of The Other Club, and again six days later, on Thursday 25 May. The familiar music of Strauss and Lehar and the quadrille, waltz and polka on the dance programme seemed more than a little tired to Winston, who lacked any enthusiasm for such social occasions. Without his wife by his side he would much rather have stayed at home. The French Ambassador was also bored – in Paris they were learning to tango.

Winston was not known for his elegance of dress (the *Tailor and Cutter* magazine had described the clothes he wore at his marriage as 'one of the greatest failures as a wedding garment we have ever seen, giving the wearer a sort of glorified coachman appearance'), but arrived at Buckingham Palace wearing 'full dress uniform', according to Lady Ottoline, wife of the MP Philip Morrell, at whose house in Bedford Square in Bloomsbury he had dined earlier. Lady Ottoline thought he looked like a 'Mock Napoleon'. Among the other guests at dinner that evening were a young and beautiful writer, Virginia Stephen, and Roger Fry, the artist responsible for bringing the controversial Post-Impressionist exhibition to London the preceding winter. Winston dominated the party, speaking of politics in detail and making the subject sound to Ottoline 'like high mathematics for he is very rhetorical and has a volcanic complicated way of talking.' Winston did manage to abandon politics for long enough to placate her by admiring two etchings by Picasso that were hanging in her hall. Later, at the Palace, he had an agreeable conversation with the King, who promised him a seat for Clemmie in the Royal Box at the Coronation. She did not expect to feel well enough after the baby's birth to sit through the ceremony in the packed, claustrophobic pews of Westminster Abbey, and was very touched when she learned of the King's thoughtful gesture.

Two distressing pieces of news over the next couple of days momentarily distracted people from parties and politics. On Sunday 21 May, at the French end of the Paris–Madrid aeroplane race, one airborne competitor banked too steeply over the heads of those watching on the ground, and lost control. One blade of the propeller came loose and flew into the crowd, shearing off the arm of Monsieur Berteaux, the French Minister of War, and killing him outright. *The Times,* aware that British Royalty frequently attended demonstrations of new breakthroughs in the science of flying, warned of 'the consequences of the slightest mishap when machines of such terrific energy are forced through the air.' Winston was one of many who had began to develop a passion for flying, and in a rare moment of united concern Clemmie persuaded F.E. to beg him to give up this hazardous hobby. Winston was not convincing in his reluctant agreement to look out for his own safety, but the next day tabled a motion in the House that the flying of aircraft over central London during the Coronation celebrations should be banned. Flying technology was clearly not reliable enough, and it would be folly to risk the annihilation of most of the crowned heads of Europe, shortly to be gathered in the capital. Stately-home owners were also given a cautionary scare when on 23 May a dreadful fire destroyed Sledmere, the Yorkshire home of Sir Tatton Sykes. The aged baronet, who appeared more corpulent than he really was from his habit of wearing four or five overcoats at once, sat on the lawn in an armchair lamenting his unsalvageable luncheon cutlet and watching as servants, farmers, villagers and children lugged 'a marble statue of Apollo weighing a ton' from the flames.

On Sunday 28 May at Eccleston Square, four days after the fancy-dress ball at Claridge's, and conveniently for the demands of a sitting Parliament and a husband who was a busy Minister, Clemmie at last gave birth to a boy, a brother for Diana. Although officially the baby was to be called Randolph, after Winston's father, he was nicknamed the 'Chumbolly', the name of a beautiful flower found in north-west India and also the Persian word for a healthy and chubby new-born baby. The Churchills were liberal with affectionate family nicknames, and now there were four: Randolph the Chumbolly, Diana the Puppy Kitten, Winston the Pug, and Clemmie the Kat.

The day after Randolph was born Clemmie wrote to thank her mother-in-law for the lovely roses she had sent, and tell her that 'the baby is sweet and another little Winston with fiery hair'. The delivery had been long and difficult but Clemmie managed to write with some sympathy, for Jennie's second marriage, to George Cornwallis-West, had begun to founder. American-born Jennie Jerome was a dazzling beauty in the eyes of everyone who saw her. According to the Queen of Romania, 'her eyes were large and dark, her mouth mobile with delicious almost mischievous curves, her hair blue-black and glossy.' Meeting her at Vice Regal Lodge in Dublin as recently-married 22-year-old Lady Randolph Churchill, Lord D'Abernon wrote of her as one in a state of hyperbolical trance: she was 'Radiant, translucent and intense. A diamond star in her hair, her favourite ornament – its lustre dimmed by the flashing glory of her eyes. More of the panther than of the woman in her look but with a cultivated intelligence unknown to the jungle.' To her son she was a heroine from a children's story: 'Like a fairy princess, a radiant being possessed of limitless riches and power,' he wrote. 'She shone for me like the Evening Star. I loved her dearly – but at a distance.' Before his marriage she was friend, sister and sweetheart to Winston, as well as his mother. She also became his literary tutor, encouraging his reading by sending him all of Gibbon and Macaulay, guiding his mind towards the great writers and historians. His loyalty to her remained undimmed, but Clemmie was aware that Jennie might just now be feeling neglected by her adored and usually adoring son, and took care to explain that 'Winston is in the House all the time this week – no dinner – no time for anything,' adding her own gesture of affection: 'I can't bear that you should be sad.'

The first politician to send Winston 'hearty congratulations' on Randolph's birth was Austen Chamberlain, former Chancellor in Balfour's Conservative Government. For a day or so at the end of May 1911 politics were not Winston's priority, as he boasted to Clemmie with all the pride of a new father that 'many congratulations are offered me upon the son. With that lack of jealousy which ennobles my nature, I lay them all at your feet.' Two days later he was back in the House, attacking the judges who had been harsh on trade union leaders and arguing the case for securing 'freedom of political opinion' for the individual worker, 'and for the trade union organisations freedom from the embarrassment of perpetual litigation'.

Winston realised that the momentum of the unions' discontent was growing in power and intensity. F.E. Smith was one of the advocates for the restriction of trade union powers, seeing more advantages in the power of unorganised protest. That day in the House he argued his point against Winston with characteristic tenacity and eloquence; immediately afterwards the two men left London together for a few days, their personal relationship as harmonious as ever. Reluctant as he was to leave Clemmie so soon after Randolph's birth, Winston always looked forward to the annual week's summer camp of the Oxfordshire Yeomanry at Blenheim – a military exercise the military-minded ex-soldier found hugely enjoyable, and by no means all work. F.E. also enjoyed these camps, which he attended in his capacity as an officer of the Buckinghamshire Yeomanry. Margaret Smith knew what went on: 'They behaved like Regency rakes,' she declared. In the early hours of a summer morning the two friends had been sitting on upended barrels in F.E.'s bell-tent with Winston's cousin, the Duke of Marlborough. The tallow candles that had illuminated the evening's gambling were no longer required; dawn was breaking. F. E. had moved into his camp bed but was still awake. The Duke asked what were to be the stakes for the final game of poker. 'Your bloody palace if you like?' suggested F. E. to the Duke from beneath the bedclothes. Instead they all fell asleep.

F. E. and his family loved their weekends at the house Winston had described as 'an Italian palace in an English park without apparent incongruity'. F.E.'s son wrote that 'our pulses quickened every year as we left the torpid streets of Woodstock and passed under the first grey arch into the domain of the Duke of Marlborough.' The three-acre house was magical for children, with endless rooms to explore, including the magnificent library where Perkins, the resident organist from Birmingham, would play a Bach fugue oblivious of the high chatter of the assembled adults and the children who lounged on their backs on white bearskins, staring at the painted, star-spattered ceiling. F. E. also loved his solo visits for the yeomanry summer camp – but had been known to fall asleep for hours beneath the lookout tree in which, as their commanding officer, he had directed his soldiers to hide. This year a loving but cautionary letter addressed to Winston arrived from Eccleston Square: 'Please be a good Pug and not destroy the good of your little open air holiday by smoking too many fat cigars.' But Clemmie was aware that her request might prove futile: 'This recommendation comes rather late,' she conceded, a wry smile barely concealed within her words.

On the last day of May the *Times* reporter in Belfast filed a three-line story: 'In brilliant weather and in the presence of hundreds of spectators the new eight hundred and fifty foot White Star liner was successfully launched from the shipyard of Messrs Harland and Wolfe a few minutes after noon.' The ship was described in the current issue of *The Shipbuilder Marine Engineer* journal as 'practically unsinkable'. A fourth funnel had been hastily added when White Star realised – a little late – that the rival super-liners *Mauritania* and *Lusitania* carried four. The last-minute 'steam' pipe on the new ship, while purely cosmetic, provided convenient extra space for ventilation and for the storage of pets. The ship steamed her way towards Portsmouth, where she would join her sister ship *Olympic* for the first of their sea trials. *Olympic*, which had set out a few weeks earlier, was equipped with a roller-skating rink, a gym, and a goldfish pond to keep the anglers on board happy.

The technological innovations of the eleventh year of the century seemed increasingly impressive, while certainties belonging to the earlier century were vanishing. The horse-drawn buses had all but disappeared, and the mood of the third gathering of The Other Club in the Pinafore Room at the Savoy was somewhat dampened by the announcement on 31 May of the death of Sir William Gilbert, the Savoy Opera's librettist. Sir William, aged 75, in apparent good health, had been taking an early summer swim in the lake at his home at Harrow Weald when the lady friend accompanying him ran into trouble in the water. Sir William had drowned while trying to save her life.

Temperatures had dipped a little since 20 May and a breeze had been building, but on the last day of the first month of the summer the heat had returned, beneath skies 'sultry, oppressive and dull'. The *Daily Mail* observed that 'even ladies did not succeed in looking cool', but nothing would deter the race-goers travelling down to Epsom for the 1911 Coronation Derby, and the forecast had contained nothing to alarm them. Winston remained in London, spending the afternoon in an almost empty House of Commons. The fine racing weather had tempted many MPs to Epsom, but one of those who remained behind, Mr Lyttelton, a Tory, raised the rumbling question of the proposed restrictions on the legal power of the Union leaders that F.E. supported and Winston opposed. It seemed to Winston that Lyttelton had a reprehensible lack of sympathy for and understanding of the appalling conditions under which non-unionised labourers worked. He lost his temper, and according to one report was driven into a 'passion of fury'. Scribbling a few short words on a piece of paper, he passed it in silence across the floor to Lyttelton: his response to Lyttelton's 'monstrous allegations' was couched in terms the Home Secretary was 'unable to use openly in the house'.

When Queen Mary arrived at the Epsom racecourse there was scarcely enough wind to lift the Royal Ensign over the grandstand. Wearing a gown of delicate mauve and carrying her by now familiar posy of pink carnations, she watched with her husband as the horse Sunstar won the big race by a head, although he stumbled so severely at the moment he reached the winning post that he was led into the winner's enclosure limping badly. Newspaper sketchers rushed to the enclosure with their pads and pencils – press photographers, regarded as excessively intrusive, were banned from Royal race meetings. Race officials were on their guard, however, as some enterprising punters had been caught with cameras disguised as race glasses.

As the race-goers left the Epsom stands the sun was just visible through the veil of clouds, a shimmering ball of hot metal. Early that evening the stable lads taking the horses for a final gallop on the Downs heard a distant rumble, and as dusk began to settle there was a stupendous crash, followed by lightning which landed in flat white patches, irradiating rooms with a 'ghastly illumination'. Hailstones the size of sovereigns began to fall, and rain hissed and whipped against windowpanes. Forty-five cars travelling back to London had to be abandoned between Epsom and Sutton. Four horses were killed by lightning that evening and seventeen people died, including a stable lad in a van at the course, two policemen, and Mrs Hester, a gravedigger's wife, who had slipped out to the village churchyard to take her husband a cup of tea as he worked. She died in front of him, crushed by the graveyard wall that collapsed under the force of lightning and fell on top of her.

The summer was turning bad. For the preceding two weeks the press had been reporting the ship owners' view that the threat of a new dock strike was unlikely to come to anything, and on 18,

23 and 31 May reports indicated that the dock workers' discontent was being defused. But the strength of feeling in the ports up and down the country had been underestimated. Discontent over poor pay, irregular employment and unpaid overtime had been simmering for a generation, and expression of these grievances had begun to resurface during the last couple of years. In the early summer of 1911 the press was taken in by the confidence of the dock owners, who felt they could contain their unsettled work force. But the dock owners had failed to reckon with Ben Tillett, an impressive, implacable and seasoned trade unionist, leader of the Dockers' Union and a man bent on seeing justice for the men he represented. Ben Tillett was viewed by the Government with particular caution, for he could also command the potentially powerful support of other fledgling transport unions – including the Railway Union, representing the men on whom the efficient flow of food, drink and other goods to all parts of the country depended. It was predicted that temperatures would continue to climb during the summer, and Winston feared the consequences of strikes in very hot weather. He was determined to keep the unrest under control, at least until after the Coronation, and for the next few weeks he was successful.

But if Winston feared the pervading aura of unpredictability, unpredictability was exactly the state of affairs that Lady Diana Manners embraced. Considered one of the most striking of the season's debutantes, she was looking forward to the summer ahead when she would be 'out' and licensed to behave exactly as she wished.

4

Early June

We were on the go with a sort of frenzied madness of
pleasure-seeking throughout every one of our waking hours.
Mrs Hwfa Williams

We were half-mad with hilarity.
Lady Diana Manners,
The Rainbow Comes and Goes

LADY DIANA MANNERS was exhausted. On Thursday 1 June
she emerged from her latest ball into the sunlight of a summer
morning and was helped across the few steps from the door of
Devonshire House in London's Park Lane to her carriage by the
famous red-breasted, top-hatted 'linkman' Mr Piddlecock, who
gave her a cheery 'Good morning'. As she was driven the short
distance *en chaperone* with her mother from Devonshire House to
her family's London home in Arlington Street off Piccadilly, she
watched the dawn ritual of the streets being hosed down by men
in rubber boots and rubber hats. She had been dancing for six
hours in the white silk evening dress she had made herself, with
coloured scarves wound turban-style around her curly hair. Her
feet, tightly encased in pointy shoes, hurt as she stepped down
from the carriage onto the cobblestones. Diana thought back on
the relentless partying of the last two weeks, the first of her first
Season as a debutante, and knew that with all the lunches, dinners,
theatres and balls of the forthcoming month, she would be writing
at least five 'Collinses' a day. These thank-you notes, requiring

extensive consultation of a recognised dictionary in order to make them sufficiently original, accurate and ingratiating, took their nickname from the obsequious gratitude that flowed from the pen of Mr Collins in Jane Austen's novel *Pride and Prejudice*. These letters were a great drain on time and imagination.

Diana had recently attracted some comment for wearing the same Velásquez 'Infanta' dress to two costume balls in a row. But she did not care. With its off-the-shoulder boned bodice and full hooped silk skirt it was spectacular enough to merit a second outing, particularly when enhanced by a thick black feathered hair-piece and a double layering of crimson lipstick (which raised more eyebrows), and had brought her triumph in the competition at the Savoy Ball for 'best lady's costume'. She had been presented with a prize of 250 guineas – roughly the equivalent of five years' pay for the average labourer – and a four-hundred-stone diamond and gold pendant. Diana thought the money would come in useful for buying books.

The press was jubilant on her behalf, because the opposition had been stiff. The runner-up was the beautiful Russian dancer Anna Pavlova, who won a sixty-guinea beauty case for her wonderful costume from her native land. The prize for the most effective costume worn by a man had gone to the Hon. Wilfred Egerton, dressed as a Chinaman. Winston Churchill's mother Jennie Cornwallis-West had made a stunning entrance as Empress Theodora, in an embroidered Byzantine cope; the Duchess of Marlborough was splendid as Madame de Pompadour; the Earl of Shrewsbury was menacing as an Apache Indian with full feather headdress and glinting knife; and Lady Northcliffe, wife of the multi-millionaire newspaper proprietor, had thought it would be amusing to step out of her life of privilege and wear a simple pale blue gown inspired by Gertie Millar, currently playing the lead role at the Gaiety Theatre in *The Quaker Girl*. Diana's own mother, the Duchess of Rutland, looked sensational in a rich velvet medieval gown; and Princess Kawananako of Honolulu chose a cape of yellow feathers worn over a black dress to combine the colours of the Honolulu flag. These feathers occurred singly on the heads of a native bird, a species already so endangered that this one coat ensured its extinction. Diana had been on her best behaviour that night, presenting the lady guest of honour, Princess Alexander of Teck, with a spray of orchids. The proceeds of the ball were to be donated to the Prince Francis of Teck Memorial Fund at the Middlesex Hospital, founded in tribute to Queen Mary's younger brother who had died the year before.

Diana had received her prize very prettily from Prince Alexander, Queen Mary's youngest brother, and from Philip Burne-Jones, the not-so-well-known painter son of the distin-guished pre-Raphaelite Sir Edward Burne-Jones. As a firm tradi-tionalist, Philip Burne-Jones delighted in Lady Diana's choice of costume. Flattered by the *Daily Sketch*, who singled her out in their 'Gossip about Prominent People' column (it was 'unlikely that Lady Diana has ever worn an ugly or commonplace garment'), she had not been able to resist wearing the dress again to Lord Winterton and F. E. Smith's party at Claridges the following week.

Diana was the golden girl of the summer, and as far as an in-fatuated press was concerned she could do no wrong. She was amused by the reaction of other guests at the Claridge's ball when they realised that one society rag had smuggled in a journalist, C. P. Little, disguised as a wooden soldier who stood motionless at the entrance shouldering his musket. Diana felt he had not properly thought through the implications of his character, and joined other ladies in prodding his 'wooden' exterior freely with the wing of a lorgnette. The soldier remained immobile, his scope for journalistic snooping frustratingly restricted.

The *Aberdeen Journal* had pronounced that 'no fancy dress ball was complete without the presence of Lady Diana', and her appearance a few days earlier at yet another charity ball, held this time at the Albert Hall, had disappointed neither her fans nor her critics. A procession of 'dancing princesses' – some of the season's most gorgeous girls, dressed as virginal white swans – had already set off round the specially-built circular platform, each accompanied by a prince (among them a young journalist and short-story writer, A. A. Milne). All the young men had succumbed to the suggestion that they wear silver smocks, voice-strangling tights, and golden wigs. They looked ridiculous. Diana was late, and when she eventually arrived Lady Sheffield, organiser of the event, made her displeasure perfectly clear: Diana, choosing to ignore the 'all-white' dress code imposed by Lady Sheffield, had come as a black swan. Icily forbidding her to join in, Lady Sheffield explained to the assembled guests through a rictus smile Diana's thoughtfulness in dressing so considerately in order not to outshine the other girls in white.

Diana was enjoying herself, though very much on her own terms. The life of London Society was not new to her. Indeed *The Lady* magazine had announced on 18 May with a small sniff that the beautiful 18-year-old Lady Diana Manners, youngest daughter of the Duke of Rutland, was coming out, not before time. *The Lady* reminded readers that Lady Diana 'while still in her teens had already been allowed to share the pleasures and pursuits of her two elder sisters', and had 'never been kept entirely in the background'. Like her sisters, she had 'inherited the artistic tastes of her brilliantly gifted mother, and being exceptionally musical has been encouraged to go to the opera. Tall and ethereally fair with a beautiful complexion and charming unaffected manners' – *The Lady*, abandoning its haughty manner, gushed – 'she draws, paints, is extremely well read, rides, plays games and is a marvellously clever mimic.' Mrs Hwfa Williams, still filling her notebook with observations for her forthcoming memoir, knew Diana as 'the White Baby' because of her 'extraordinary white skin and beautiful blue eyes'. And never had Mrs Williams come across a bridge player so accomplished.

A hint of scandal had hovered about Diana's elegant head ever since a dinner party the year before at which one suitor, the novelist Maurice Baring, had felt it worth his while to set his hair alight, until it fizzed and singed. He had asked Diana to join him in 'the game of risks' in which, blindfolded and with increasingly trembling hands, he hacked off crusts of bread from a loaf with such a sharp knife and at such speed that he sometimes missed the bread and hit his fingers, which began to bleed. Diana was supposed to express horror, but Baring felt himself better rewarded when he took off the blindfold to see the expression of amusement on her face. She felt 'half-mad with hilarity'.

By the time she was 17 Diana had been banned from the distinguished hostess Lady Desborough's house because her excessive behaviour made her parents' friend shudder. But her intelligence, her sense of fun and her beauty enabled her to get away with almost anything. Violet Keppel, a fellow debutante, inspired perhaps by reading too many of Elinor Glyn's best-selling romantic novels, wrote that Diana's beauty lit up the room. 'So must the angel have looked', sighed the envious Miss Keppel, 'who turned Adam and Eve out of the Garden of Eden. With a face like that she should, I thought, carry a sword or trumpet.'

The Devonshires' Derby Night Ball on 31 May had been (as it was each year) hugely 'jolly'. Lady Curzon, a cousin of the former Viceroy, came as the self-proclaimed 'Queen of Beauty', a turquoise crown on the small golden head that 'flowered proudly on her long throat', one of several hundred guests, including Queen Mary herself, beginning to revive in the gay atmosphere after a long day on their feet at the races. Diana and her family had dined with the Marlboroughs and arrived at Devonshire House at about eleven. The house was hidden from the street by the high brick wall built as protection from a potentially threatening mob whose homes were destroyed after the Great Fire in 1666. The casual passer-by could have no idea of the size of the eighteenth-century yellow brick Venetian-style house and huge forecourt by William Kent that lay behind it, large enough to entertain seven hundred Royal persons, aristocrats, politicians, writers, artists and self-made millionaires. It seemed that only the poor were excluded.

Guests were invited to walk up the crystal staircase to the first floor, where the Saloon, the Great Ballroom and the Smaller Ballroom had all been decorated for the evening. That night, beneath two enormous chandeliers hanging from giant rosettes in the white, gold and yellow room, Cassono's popular orchestra was already belting out the new hit of the summer, 'Alexander's Ragtime Band'. At some parties a military band ablaze in the red and gold emblazure would be asked to play, moonlighting from official Army tattoos. The Earl of Lonsdale and the Rothschild family had their own private bands. Lord Rothschild was known to enjoy wielding the conductor's baton himself. Vorzanger's Austro-Hungarian musical group were Diana's favourites, and her young men friends were invited to practise the czardas, a Hungarian folk dance, in the ballroom at Arlington Street.

The standard of dancing at parties was not always high, though many of the debutantes had taken dancing lessons from the current master of the correct step, Monsieur d'Egville, who impressed on them the importance of never reversing during a waltz when Royalty was present. But the older generation were oblivious to the inhibitions of the modern style, anxious to per-petuate the gaiety of the first decade of the century. 'We were on the go', exclaimed Mrs Hwfa Williams, 'with a sort of frenzied madness of pleasure-seeking throughout every one of our waking hours.' For Mrs Williams and her friends there was 'an infinite sweetness in the air they breathed', and while as Diana observed, 'gambolling does not go with weary faces and unlimber limbs', nevertheless elderly bejewelled peeresses swept by on the arms of their 'dear old prancing partners jangling with orders and deco-rations, coat tails flying.' One young guest, Osbert Sitwell, thought them 'like roses that linger in flower well past September, as if refusing to relinquish one of the last summers of their lives.'

After a few hunger-inducing hours of dancing, guests left the ballroom in search of the red-and-white-striped marquee reached by a special temporary staircase constructed from inside the house for the night. Filling a corner of the three-acre garden, and on the opposite side from the tennis court where the Duke enjoyed a daily game, the supper tent was lit with twinkling red, white and blue fairy-lights. The supper menu for balls never varied, prepared by a stretched kitchen staff supplemented with chefs from local restaurants, and Diana was wearily familiar with the dishes before her. The choice was guaranteed to include 'quails too fat to need stuffing, and chaud-froids with truffle designs on them, hot and cold soup, lobsters and strawberries, ices and hothouse peaches', all piled high on Sèvres plates.

Occasionally Mrs Rosa Lewis, proprietor of the Cavendish Hotel in Jermyn Street, was engaged to provide a more varied and mouth-watering supper. The most celebrated cook in the land, she often commandeered Number 27 Grosvenor Square, an empty house that could be rented out for private parties. Here, at Lord Ribblesdale's ball for his daughter, Rosa not only cooked for the seven hundred guests but organised the flowers, the lighting, the servants, and the wine. She was much in demand for balls, dinners, wedding breakfasts and christenings, as well as country Saturday-to-Monday house parties, where meals were prepared in kitchens the size of small cathedrals. At Mr Waldorf Astor's Hever Castle in Kent, where much of her time away from her London hotel was spent, Rosa was proud to boast that the menu always included foie gras. She had become a great favourite of Sir Edward Grey and had been working at the Foreign Office since 1909, catering for ambassadors' dinners. A party at the Colonial Office on 27 May was considered a particular triumph because Rosa had provided a budget-conscious Government department with an eight-course dinner at the bargain cost of £1 7s. a head. For this excellent price, she had ended a diplomatically thought-out menu triumphantly with 'Canapés à l'Américaine'. Guests invited to pre-ball dinners by Mr Lloyd George, Mr Balfour, Lord Ribblesdale or the painter John Singer Sargent could always look forward to Rosa's cooking. Regulars at her hotel took special pains to show this pretty, vibrant cockney woman their appreciation. She had her own favourites, among them Lord Northcliffe, who would send her French scent and soap from his annual holiday in Cannes. That summer of 1911 Lord Ribblesdale, more than just a good friend to Rosa, was travelling abroad with an unchallenging

lady named Miss Willing, and had lent someone else his room at
the Cavendish. 'You can make love in this room because that's
beautiful,' Rosa told the interloper, forgiving and protective of her
errant lover, 'but you can't drink beer in it. He hates the smell.'

The most exalted 'customer' of them all had died the summer
before, however, and the new King was not expected to become
a patron of Rosa's establishment. When she heard the news of
Edward VII's death, Rosa gathered all the guests and servants in
the hall and led them in procession down to the wine cellars. She
unlocked an inner door, and the small group could just see the
priceless bottles racked up along the dim, cool walls: Veuve
Clicquot 1904, Château Pontet Canet, Château Haut Brion,
Cachet du Château 1888, an 1820 Martell brandy, a Courvoisier
from the year of the Battle of Waterloo. Rosa could see the light
glinting on the foil of the Irroy 1904. These bottles had been
reserved for the late King. The group stood in solemn silence,
allowing the memory of the hotel's most distinguished guest to
fill the cellar, then Rosa locked the door and led the procession
back out of the cellar, leaving instructions that at least in her lifetime the small inner door should never be opened again.

A less rare wine, the delicious pink champagne 'Oeil de Perdrix',
fizzed temptingly in crystal flutes at the Devonshire House Ball.
Debutantes were not supposed to drink alcohol, but behind her
mother's back Diana accepted her first cocktail of cherry brandy in
a sugar-rimmed glass. It tasted so delightfully amusing and daring
that she helped herself to another and found herself propelled away
from her peers and into the adult world, 'all my old fears allayed,
confident in high humour and ready for the world and whatever it
gave.' The huge rooms of Devonshire House had been filled with
flowers collected from the Chatsworth gardens and greenhouses
earlier in the day and brought down by rail from Derbyshire. There
were rose trees in full bloom draped with rose-coloured electric
lights, and bamboo palms with their stems bound in alternating
pink and scarlet ribbons. In the centre of the room hung a gleaming electric star. Candles still shone their gentle muted light on the

tables, and neither Diana nor the older Countess of Fingall liked the new electric bulbs which had come to dominate and coarsen the atmosphere of most large parties, making it 'much less beautiful' and giving it a 'crude blaze' that robbed 'the fabulous crowns and jewels of their smoulder and sparkle.'

Every night during the month of June there would be three or four 'Bals Blancs', given by the parents, grandparents, aunts and uncles, guardians and benefactors of the girls making their debut that year. Some thought it curious that the Duchess of Rutland had planned no special party for her youngest daughter, but there were not many rules or expectations by which Diana or her mother felt bound. In the spring, in the country, Diana had attended the occasional Hunt Ball, occasions intended to provide a dress rehearsal for innocent and inexperienced girls only recently released from the schoolroom and not yet introduced to the conventions of smart London social functions. 'Overnight one was magically transformed,' recalled Violet Asquith, who had made her debut a few years earlier, '. . . from a child into a grown-up person.' Lady Cynthia Asquith remembered how the whispering sound made by the train of her first long dress seemed to suggest that it had a life of its own as it pursued her heels down the stairs, producing the 'queerness of suddenly no longer being able to see my feet.' Reluctantly coiffed and evening-dressed, Diana endured the hour-long journey to her first Hunt Ball with eleven other girls who lived nearby, all of them squashed into the Rutland family's own horse-drawn bus. For Diana 'there was no pleasure in it'.

Diana despaired of her 'deplorably dressed' fellow debutantes, 'innocent of powder with their shapeless wispy hair held by crooked combs.' None of them seemed to have any sense of style, or to know how to dress. Gloves reaching above the elbow to the upper arm were obligatory, and as it was expensive to have a new pair every night, they usually reeked of cleaning fluid. Shoes of pink and white satin, too difficult to clean, were scuffed and smudged from the accidental tramplings of clumsy dancing partners. Some of the debutantes' mothers shopped at the new department stores of Debenham and Freebody, Selfridges, and Peter Robinson. Sometimes a dressmaker was employed to come to the house and copy magazine illustrations of designs by the celebrated first couturier Charles Frederick Worth, dead for more than fifteen years but still popular with the older generation. Diana, however, had her eye on the far more pacey clothes produced by his apprentice and successor Paul Poiret, the current French arbiter of fashion, who had established a considerable following with his sexy, clingy dresses. Curiously, Poiret was also the designer responsible for the inhibiting and controversial hobble skirt and, paradoxically but 'in the name of liberty', the man who 'proclaimed the fall of the corset and the adoption of the brassière.' The freedom he offered was eagerly welcomed behind locked bedroom doors, where time was often precious to illicit lovers. Poiret well knew that in the era of the elaborately laced corset, 'undressing a woman is an undertaking similar to the capture of a fortress'.

Many of the grandest women shopped at Lucy Duff Gordon's salon, Madame Lucille in Hanover Square. Royalty, Ellen Terry, Mrs Asquith and duchesses crowded into the soft, rich-carpeted and grey-brocade-curtained rooms for the innovative 'fashion shows' in which the models Dolores and Hebe wafted up and down Lucille's catwalks wearing gowns with names like 'When passion's thrall is o'er' and 'The sighing sounds of lips unsatisfied'. There was a special underwear room where customers could try on Lucy's silky nothings while reclining on an exact copy of a bed that had belonged to Madame de Pompadour. As some women had begun to flout convention by smoking in public, the matching accessories and evening purses that now appeared on the arms of the models were designed to contain not only the essential inquisitive lorgnette but also the new smoking apparatus of cigarette lighter and long holder. There was a practical side to these elegant holders, for they prevented flakes from the loosely rolled cigarettes attaching themselves unattractively to the lips.

There were other establishments run by titled ladies, their motive not always simply financial or the alleviation of boredom but sometimes the satisfaction of charitable instincts. Both Lady Auckland with her millinery shop and Lady Brooke with her underwear shop provided employment for women who would otherwise have been working in the atrocious conditions of London's factories and workshops. The Countess of Warwick had a much-visited underwear shop in Bond Street, and so that customers might be quite certain of the exclusivity of the service to be found there the words 'The Countess of Warwick' were painted in large letters on the shop window. Lady Angela Forbes called her George Street flower shop 'My Shop'.

Diana and her two elder sisters Marjorie and Lettie were passionate about clothes and dressing up, and relished any opportunity to put on a costume remotely theatrical. The arrival at Rutland House one day of a new and exotic guest, Princess Murat, 'a fascinating surprise and totally different from anything we knew', was responsible for Diana becoming 'an inspired dressmaker'. The Princess made her entrance in a Poiret-designed chiffon evening shirt worn over a skirt cut like an eastern djellabah (the Islamic gown with long sleeves and a hood), and edged at the hem and neck with braid. Diana copied Princess Murat's clothes for her friends, adding a customising touch of her own, using fur at the cuffs instead of braid. She charged a 25 per cent mark-up on the cost of material, and with the profits bought herself much-wanted first editions of her favourite writers Meredith, Wilde, Conrad and Maupassant.

Most of Diana's ill-dressed fellow debutantes were intimidated by the prospect of being launched into an unknown society containing the unfamiliar presence of boys. Here Diana had the advantage: not only did she have an elder brother (a second had died when she was two years old), but her elder sister Marjorie had held hair-brushing sessions during her first season to which Diana and the young men who admired Marjorie most were invited. But even Diana was a little intimidated at the beginning of the season, describing herself as 'extremely insecure but could not help showing off, a surface glitter, wanting and trying to shine through thick miasmas of shyness.' She also considered herself conspicuously tall and fat. In an attempt to lose weight and become more streamlined she would strap herself into a jockey's rubber jacket and a light boxing-glove and shut herself into her black-painted bedroom at Belvoir where she battered away at a punch-ball hung from a hook in the ceiling. There too she danced alone to records on the gramophone with 'a mahogany megaphone three feet across' that Nellie Melba, a friend of her parents, had given her as a present. 'I felt that I wasn't clever which I so longed to be. I felt that people over-estimated me and that I should be found out and cause disillusion.' During the first parties of her official 'Season', the horror of being a wallflower in the 'confused mass of seething people, where everyone seemed to be being crushed or pushed or complaining of the heat or making banal conversation', was 'unendurable'. Diana and the other rejects would creep away from the dance floor and skulk downstairs to the cloakroom, pretending to look for their maids to have a stitch or two sewn into a torn dress. Lady Desborough's daughter Monica Grenfell considered the 38 balls she was to attend that season to be little more sophisticated than 'glorified children's parties'.

Neither did the chaperoning parent always enjoy herself. The Countess of Fingall went 'as a dutiful mother', but it was with reluctance that she 'shook hands with people I had never seen before and ate their wonderful food in their own houses or at The Ritz and sat on the bench with the other dowagers.' She felt like a guilty parasite. And there was little opportunity for the older women to relax, for they felt compelled to keep an eye on their daughters at all times. 'All the girls collected after the previous dance and the sitting out interval in a cluster to be claimed by their next partner,' explained Monica Grenfell, 'so our mothers knew who we were dancing with, and who we were dancing with too often.'

Nor were the men always up to scratch. Some were terrified of the ritual to which they were involuntarily committed on the chance of finding a wife. Lady Fingall watched as a Mr Charles

Hervey, white as a sheet, was dragged onto the dance floor by his mother. Diana had decided views about many such 'eligibles' who were steered in her direction. Lord Dudley was 'slothful', Bobbety Cranborne wholly unacceptable with his 'loose gaping mouth and lean mean shanks'. Lord Rocksavage, despite the glory of his looks, was dismissed without a thought: he had no conversation and had only ever been heard to say 'Oh', 'Really' and 'Right-Ho'. An admired and alarming fellow debutante, Vita Sackville-West, had scuppered that peer's chances of being taken seriously. 'Dim to a degree,' she had pronounced as she sloped off in secret to spend the evening in bed with her friend Rosamond Grosvenor.

Women of a certain class and upbringing were expected to be 'gorgeous, decorative and dumb' until their engagement, and thereafter 'married, matronly and motherly': so Agatha Evans, a well-known feminist, told her 25-year-old niece Edith in a tone of high disgust. From her unwavering position as suffragette agitator on her local MP's doorstep, waiting daily to ambush the poor man as he went in or out of his own house, filling the hours in between by reading *The Times*, Aunt Agatha never ceased to warn young Edith of the perils of a pompous husband. Lady Diana Manners's views were in total sympathy with Aunt Agatha's.

That June, despite her objections, Diana received her first bona fide proposal. But Sir Claud Russell, a grandson of the Duke of Bedford, was twenty years older than her, and his present of a diamond and ruby pendant – her second of the early summer – did not prevent her laughing off his declaration as a huge joke. Her mother tried to encourage a romance with the unsophisticated, soon-to-be-invested Prince of Wales, but Diana considered the heir to the throne little more than a 'snivelling cub', and declared she had no intention of 'marrying a country house'.

By the end of the first week of June, London had become extremely hot after eight consecutive days of fine weather. A sun-bronzed colonel with the experience of many summers behind him was leaning over the parapet of Westminster Bridge near the House of Commons when he told a passing *Daily Sketch* reporter that he forecast a 'long fine summer'. On the same day Mary Anne Sudworth, a typist who worked at the British Electrical Foundation in Kingsway in London, poisoned herself. Her mother said the abnormal heat had caused her daughter's death, and a verdict of 'temporary insanity' was brought in. It was a week during which the novelist Thomas Hardy celebrated his 71st birthday, the King's daughter Princess Mary visited the sweltering sea lions at London Zoo, and Churchill attended a ball at Blenheim. Diana, with too many parties both behind her and ahead of her, needed a rest. She removed her aching feet from the London cobblestones and the 'iridescent season of music, dance, pageantry and fluttering flirtations', and left for 'the calmer joys of the country'.

Belvoir (pronounced 'Beaver') Castle was the Rutland family's principal country seat, set in thirty thousand acres of Rutland-family-owned Leicestershire. There, with the encouragement of forty gardeners, the *Clematis* 'Montana' was still in full flower in the middle of June. During the day larks filled the air with the same sound of 'shrill delight' that had been so familiar to the poet Shelley, while at night 'from the deepest wells of silence the wood pigeon drew its bubble of sound'. Visitors, privileged, rich and connected, arrived to spend their ends-of-weeks, their Saturday-to-Mondays in the early-nineteenth-century castellated and turreted house, in drawing rooms hung with paintings by Gainsborough, Reynolds and Holbein. Extra night-watchmen were employed to circle the castle walls in case any intruder should seek to make off with the tiaras and precious jewels that had arrived in their own velvet-lined trunks earlier in the day.

There was a familiar rhythm to these end-of-the-week days, for they were largely punctuated by meals. Guests were woken by their maids and manservants bringing cups of tea accompanied by biscuits for the gentlemen and plates of wafer-thin bread and butter for the ladies. Soon afterwards the housemaids, helped by the footmen, would either struggle up the stairs carrying tin baths which to Osbert Sitwell resembled 'Egyptian coffins, and hip baths like gigantic snail shells', or heave the baths out of the huge nearby cupboards in which they were stored. Heavy, slopping cans of hot water had to be lugged up from the kitchens: at Belvoir, special 'watermen' were employed for this sole purpose. In the most avant-gard houses there were bathrooms where a man might find 'the scented smell of his predecessor's indulgence'. The writer Harold Nicolson winced at the sight of a signet ring, left floating in the grimy soap dish. However, Nicolson was quite unashamed to admit that he too, like all smart male guests when compelled to share a bathroom, would shave in his bath. 'All Edwardians,' he later confessed, 'being at heart dirty folk, shaved in their baths.'

Lavatories or water-closets had been familiar fixtures in rich people's houses since the 1880s, long enough to have acquired an upper-class euphemism. Lady Louisa Anson, an intimidating guest at Viceregal Lodge in Ireland, was so rude to the Viceroy's children that in revenge they stole the name card from her bedroom door and slid it into the holder on the door of the water-closet: Lady Louisa was not amused to find her maid persistently mis-delivering her early morning tea. The story spread, and from then on people needing a discreet reason to excuse themselves would announce that they were off to visit 'Lady Loo' or as it became known, simply 'The Loo'.

Not every house met the luxurious standards that were coming to be expected. At Stanway in Gloucestershire, home of Lord and Lady Wemyss, Diana noted with amusement the 'lukewarm water, blankets that are no prison to ones wayward toes, and every horizontal object wear[ing] a coat of dust like a chinchilla. It's a wonder the inmates look as clean as they do.' Even at Chatsworth the only fixed bath was in the sculpture gallery, convenient only for the already gleaming marble Greek goddesses who overlooked it.

Breakfast included several cooked dishes both hot and cold: porridge, whiting, devilled kidneys, cold grouse, tongue, ham, omelette, kedgeree, and cold sliced ptarmigan, a sort of large mountain grouse. That summer an electrical gadget for grilling waffles and a new breakfast food, called Post Toasties, made from crisped flakes of corn, had arrived from America to take their place on the already laden sideboard, next to the scones, honey, and bowls of golden butter. At Belvoir the butter was fashioned by Miss Saddlebridge the dairymaid (whose face, Diana lamented, was not her fortune) into round yellow pats bearing the imprint of the Rutland peacock. Hot-house nectarines, grapes and summer fruits ended the meal. To drink there was coffee and a choice of tea, the Indian variety identified by a little Empire red flag, its string wrapped around the handle of the pot, China tea came with its own fluttering yellow indicator.

After church (the Belvoir service was always conducted by the resident chaplain, who was also the captain of the Belvoir fire-brigade) the ladies went to their bedrooms to change from the formal dress suitable for church into day dresses, reappearing in time for lunch. In the dining room the tables were decorated with heavy glass vases filled with red roses, and white geraniums spilled over the edges of silver bowls. Sometimes home-made wines were served at lunch, and the Countess of Fingall was once quite overcome by home-brewed cider. Her legs would no longer support her, and, sober enough to be mortified, she had to be carried from the table by two footmen and settled down in a corner of the drawing room to recover.

Not everyone aspired to the munificence of Belvoir. Mrs Arthur James, a hostess with a reputation for meanness in a world where such a thing was gasped at, usually served fish, but when she felt like pushing the boat out, chicken appeared on the menu. Nevertheless Mrs James kept a vigilant eye on her guests, and if they seemed satisfied with small helpings, would pass a coded note to her butler – 'DCSC', meaning 'Don't Carve Second Chicken'.

After lunch there was the garden to tour, and lawn tennis to play, in dresses so long that sprained ankles caused from tripping were not unusual. An expedition in the Daimler to a local site of inter-est and for antique-shopping in the nearest town would persuade the women to wrap up their faces in a claustrophobic veil to prevent too much dust flying into their already goggle-covered eyes. Other parts of the body were ill-protected from the all-pervading dust, until the mackintosh makers Burberry devised a discreet 'Dust Wrapper', to be worn over underwear to insulate ladies from the invasive dirt of the rough country roads. Outer garments were covered in rather ineffectual protective rugs.

On returning to the cool of the house the ladies consulted Mrs Eric Pritchard's excellent guide to fashions *The Cult of Chiffon* and retired to their bedrooms to change into floaty tea-gowns – because, as Mrs Pritchard advised, 'when the tea urn sings at five o'clock we can don these garments of poetical beauty.' After tea – ginger biscuits especially brought in from Biarritz (they had been Edward VII's favourite), scones, egg sandwiches and three sorts of cake (including chocolate) – a rubber of bridge, with a plate of nourishing 'bridge-rolls' on the side-table, relieved the tedium before it was time for the ladies to change again, this time into something described by Diana as 'a little less limp'.

A good hour was required for the evening toilette, since the fashionable brilliant white skin was achieved with the help of liquid creams and white rice powder, while to indicate sensitivity the naturally bluish-violet veins at neck, temple and cleavage were emphasised with a blue crayon. Elderflower berries or a cork singed in the flame of a candle darkened eyebrows and eyelashes. On 14 June the *Daily Sketch* printed a series of photographs from an American magazine under the heading 'Decoys for the Affections: Beauty's Artful Aids'. Here were devices to enhance the appearance. A double chin could be suppressed using a tightly-wrapped leather chin brace that resembled a dislodged muzzle or a miniature feeding trough that had slipped too far below the mouth. Other photographs showed how to enliven the cheeks with what looked like a small tarmacadam-road pounder. English ladies were also let into the secrets of a contraption for eradicating the lines on the forehead caused by bad temper, and an alarming nasal clamp said to 'pinch the offending member into an Aphrodite contour'.

The English country-house beauty routine was less complicated. Wavy locks were created nightly with curling tongs,

straight hair being thought to indicate obstinacy. False braids or
chignons known as 'rats' were often added, though they only
stayed in place properly on rather grubby, sticky hair. Small silver
rings clamped into the nipples deepened, enhanced and raised the
cleavage by providing a sort of ledge on which the evening gown
rested precariously. Fresh flowers – a carnation or gardenia for a
man, a spray of stephanotis for a woman, provided by the Belvoir
greenhouses and brought round on a silver tray by a servant – gave
the finishing touch. And so the finest of Edwardian society made
their way downstairs for dinner, the men smelling strongly of Mr
Penhaligon's Hamman Bouquet, undercut by inescapable body
odour and cigar smoke, the ladies wafting down in a cloud of lavender and rose-water that helped disguise the whiff of dirty hair,
while the rubbing of the unseen rings against the dress afforded a
secret frisson of pleasure.

The dining table would be decorated with orchids and cycla-
men, and after an eight-course dinner at a grand house like
Belvoir, eaten off Charles II silver and Charles II gold, the ladies
would leave the gentleman for a period that if extended too long
could lead to a row between enthusiastic port-dispensing host
and weary conversation-sustaining hostess. Later there might be
more bridge in the study, or an amusing session of charades
in the gardenia and stephanotis-scented drawing room. A large
dish of crystallised violets often sat on the piano in case an
impromptu player or his accompanying singer should suddenly
feel peckish.

At the very, very grandest of houses a more elaborate entertainment was laid on – at Renishaw in Derbyshire, home of the
Sitwells, a full orchestra for dancing was imported from London.
At Chatsworth, not far away, the guests themselves might put on
a play in the private Bijou Theatre. Crossing through the long
Hall of Statues, the audience would enter the theatre by the small
staircase at the back. A total of 200 could be seated downstairs, a
further 150 could be squeezed in on the balcony above. Local
worthies would be invited in for the evening, and the first thing

they saw was the safety curtain painted by the master set designer and painter of the day, William Hemsley, with a sweeping panorama of the original Elizabethan house that had belonged to Bess of Hardwick. The footlights were provided by dangerously flickering candles, and an elaborately coiled wire was stretched across at the front to prevent the flames catching the lady actors' gowns as they moved about at the edge of the stage.

When the exhausted house guests finally dispersed to their own or other people's bedrooms they would find fires lit by sleepy housemaids, the gentlemen's loose change washed and dried by the valet and put on the table next to a vase of sweet peas. The latest novels and biographies, their pages still uncut, were stacked beside the bed, and a plate of sandwiches left on the dresser lest hunger strike in the night.

Saturdays-to-Mondays were a heaven-sent opportunity for sex. Although a contemporary academic claimed that 'nine out of ten women are indifferent to or actively dislike it', the evidence pointed the other way, and most agreed with the writer Arnold Bennett who advised that 'the most correct honeymoon is an orgy of lust and if it isn't it ought to be'. Lady Diana Manners's mother the Duchess of Rutland was generally known within her own circle to have ignored her marriage vows. Nearly nineteen years earlier she had enjoyed an affair with Harry Cust, the extremely handsome and clever editor of the *Pall Mall Gazette*. Diana, though brought up as the Duke of Rutland's daughter, was in fact the result of her mother's teatime liaison with the charming Harry Cust.

In a world of marriages of convenience, one in which divorce was both expensive and ruinous to the reputation, an illicit couple was challenged to find somewhere private to take their clothes off. A few restaurants, among them Rules and the Café Royal, rented out private dining rooms by the hour, but a large country house and a complicit hostess eased the problem beautifully. During the day, a clandestine affair could develop unobserved while family portraits were being admired in the picture gallery, or in a dark corner of the library, or out walking in magnificent gardens in which enclosed gazebos scattered the landscape with convenient regularity. At night, the names written on cards slotted into brass holders on the bedroom doors were as helpful to lovers as to the maids bringing early morning tea. Assignations confirmed by the squeeze of a hand beneath the bridge table, a whispered exchange over the candle that lit the way up the stairs, a note left (in collusion with the maid) beside the bottled water on the bedside table, or the placing of a code-laden flower outside a bedroom door ensured that extra-marital sex went on with ease. Confusions occasionally occurred. Lord Charles Beresford became particularly vigilant after leaping with an exultant 'Cock-a-doodle-do!', onto a darkened bed, believing it to contain his lover, only to be vigorously batted away by the much startled Bishop of Chester. At six in the morning a hand-bell rung on each of the bedroom floors gave guests time to return to their own beds before the early morning tea trays arrived.

The general tedium and vacuity of the usual country-house Saturday-to-Monday held no appeal for Diana. Her childhood had prepared her for eccentricity and bred in her a horror of bores, and she later acknowledged gratefully that 'everything Society criticised me for I now realise my mother encouraged'. Many of the guests at Belvoir were among the group of the Duchess of Rutland's friends known to all but themselves as 'The Souls': they referred to themselves as 'The Gang'. These were clever people who had rebelled against the bored indolence that characterised the usual country house set. Instead of spending these weekends drinking and eating to excess, the Souls used their brains, indulging in wit and revelling in conversation. Words were fundamental to the Souls' enjoyment of life, and at Taplow Lady Desborough ensured that an hour and a half was set aside for the reading of *The Times*. They developed a private language – 'diskie' was disgusting, 'deevie' was divine, and 'utterly utterly' was used to describe a subject deserving of the most extravagant compliment, or simply the most emphatic feeling known to mankind, whether good or bad; further private language involved leaving the 'G' off the ends of words – borrowing money from friends was 'lootin'; and unlikely words were substituted for others, so that 'spangle' meant 'flirt', and 'backstairs' meant 'homosexual'. An Italian ending was often added to nouns, so that 'after dinnare' one might have a little 'dansare' with one's chosen 'partnerino'. They loved games which included acting, or ingenious plays on words. A favourite was 'In the manner of . . .', which might involve the writing as well as the reading of an essay 'In the manner of Ruskin'.

The Souls also played outdoor games and took up physical activities, as a relief from that constant cerebral intensity. The Crabbet was a club formed among The Souls with the purpose of playing 'lawn tennis, the piano, the fool and other instruments of gaiety', exemplified by Harry Cust joining Lord Curzon in a nude tennis doubles match against George Wyndham and Wilfrid Blunt. Days were spent at Lady Rutland's sister-in-law Norah Lindsay's beautiful house, Sutton Courtenay, drifting about on the Thames in boats crammed with poetry books while Norah, pearls and emeralds roped round her neck and dressed 'mainly in tinsel and leopard skins', watched with delight from the river bank. They would have lunch 'under a loggia from great bowls of chicken in rice and kedgeree and mushrooms and raspberries and Devonshire cream and gooseberry fool and figs – all in abundance.' Other favourite Souls meeting places included any one of the several marvellous houses in the Home Counties owned by the Rothschild family, among them Waddesdon, Mentmore, Halton and Tring. Walter Rothschild would send round a carriage drawn by two zebras to collect his guests to view his extensive menagerie, which included a collection of kangaroos, cassowaries, giant tortoises, a wolf, and several bad-tempered glis-glis, a variety of succulent edible dormice.

Two love affairs involving the older generation were the subject of much Souls talk that June. Lord Curzon, a leading Soul whose house at Hackwood in Hampshire was one of Diana's favourite places to stay, was not being kind to the writer Elinor Glyn. He was to her 'the sun, moon and stars', but the former Viceroy was not prepared to introduce the best-selling romantic author to the inner circle of his clever friends. Poor Elinor considered her lover to have been 'the noblest ruler since Augustus Caesar', but she was always invited down to Hackwood on a Tuesday and asked to return on a Thursday. The slight that hurt her most was her discovery that although on leaving she would carefully sign her name in the visitors' book, by the Friday it would have been scratched out. But at least *her* husband had not discovered her liaison. Lady Cunard, on the other hand, having tired of her hunting, shooting, fishing, shipping line-managing baronet husband, Sir Bache Cunard, then made the mistake of getting caught, despite the six o'clock morning bell. One morning at her husband's Leicestershire house, Neville Holt, near Belvoir, her bedroom curtains had fluttered open just wide enough to allow a workman, high on his ladder repairing the clock tower, to peer in and spot her ladyship tucked up in bed with the distinguished conductor Thomas Beecham. The ensuing scandal threatened to overwhelm her reputation, and that June Emerald Cunard packed her bags for a single life in London, renting the Asquiths' house in Cavendish Square, conveniently unoccupied while its owners were resident at Number 10 Downing Street.

Diana's generation took things a little further. All through the summer of 1911, that year of her entrée into polite society, Diana was running close to the limits. Nowhere was she better able to indulge her impulse to challenge convention than among her sisters and her own special group of friends. The Manners girls were collectively known as The Hothouse or The Hotbed, for their exotic, undisciplined and affected behaviour, and Raymond Asquith, the Prime Minister's son, singled Diana out as 'an orchid among cowslips, a black tulip in a garden of cucumbers, nightshade in the day nursery'. Another sceptical friend was Julian Grenfell, Lady Desborough's son and brother of Diana's fellow-debutante Monica. Julian was so beautiful that an Eton master who had taught him said merely to pass him in the street made his eyes fill with tears. But Julian thought the Manners girls 'born professionals' and took this to be the secret of their 'coldness and their enthusiasms and perhaps their second ratedness'. Julian's brother Billy Grenfell felt differently. Writing to Diana after one June weekend, he awarded her 'one hundred out of a hundred for companionship, beauty, wit, intelligence and intellect, seventy seven for athleticism and seven and a half for lawn tennis.' The notorious group, known also to themselves and others as the 'Corrupt Coterie', had become friends during one summer holiday in Diana's mid teenage years. She had been invited to stay with the Trees, friends of her parents whose children were slightly older and more worldly. Impressed by their sophistication and by the visiting 'Oxford boys' Patrick Shaw Stewart and Edward Horner, she had bought a bottle of peroxide and secretly dyed her hair, crediting the rays of the sun with her golden transformation. Her audacity pleased her, as did her increasingly slim body. The Coterie's 'devil may care' attitude to life was summed up by Vita Sackville-West, whose own ethic was somewhat similar: 'Why worry? Why not enjoy the present?' she wrote. 'We may all be dead tomorrow, or there may be a war or an earthquake . . . I think one never enjoys life so much as when it becomes dangerous.'

Diana admired the slightly older Vita enormously. 'She is an aristocrat, rollingly rich, who writes French poetry with more ease than I lie in a sofa,' Diana herself wrote in awe. To many of the younger generation of the upper classes, this only child of the Sackvilles of the enormous and ancient house Knole, in Kent, was an impressive figure. She had been photographed that summer with her pet Russian bear cub, Ivan the Terrible, a gift from an admirer to add to the baboon and two tiger cubs that she already walked on leads round the garden at Knole. For an interview she gave the *Evening Times* she wore a white tennis dress with a scarf wrapped round her head 'in Corsican fashion'. What neither Diana nor anyone else knew was that Vita was already rebelling in ways beyond even Diana's vibrant but virginal imagination, by sleeping with women; Diana and her friends would, however, have been delighted, had they known. The Coterie made a common pledge to be 'unafraid of words, unshocked by drink and unashamed of decadence and gambling. In other words, Unlike Other People.' They revelled in drink, blasphemy, gambling, drug-taking, chloroform ('chlorers') sniffing, and decadent behaviour of every kind imaginable. Diana boasted that 'they prized honesty whether or not it offended'. They were healthy, beautiful and exceptionally clever, and the young men 'carried off prizes and fellowships with as much ease as they could win a steeple-chase'. On leaving university they planned careers in the law or in the City, determined to remain rich enough to maintain the only way of life they knew or cared to know about.

They played a parody of the acting games so beloved of the Souls' evenings. In the Coterie's 'Breaking the News', the effect of the announcement of the death of a child to its mother was acted out for fun. Margot Asquith was deeply upset on hearing of it. 'A more terrible game I never could imagine,' she cried, 'heartless and brutal.' She believed Diana to be the ring-leader, and thought she suffered from 'Love of notoriety and stainless vanity – her boredom with the country, her blasphemy, her entire want of sensitiveness, no imagination, and no compassion.' At a party at Billy Grenfell's rooms at Trinity College, Oxford, fifty rabbits were lowered out of the window in baskets, released, and then chased by a hundred humans and a bulldog, pursued in turn by several horrified dons who collected up the dead rabbits for burial. Raymond suggested that God had played his cards wrong, and that Jesus Christ would have been appreciated more if he had been clean-shaven and the Virgin if she had worn rouge. Diana was aware that they were 'very irritating to others and utterly satisfying and delightful to themselves', but even she knew she had gone too far on the occasion when the former Prime Minister and Conservative leader Mr Arthur Balfour hesitated for a moment during a guessing game and Diana shouted at him in exasperation 'Use your brain, Mr Balfour, use your *brain!*' The Duchess of Rutland was an indulgent mother, but even she drew the line at one activity: Diana was not permitted to fly in her golden-haired Swedish friend Gustav Hamel's plane. Obedient but frustrated, she watched from the ground as her friend Sybil Cooper, a sister of her brother John's friend Duff, rose into the air, two small squealing pigs in her pockets to prove to the world that such animals really could fly.

Without the occasionally moderating influence of Raymond Asquith the Coterie's behaviour might have been even more unacceptable and out of control. He was fourteen years older than Diana and respected by the entire group. His sister-in-law Cynthia Asquith realised that there was 'an insidiously corruptive poison in their midst', the flagrant decadence was 'brilliantly distilled by their inspiration, Raymond', and Diana declared that 'he was the one we liked best'. He had married her best friend Katherine Horner in 1907, but even so Diana could not help herself: he was the first love of her life. Ottoline Morrell had known him when he was an undergraduate and saw him as the leader 'of all that was clever and reckless and contemptuous', and while she confessed herself intimidated by his cynicism and intellectual dexterity, she also recognised a 'charming gentleness and tenderness', adding 'but it was not easy to find the way to it through the armour of sceptical cleverness.' Under Raymond's direction the friends often behaved quite sensibly – dressing up and producing an entire Shakespeare play, for example. Duff Cooper, who had graduated from New College at the beginning of June, was invited to stay at the Manners' house by the sea at Clovelly in Devon. There, with the core of the Coterie as fellow house-guests, he was entranced by the life of 'picnics, games and charades, midnight bathing and clandestine suppers, singing and repetition of poetry.'

In the middle of June Diana briefly left behind the amusements of the Coterie and returned to London to continue with her summer debut. In Hyde Park the familiar stink of horse and car was alleviated a little by the distinctively summery smell of fresh hay that filled the nearby mews, and the cobblestones were alive with the little voles and field mice that arrived buried in the hay carts that rumbled into town from the country fields.

The Duke of Rutland was preoccupied with the proposed National Insurance Scheme and its compulsory contributions from all employees, which he felt ill-thought-through. Mindful of the number of servants in his own employ across the 65,000 acres of England in his possession, he wrote in anger to *The Times* that the new arrangement 'would undermine the harmonious relationship currently enjoyed between employers and servants.' But Diana would not allow a politically agitated adult world to derail her summer. For her presentation at Court, an ordeal she had not been looking forward to, she conformed to the obligatory white satin dress. She felt her own version only 'adequate', though she was pleased with her imaginative design for the accompanying train, sewn by herself, with its three yards of cream net 'sprinkled generously with pink rose petals, each attached by a diamond dew drop'. Even the mandatory three ostrich feathers fastened to her head looked less ridiculous than she had feared. For Diana the proceedings were not as tiresome as they might have been, for the Duchess had been granted the 'entrée' by Queen Victoria, and this still-valid privilege meant they could avoid the three-hour queues at the front door of Buckingham Palace and 'stalk in through a smaller but nobler entrance.' The culmination of the presentation was the low curtsey to the monarch. Though Poiret's fashionable hobble skirt was banned, courtiers were always in attendance to catch a toppling deb. Violet Asquith only achieved her smooth descent and rise after hours spent practising in front of the nursery rocking-horse.

As the Season continued there were daily excursions from London to the race meetings at Royal Ascot. *Tatler* recorded that on Ladies' Day Lady Diana Manners wore a 'picturesque dress of delicate pastel with a hat full of feathers, and a toilette of shell pink veiled in cloudy grey.' Indeed, after the sombre beauty of the previous year's mourning dress the clothes all seemed gayer than ever before. And still the ceaseless partying went on. There was a ball at Grosvenor House in Park Lane, where Gainsborough's *Blue Boy* hung over a golden mantelpiece and his glorious *Mrs Siddons* watched as the *jeunesse dorée* danced below her. The sadly untitled but socially generous Mrs Hwfa Williams held a dance in the studio of her Ovington Square house, honoured by the 'vision' of Lady Diana with her 'perfect face and figure'. The actor-manager Sir Herbert Beerbohm Tree, half-brother of the novelist Max Beerbohm, was dressed, to the immense satisfaction of his hostess, in a manner 'as immaculate and spruce as ever, an invaluable acquisition to a party'. He was much amused by the sudden appearance of a panicking horse belonging to Mrs Williams's milkman that unknown to her had been locked up for safekeeping in the stable off the courtyard and was whinnying loudly in protest at the heat and noise generated by the energetic dancing to the band. Luckily, with the arrival of the Russian dancer Pavlova (in Mrs Williams's words 'the marvel'), who danced an impromptu *pas seul*, the harmony of the interrupted evening was restored and it turned out to be 'one of the most successful and delightful dances' Mrs Williams had ever given, though she said so herself.

That week Diana was being painted by the society portrait painter Philip de László, the sitting itself recorded in a charming pencil drawing by her mother. At the same time Diana was sketching in her own notebook a tubular skirt in brilliant yellow with a chiffon overlay. There was a belt of tasselled cord, and the clinging skirt was edged in orange and yellow beading, with a low-draped cowl-necked top. The model was clearly herself, her hair *en bandeau*. De László was not the only person for whom she was posing. For her brother John she stripped in private to nothing more than a sheer silk veil of cream lace, which she allowed to slip far below her waist, revealing a long naked back. Her left hand, braceleted above the elbow, held a mirror into which she gazed steadily back at John as he photographed her on an Arlington Street sofa. In another picture the protecting veil was removed entirely as she imitated Velásquez's exquisite *Rokeby*

Venus, a long strand of pearls creeping erotically down her back and round to the front of her body like the familiar and lingering hand of a lover.

And then, right in the middle of Royal Ascot, the swelling dissatisfaction in the docks suddenly erupted. On Wednesday 14 June the entire crew of the *Olympic*, moored at Southampton docks, went on strike, followed by the men of five shipping lines and the National Sailors' and Firemens' unions. By the end of the racing week dockers in Glasgow, Newcastle, Hull and Goole had come out in sympathy. In the last week before the Coronation, uncertainty suddenly filled the air. Churchill embarked on a series of urgent talks with the dock owners and the union leaders in an attempt to address the men's concerns.

But Diana's attention was concentrated on the impending arrival of the Russian Ballet.

5

Late June

The ballet made my hair stand on end.
Duncan Grant in a private letter

AFTER LOOKING INTO the face of the Marchioness of Ripon, things appeared green-coloured, as if one had stared directly into a blinding light. Gladys Ripon, patron of the opera and beloved of the accountants responsible for the cash takings at Covent Garden, was so beautiful that she made most people appear dumpy and, according to one admirer, the writer E. F. Benson, 'a shade shabby'. He felt that in Lady Ripon's presence even the glamorous 'wanted the touch of the sponge or duster'. Six foot tall, smoking a cigarette in a long amber holder, she presented a figure of unequalled elegance. She wore her hair piled vertiginously above her head (a diamond brooch flashing at its summit when it was dressed for a ball), the dark waves swept back to reveal a broad and, for a woman in her fifties, curiously unlined forehead. From beneath thick eyebrows she would return a look with her head tilted at a slight and disconcerting angle. Her Russian ancestry was evident in her high cheekbones, and her 'distinguished features of so pure a cut' marked her out for Osbert Sitwell as 'the most striking individual to look at in any room she entered.'

Gladys had collected a succession of names from her two marriages that Henry James, always so scrupulous about the appropriate naming of his heroines, would have envied for their pertinent beauty.

Born Lady Gladys Herbert, daughter of Lord Herbert of Lea and niece of the Earl of Pembroke, she married first the faithless Earl of Lonsdale, a man apparently incapable of enjoying a healthy sex life with a member of his own class: he collapsed, dead of a heart attack, while in action in his own private brothel. His resilient widow's next choice was Lord de Grey, heir to the Marquess of Ripon and famed for his grouse-shooting prowess. When in 1909 he inherited his father's title, the new Marchioness found herself a peeress again, but this time very rich. She was the granddaughter of a Russian prince on her mother's side, and therefore one-quarter Russian; her father had helped Florence Nightingale establish her hospital at Scutari. Her own encouragement and support of Oscar Wilde was rewarded when he teasingly dedicated his play *A Woman of No Importance* to her. She embodied something of the exotic, entrepreneurial and rebellious spirit that Lady Diana Manners sought to emulate. Diana and Gladys were indisputably rooted in the bosom of their aristocratic birthright, but these two beautiful women shared a spirit of mutiny, and in Diana's eyes Gladys was well qualified to be her mentor: she had a 'past'. She was indeed notorious for her many affairs, in particular with Harry Cust, witty and compulsively attractive but also sexually voracious and careless. (Diana, result of his earlier liaison with the Duchess of Rutland, was at least three when his affair with Gladys began.) Alone in her lover's house one day, Gladys discovered a pile of wonderfully indiscreet love letters written to Harry by one of her social adversaries, Lady Londonderry. Perversely delighted with her discovery and especially relishing Lady Londonderry's disparaging remarks about her husband, Gladys pocketed the lot, realising she was sitting on a source of irresistibly diverting material. Her friends and Theresa Londonderry's enemies were cock-a-hoop with the instalments Gladys would read to them with her mischievously exaggerated delivery on rainy afternoons during lulls in the bridge game.

After the fun had exhausted itself, Gladys arranged for the letters to be delivered by her own footman to Londonderry

House in Park Lane on an evening when she knew both husband and wife were dining alone at home. The butler approached his Lordship's end of the table and solemnly handed him the ribbon-tied bundle. After a moment or two spent in absorbing their contents, his Lordship beckoned to the butler and directed him to carry the opened package to the other end of the table. Silence filled the large dining room, a silence so terrible that husband and wife suspected it might never be broken. Lord Londonderry had been shattered not just by the knowledge that his wife was being unfaithful but also by the realisation that, thanks to Lady Ripon, her affair was the stuff of common gossip. From that day onwards, the Londonderrys stood yards apart whenever they appeared together in public, and not a word passed between them. Society whispered for months afterwards, not of the immorality of having an affair but of the terrible consequences of being caught. Few considered Gladys in any way at fault for actions prompted by little more than spite.

Gladys found politics dreary and the personalities involved in them unattractive, so her party guests never included the political luminaries who attended the packed soirées at Londonderry House. Nor was she remotely interested in sport, although her husband was a legendary shot. For her, the chitchat of winter shooting parties and of summer tennis gatherings at Studley Royal, her father-in-law's huge house in Yorkshire, was equally and thoroughly tiresome. She did not really like going outside at all – the relentless sound of the cuckoo during the summer months made her feel faint. Card games induced fits of yawning but had to be endured. The emerging Bloomsbury intellectualism she considered too blue-stocking. But she was intelligent and she disdained the frivolities that consumed Society: she needed an occupation. E. F. Benson, certainly a friend and admirer, though a little less dazzled by her than some, had the perception to recognise that in the early years of marriage Gladys was casting round for something original to do, in his words, for 'a stunt'.

Among Gladys's gifts was irresistible enthusiasm, and a talent for apparently artless salesmanship. According to Osbert Sitwell, her conversation was 'fascinating and spontaneous', and she spoke as a wise and genuine observer of 'the behaviour of human beings'. She could not have been described as a woman passionate about music – in fact she knew nothing much about it at all, and E. F. Benson believed she would not have willingly listened to a Beethoven symphony 'unless she had been a personal friend of the composer' – but she had been seduced by the opera, the drama of it all rather than the singing. The staginess of a full-blown operatic performance and its 'pageantry and artifice' exemplified just the sort of sophisticated bohemianism that attracted her, and over the past few years she had promoted the Covent Garden Opera so effectively that attending a performance there had become the *de rigueur* way of spending an evening. Her recruiting methods were subtle. At a dinner party she would mention, in a voice full of hushed theatrics, how gloriously Nellie Melba had sung in Drury Lane the night before, and how difficult it had been to reserve a seat for the performance. The next morning her guests would rush to buy tickets for the next available performance. The tiaras that packed the velvet tiers night after night confirmed her instinct for the effectiveness of word-of-mouth recommendation.

In the spring of 1911 Gladys sold her huge house in Carlton House Terrace and moved to Coombe Court, a handsome house with a large garden near Kingston, a convenient hour by car from London. Privileged guests would find the stars of Covent Garden mingling on the Surrey lawns with Gladys's long-standing friend Queen Alexandra and other members of the Royal Family. The press were never tipped off about these gatherings, but not because Lady Ripon thought them '*canaille*', too vulgar to be invited to cover her parties. Gladys spared neither the time nor the energy to think about common journalists at all. She hated the tastelessness of self-promotion, and was on occasion surprisingly reticent about drawing attention to herself. On visits to the

Niagara skating rink, next to St James's Park underground station and 'scene of the most amusing parties', according to Mrs Hwfa Williams, she persuaded her women friends to stack the heels of their shoes with 'elevators' so that her height did not make her conspicuous. Her accommodating friends hobbled stilt-like 'in utmost discomfort' across the pavement while Gladys glided gracefully towards the rink, at ease with her anonymity.

By 1911 the popularity of the Australian diva Dame Nellie Melba was such that the celebrated French chef Georges Auguste Escoffier (whose fourth cookery book, *Le Carnet d'Epicure*, had been published that year) had been inspired to name an ice-cream and peach-based pudding after her. One gala night Osbert Sitwell was in the stalls when she sang with the celebrated tenor Enrico Caruso, 'fat as two elderly thrushes as they trilled at each other over the hedges of tiaras.' But Dame Nellie was spending much of the early summer in her native Australia, and the voices of Gladys Ripon's two favourite Polish male singers, Édouard and Jean de Reszke, were beginning to sound a little raspy: Covent Garden's seats were half-empty, and Gladys was becoming worried. She had to come up with a plan sufficiently marvellous and original for the Coronation summer.

Over the course of the past two years the Russian producer Sergei Diaghilev had been introducing the opera singers, dancers, music and startling choreography of his Ballets Russes to amazed European audiences in France and Italy. In April 1911 in Monte Carlo Gladys's married daughter Lady Juliet Duff had attended the world première of a new ballet, *Le Spectre de La Rose*, based on a poem by Gautier with music by Carl-Maria von Weber arranged for the orchestra by Hector Berlioz. Lady Juliet had been astonished by the performance of the 22-year-old Ukrainian, Vaslav Nijinsky, who danced the leading role. Gladys had seen Diaghilev's dancers several times in Russia and Paris, and had made a point of getting to know Diaghilev himself. When Lady Juliet rushed breathlessly home from Monte Carlo with news of his latest creative spectacle, Gladys knew she had her next 'stunt'.

She had once told Mrs Hwfa Williams that her enthusiasm for 'discovering a new stunt' meant that 'where the ballet goes I go too', but there was no need for her to go to Monte Carlo if she could arrange for the ballet to come to London.

For all the frenzy of the Coronation year, Gladys Ripon was not alone in her awareness of a void in her life and a yearning to fill it. Furtive assignations in rooms off darkened corridors were no longer enough. Dissatisfaction and unease riddled every layer of society, and that included the ambitious, bored, unfulfilled intellectuals, who felt at a loss, waiting, longing for something to happen. For those with the insight or the courage to admit it, it was a life that despite the 'fun' currently signified nothing. In November 1910 the art critic Roger Fry had organised an exhibition of European paintings at the Grafton Galleries, a few hundred yards from the Royal Academy. Pablo Picasso from Spain and Henri Matisse from France were among those whose work Fry had chosen to exhibit in 'Manet and the Post-Impressionists', but most of the paintings were the work of two French artists and one Dutch. The 21 paintings by Paul Cézanne, 37 by Paul Gaugin and 20 by Vincent van Gogh dealt with the fundamental issues of life, death and passion, executed in bold colour and daring, defined strokes. They contradicted what Fry thought of as 'the fatal prettiness of British art'. The critics who defined the conservative taste of the British art world, applauding the elegant barometers of taste as exemplified in the appealing and flattering portraits of Philip de László and John Singer Sargent, considered Fry insane. The *Morning Post* said the 'primitive and sinister paintings' he exhibited were intended for 'students of pathology and the specialist in abnormality.' *The Queen* magazine called the show 'barbarous', the *Daily Telegraph* said it was 'weird and uncouth'. The Establishment painter Philip Burne-Jones wrote to *The Times* full of anti-French scorn, suggesting that the whole thing was a 'huge practical joke organised in Paris at the expense of our countrymen.' Old ladies had to be carried from the gallery after fainting in shock. An acquaintance of Lady Sackville confessed that she had been physically sick at the sight of the paintings. But the young writer Virginia Stephen, at work that summer on her first novel *Night and Day*, went so far as to feel that with the exhibition in December 1910 'human character changed'. And one lone critic, Hugh Blaker, predicted that 'cultured London is composed of clowns who will by the way be thoroughly ashamed in twenty years' time and pay large sums to possess these things. How insular we are still.' And yet for the three months of the exhibition, more than four hundred visitors a day travelled to Mayfair to see and buy the pictures. Roger Fry wrote later of how 'the English public became for the first time fully aware of the existence of a new movement in art, a movement which was the more disconcerting in that it was no mere variation upon accepted themes but implied a reconsideration of the very purpose and aim as well as the methods of pictorial and plastic art.'

Many of Roger Fry's group lived in London's Bloomsbury. Among them his new lover Vanessa Bell and her painter friend Duncan Grant, a cousin of the biographer and critic Lytton Strachey. All were exhilarated and inspired by what they saw happening on canvases in Europe. That summer, several of these young English painters formed the Camden Town Group, and on 19 June the directors of the Borough Polytechnic near the Elephant and Castle invited Fry and Grant and a couple of other members of the Group to paint the students' dining room. The striking murals, based on an appropriately sunny summer theme of 'London on Holiday', transformed the dull Victorian walls: painting had become indistinguishable from decor. The students were delighted.

The Russian ballet too was soon to demonstrate the stimulating possibilities of this overlapping and merging of art forms. The appeal of things Russian was not unknown among British intellectuals seeking some meaning to life, spiritual or otherwise. A vogue for Russian literature was promoted in part by the novelist Arnold Bennett's encouragement of the publication of English translations of the works of Chekhov and Dostoevsky, Tolstoy and

Turgenev. And in the late 1880s the Ukrainian-born mystic Madame Helena Blavatsky had introduced to European consciousness the concept of 'Theosophy', the intuitive insight into the nature of God. Inspired by the teachings of Hinduism and Buddhism and by the writing of William Blake, Blavatsky devoted her life to demonstrating her conviction that the simple, inner truth of religious thought had been corrupted and complicated by the inadequate interpretations of man. 'I am an old Buddhist pilgrim,' she wrote, 'wandering about the world to teach the only true religion, which is truth.'

A cult following for Blavatsky's teachings grew up in Europe, and the writers William Butler Yeats, James Joyce and Edwin Arnold were among those who felt her influence. Other forms of spiritual stimulation became popular, including séances and clairvoyance, necromancy (the summoning of the spirits of the dead), palmistry, and all varieties of crystal-gazing mysticism. In England Annie Besant, convincingly passionate and outspoken, adopted Blavatsky's beliefs, became President of the British Theosophical Society in 1907, was an advocate of birth control for women, fell in love with the playwright Bernard Shaw, and was scheduled to speak at the suffragette rally planned to take place (with Asquith's reluctant permission) a few days before the Coronation. Under Annie's leadership membership of the Society had reached 16,000 by 1911. Lady Emily Lutyens, wife of the architect Edwin and sister of a notoriously active suffragette, Lady Constance Lytton, was fascinated to find a religion that combined the psychic and the spiritual. In the Society's Bond Street headquarters she met their secretary, the shy Miss Sharpe, and was overjoyed to discover that she had known Miss Sharpe in her previous life as a mouse. When squeaky-voiced Miss Sharpe introduced her to Mrs Besant, all white-robed, silky-seductive-sounding, Emily felt herself 'face to face with something immeasurably greater than anything I had ever known.'

In the same way that Roger Fry had recognised the potential impact of the stimulating and imaginative vision of the European painters on British taste, so Gladys Ripon identified a similar potential in Russian dancers. In their raw energy, their gravity-defying movements and their unashamed sexuality she saw something that was sure to divert a sophisticated London audience from the dreariness of familiarity, even of emptiness.

Russian ballerinas were by no means unfamiliar to London audiences, for several had already appeared in the mixed bills of variety shows at the music halls. Tamara Karsavina had danced at The Coliseum in 1909, and in the spring of 1911 Anna Pavlova was invited to renew her contract of the previous year at the Palace. She had shared a programme there with a four-foot six-inch singer of comic songs, the phenomenon Harry Relph, popularly known as 'Little Tich', and through her recommendation he became a favourite with Nijinsky.

Lady Diana Manners was mesmerised by the slight Russian figures she saw performing at the Palace. Explaining that dreary blocked toes and tutus were not all the new ballet had to offer, she persuaded her sceptical mother to accompany her every Saturday to lean against the golden rail at the back of the theatre with its easy access to the champagne bar, as was the fashionable custom, and watch Anna Pavlova's graceful steps. She was 'a leaf, a rainbow, a flake, an iridescent foam, her bones of music made', so aware of her own pre-eminence that any partner unfortunate enough to drop her while lifting her into an airborne arabesque risked having his face firmly and publicly slapped. Audiences longed for her to be dropped.

Just as it had been fashionable to persuade Dame Nellie Melba to sing at private parties, so a party was considered the height of chic if from a large basket of roses carried into the room there emerged, beribboned-and-pointed toe first, the fragile form of Pavlova, star of the Palace stage. During the summer of 1911 a Russian ballerina could be found dancing at all the large music halls in London's West End. The Duchess of Rutland became entranced, and her daughters needed little persuasion to agree to take ballet lessons. The Duchess of Rutland arranged for Lydia

Kyasht, the Russian girl currently dancing at the Empire, to give up some of her day off to teach Diana to 'glide like a Russian peasant'. Lady Ripon's former brother-in-law, now Earl of Lonsdale, had also been much taken with Lydia, and had offered to provide her with lodgings for the summer in St John's Wood, conveniently near his own home. Lydia and the other ballerinas would rehearse on Lord Lonsdale's lawn, to the delight of such lunch guests as Mrs Hwfa Williams. But the London audience had not yet seen the Russian male dancers, and, in particular Nijinsky.

The theatrical impresario Eric Wollheim had been responsible for bringing the French actresses Sarah Bernhardt and Madame Rejane to London, and had made the previous arrangements for the visiting ballerinas: he was delighted to help Diaghilev realise his plan to bring the whole company to London. Diaghilev had already been in direct negotiation for more than a year with Lady Ripon's good friends Sir Joseph Beecham and his son Thomas, who was director of events at Covent Garden. Sir Joseph had promised to sponsor the production, but Edward VII's death and the subsequent mourning period had thwarted initial plans to bring the ballet to the Aldwych Theatre in the summer of 1910. As soon as it was deemed decent, negotiations began again between Diaghilev and the Royal Opera House, with Lady Ripon's encouragement.

Until well into Edward VII's reign, production standards for ballet and even for opera – despite Lady Ripon's glittering influence – were 'shockingly shabby'. Little attention was paid to rehearsals either for performers or for the orchestra, and almost no thought was given to presentation. The notion of choreography was nonexistent. In one famously shambolic performance of Wagner's *Lohengrin*, the pulleys that were built into the floorboards, designed to help the swan glide gracefully off into the mist, had become hopelessly rusted up. As the orchestra ran out of music, the sparse audience could hear the sound of yanking and wheezing in the wings, then suddenly there was a loud clank and a small explosion. The swan's head shot into the air, leaving the

Knight exposed and distressed astride a decapitated swan until a couple of workmen rushed onto the stage and pulled him off.

For all her love of the life of the stage, the Duchess of Rutland was contemptuous of the ballet. She was no fan of the exquisite Danish prima ballerina Adeline Genée, Eric Wollheim's protégée and allegedly his lover, who had been for ten years the star at the Empire and whose fragile form was often compared to Dresden china. Adeline had done much to revive the ever-dwindling reputation of classical dance, but though she had introduced the longer ballet *Coppélia*, her repertoire was largely short and unadventurous, and she stuck closely to the favourite classics, *Cinderella* and *Papillon*. Nellie Melba also remained unmoved by the art form that so often shared the bill with her own. 'Our western eyes had been trained to regard ballet as merely a conventional monotonous affair of toe dancing and white ballet skirts and occasional gymnastics,' she wrote, dismissing it as an entertainment with 'little colour, little thrill, and practically no contact with life.'

Something far more thrilling had been meeting the popular appetite for entertainment. Since 1908 music halls all over the country had been introducing moving-picture screens into their theatres, and some were even being fully converted into cinemas seating several hundred people. In the summer of 1911 the roller-skating rink in Brighton's West Street became The Grand Picture Palace, the fourth cinema in the town. *The Bioscope Annual and Trades Directory* was an invaluable publication that listed cinemas county by county, and that year's volume ran to more than four hundred pages. While ballet dancers performed to small and somnolent audiences, the new films that arrived thrice-weekly from France and America were playing to packed auditoriums. Films made by D. W. Griffith were particularly popular. A young cub reporter turned amateur actor from Kentucky, Griffith worked for Biograph, a small company on East Fourteenth Street in New York and his beautifully made films, often hand-coloured, combined technical expertise with all sorts of innovative camera shots. Even the English were beginning to join in the movie-making craze. Epping Forest in Essex or Box Hill in Surrey became the background for stories of cowboys and Indians, and genteel picnickers were surprised by whooping half-naked men wearing feathered headdresses leaping on horseback over the cress sandwiches. In the cinema a piano, a full orchestra, and some coconut shells to clack together to indicate the clatter of horses' hooves intensified the drama of the silent movie. Thrilling drum rolls would fill the theatre as the bow-painted lips of an unfortunate girl tied to a railway line trembled while she waited to be rescued from her perilous position. In a uniform curly typeface, helpful plot explanations like 'The black canker in the rose of love is the moment of parting' would appear on the screen, often read aloud by their friends for the benefit of the illiterate.

The hour-long programme usually included a main feature, which might be a love story, a comedy, a thriller or a 'Western', plus the latest in current affairs from Pathé News. In June the oldest man in the world, a Frenchman aged 105, was seen shakily recounting his memories of the Battle of Waterloo to the camera, while the Kaiser, in England for the Coronation, was filmed 'visiting the tourist sights of London'. In America movie houses took their name – Nickelodeons – from the nickel (5 cents) charged for the cheap seats; in England these were sixpence, with seats at the back, where the glare was less damaging to the eyes, costing a little more. During the past year, safety rules had been tightened up and the projector, which was liable to catch fire when the reel accelerated beyond the operator's control, was now housed in a screened-off booth – a new-found privacy sometimes abused when the projectionist, looking forward to an evening date, would speed up the film so that it was out of sync with the disconcerted live orchestra who was unable to keep up.

The cinemas were filthy and smelly, and not just from the thick cigarette and pipe smoke that filled them. As the programme was only an hour long it was not thought necessary to provide public lavatories, and the theatre could be particularly foul-smelling after a screening to a full house of children unable to contain their excitement. Attendants would walk through the aisles spraying the air from huge bottles filled with bright blue Jeyes fluid in an attempt to remove or at least conceal the stench. Gradually, however, some of the hundreds of especially-built movie houses smartened up their appearance. The Lenton Picture Palace in Nottingham opened in December 1910 with room for six hundred people and seats ranging from the expensive ones upholstered in red leather that tipped up, to wooden benches at the bargain price of two pence. The screen was curtained in blue plush with gold trimmings, and the building was heated by steam and lit by electricity. Some cinemas had tea-houses, and special sitting-out rooms reserved for ladies only. A reassuring manager in a tailcoat – like a maitre d'hôtel in a restaurant or a butler opening a front door – would greet the audience as they arrived.

However, reports of sinister goings-on in the dark, of uninhibited sex in the back row, no less than the contempt of the purist for a blatant amateurishness that some saw as a mockery of 'genuine' art forms deterred many. It was probably inevitable that pornography should nudge its way into the new medium, and rumours circulated that censorship was about to be introduced. The Mutoscope, more popularly known as the 'What The Butler Saw', had long been a fixture at seaside piers, its sequence of images pasted on card providing, for a penny a go and a swiftly turned handle, a pleasing if jerky view of a strip-tease. The celluloid film makers, D. W. Griffith among them, saw ready money in the perennial desire of men to see women with no clothes on, and a small underground trade in sexually explicit films grew up. Well-heeled gentleman would buy their own projectors and invite their male friends to private screenings of what was often very poor-quality porn. A tip-off might result in such a screening being raided by the police, and subsequent prosecution.

A sensuous and daring but perfectly legal form of entertainment, the new 'Grecian frieze' movement, starring Canadian-born Maud Allen, was currently on show at the Palace Theatre at the top of Shaftsbury Avenue. Maud had begun her career in the public eye as a lingerie model, adding to her income by selling her own graphic, eye-popping sketches to the publisher of a sex manual. For the London stage she had studied the drawings on old Greek and Assyrian tablets and manuscripts and devised a costume, 'a wisp of chiffon and bare legs with pipes and cymbals', that bordered on public indecency. Lady Diana Manners and her mother found her irresistible. For a while Diana became obsessed by everything Greek. She developed a habit of pulling on her second toe to make it longer than the others, in the classical custom of sandalled goddesses, and would hang from a trapeze she had hooked up in her bedroom to stretch herself to a better height. In Maud's final dance, 'A Vision of Salome', she would appear on stage like a Raphael canvas come to life, carrying a model of St John the Baptist's head on a silver plate while giving the waxen lips a lingering kiss. The audience stood to cheer. At the invitation of Margot Asquith Maud went to Downing Street to dance to the music of Mendelssohn's *Spring Song* dressed as a nymph, in *bare feet*. It was said that her naked toes were able to express sorrow beautifully, and she was applauded enthusiastically.

Lady Ripon was not alone in her entrepreneurial plans for the Ballets Russes: between herself, Diaghilev, Eric Wollheim and the Beechams arrangements were finally made for the Russian Ballet to make its official debut at Covent Garden on Wednesday 21 June, the evening before the Coronation. The dancers would stay in London for a six-week run, sharing the summer programme with the Opera. The highlight of the six weeks would be a performance on Monday 26 June at a gala evening in front of the King and Queen, just four days after their Coronation.

Sergei Diaghilev was 39 years old, broad-chested and with a flattened nose like a boxer's. The white streak in his thick, chinchilla-like hair was often hidden beneath the homburg hat tilted over his hooded eyes. He wore an oversize tie-pin, his fingers were heavily ringed, and he was known affectionately by one of his dancers, Lydia Lopokova, as 'Big Serge'. He loved food, and the only three words Osbert Sitwell ever heard him say in English were 'more chocolate pudding'. Eric Wollheim described the distinctive way Diaghilev moved: 'You had to watch the great man in a hurry, because the more worried he was about time, the shorter and shorter steps he took, so that in the end he was at a standstill.' Diaghilev had come to the ballet through the visual arts rather than music, and as a university student in St Petersburg his friends had been the painters Leon Bakst and Alexandre Benois. The use of set designs from the artists Bakst and Benois – rather than making do with the unimaginative offerings of tired set designers – was unheard-of. Employing the choreographer Michel Fokine was an act of total originality, and the music he commissioned from the 29-year-old composer Igor Stravinsky made an unforgettable impact. Son of a Russian opera singer and a student of Nikolai Rimsky-Korsakov, Stravinsky had met Diaghilev in 1909 at a concert in Russia. Diaghilev was thrilled by Stravinsky's unique combination of folk-song-inspired music undercut with its raw primitive beat, and the two men became immediate friends. Parisian audiences had reacted with delight and amazement to Stravinsky's first two ballets, *The Firebird* and *Petrushka*. Since 1910 he had been working on a new composition, *Le Sacre du Printemps*. Diaghilev believed it would cause a sensation, but was uncertain how an English audience would respond to the unsettling drama of Stravinsky's music. Diaghilev introduced the composer to Benois, and together they would plan their collaborations over dinners of 'marinated fish, caviar, Black Sea oysters and the most delicious mushrooms in the world.'

Rarely seen without a hat, and a walking-stick with which to point instructions on the stage, Diaghilev was much valued by the Russian government in his role of impresario, exporting and promoting Russian culture. There was an energy in his eyes, the monocle in one adding to the glint, and he spoke French with wit and ease. Lady Ripon found his tendency to roar with laughter one moment and dissolve in tears the next wholly charismatic.

Standing in the empty Opera House discussing final arrangements for the Coronation Gala, Diaghilev and his patron made an elegant couple. But Gladys and all those close to him knew that Diaghilev's most intimate emotions were reserved for his lover, his lead dancer, Nijinsky.

On Monday 19 June the Corps of the Imperial Ballet arrived in London with barely a word of English between them. Some of the company, including Serge Grigoriev, the *régisseur* who was in charge of all administrative matters, took lodgings near the British Museum. Grigoriev confessed to being taken aback by the peculiarities of English customs. The Russian visitors were perplexed to find London's beautiful squares in all their full June lusciousness locked up, the green lawns behind the railings only accessible with little keys belonging to those who lived round the square. They were disappointed by the 'excessive' plainness of English architecture. Grigoriev was further amazed to discover that the most famous opera house in the world stood 'in the midst of a vegetable market and was closely hemmed in by greengrocers' warehouses and vast mountains of cabbages, potatoes, carrots and all manner of fruit', making it impossible to see its façade. And Michel Fokine was disconcerted by the flatness of the stage, being accustomed to one raked towards the audience.

The leading dancers were staying at the Waldorf because their preferred hotel, the Savoy, was full to the brim with important foreign visitors already in town for the Coronation. From his room at the back of the three-year-old Waldorf at the top of Aldwych, Nijinsky overlooked the roofs of the Opera House. For the Ukrainian son of a nomadic family who had spent the first few years of his life travelling from the Crimea to St Petersburg in the train of a troupe of gipsies, jugglers and puppeteers, it was a curious and awe-inspiring sight.

On Tuesday 20 June two full-dress rehearsals were taking place in London. On the stage of the Royal Opera House, Diaghilev's company was assembling, a group of foreigners suspected by some of being mere uncivilised, untamed Cossacks indulging in wild circus acts. No more than a mile away, on the other side of Whitehall, the Duke of Norfolk, in his hereditary role of Earl Marshal, organiser of all Royal ceremonial events since 1386, in particular funerals and coronations, was struggling with one of the oldest and grandest ceremonies in the land. A book of instructions 212 pages long had been produced, but this was no guarantee that things would go smoothly. The Duke was feeling anxious despite having delegated to Lord Kitchener the supervision of 60,000 troops, many of them already billeted in Hyde Park and Kensington Gardens, with the overspill out at Wormwood Scrubs at East Acton. On the Monday another rehearsal involving Their Majesties had gone without a hitch, except that the King had been unable to conceal his irritation at the confused seating arrangements. The Prime Minister had complained to him directly that he had been placed among the visiting colonial guests, and asked for a seat more appropriate to his office. The King consequently found himself involved in juggling a complicated seating plan just when he was most anxious to concentrate on his spiritual preparations – but he had not forgotten the chaos at the time of Edward VII's funeral, when the instruction book was discovered to be littered with spelling mistakes and errors in protocol, and four secretaries had been forced to work through the night correcting it. The Earl Marshal had been given a year's notice to get ready for the Coronation, but George V had little confidence in him. 'I love the Duke,' he acknowledged. 'He is a charming, honourable, straight forward little gentleman, no better in the world but,' he added with a sigh of regal exasperation, 'as a man of business he is absolutely impossible.'

Across town, behind the fruit and vegetable stalls, Diaghilev was not getting on much better. He had brought seven ballets with him that summer, including *Scheherazade*, *Le Pavillon d'Armide* and the new *Le Spectre de La Rose* that the *corps* intended to dance five times over the season. But the immigration officer at Folkestone had become suspicious when he opened the enormous trunks containing the brilliantly coloured and unfamiliar costumes. The security officials had not forgotten the Congress of Social Democrats held in London five years earlier, attended by Lenin, and this particular summer they were taking no chances: the huge Russian cases were impounded lest their contents incite Russian revolutionary activity. So the 'dress' rehearsal took place in plain clothes. And there were other problems. The painter Benois and choreographer Fokine quarrelled over the choice of certain backdrops; dancers tripped over scenery; and everyone disagreed about the tempo of the music. Diaghilev could only hope the audience reaction would not mirror the greyness of the rehearsal clothes.

Thomas Beecham, 32, creative and business manager of Covent Garden since 1910, famous womaniser and indiscreet cuckolder of Sir Bache Cunard, remained confident that he had a future success on his hands, and offered to conduct the music for some of the ballets himself. His father Sir Joseph was the highly successful owner of the world-famous pharmaceutical company – currently using a uniformed suffragette to advertise their most celebrated product under the tag-line 'Since taking Beecham's Pills I have been a new woman.' The pills, most effective for bowel problems, were also said to cure bilious and nervous disorders, headaches, giddiness, drowsiness, cold chills, loss of appetite and shortness of breath. The Beecham family, as it happened, also owned the Covent Garden Estates on which the opera house stood.

Thomas was a conductor of exquisite phrasing, combining power with delicacy, and any orchestra responded to his baton with intense pleasure. He was known to demand the very highest standards. He once noticed that his lead cellist was not reaching the required perfection. Sweeping his flattened hands away and outwards through the air to indicate a halt mid-bar, he addressed the white-faced young woman. 'Now, Madam,' he observed, 'you have between your legs an instrument capable of bringing pleasure to thousands . . . and', he continued in a tone of incredulity, 'all you can do is scratch it.'

As the Russian dancers tried to rest before their opening night in a country Grigoriev summed up as 'quite different to what we were accustomed elsewhere', the indigenous social whirl spun ever faster. In the past few days parties had been given by the Duchess of Sutherland, Lady Londesborough and Lady Derby, and on 20 June six hundred members of the upper classes danced from eleven at night until half past five the following morning at Jennie Cornwallis-West's magnificent Shakespeare Ball. Guests could choose their own Shakespearian character on which to base their costume. Jennie was launching an appeal to raise money to build a National Theatre, and hoped the ball would net more than £10,000 for the cause. Dressed as Olivia from *Twelfth Night*, she strolled through the Elizabethan–Italian garden into which Edwin Lutyens had transformed the Albert Hall, surveying the magnificent sight. The blue sky that completely covered the dark red-brick Victorian roof made the guests feel light-hearted as soon as they entered the hall. The lower tiers of boxes had become clipped yew hedges crested with topiary birds over which grape-laden vines tumbled. Cypress trees stood at intervals around the hall, and the boxes at the top of the auditorium had been turned into marble terraces. The pageant of the Court of Queen Elizabeth largely comprised real-life direct descendants of Shakespeare's historical characters; of the fictional characters, F. E. Smith stood out among the seventeen others dressed for the part as the most excellent Romeo of them all. In the souvenir brochure Mr H. Hamilton Fyfe concluded that 'this age has shot its bolt. Whatever the future may conceal of splendour and beauty, it will certainly not outdo this.' Some would have disagreed, anticipating the magnificence of the Coronation in two days' time. The attention and excitement of others was concentrated on the stage at Covent Garden.

British reaction to the Russian ballet was tested on Wednesday 21 June, the night before the Coronation. It was not the first time Nijinsky had danced the lead role in *Le Pavillon d'Armide* and *Carnaval*, but it was his first appearance on a London stage and things did not seem to be going well. During the interval Diaghilev watched in horror as 'at least a hundred old ladies, covered with diamonds as if they were icons,' passed him 'with a look of disgust on their faces,' prompting the business manager to come rushing over. 'You've spoilt your magnificent opening by the barbarian horror,' he panicked. 'It isn't dancing. It's just savages prancing about.' Diaghilev feared he had a disaster on his hands.

But the following morning's reviews in *The Times* and the *Daily Mail* were enough to reassure him, and to give Nijinsky the confidence to exchange his decorous carnival trousers for an infinitely more suggestive pair of harlequined tights. 'Every jump is a separate ecstasy,' exclaimed the *Times's* critic George Calderon, while the *Daily Mail* reporter thought the performances 'little less than a revelation', continuing: 'the amazing Nijinsky, bounding into air with the light joy of a Mercury with winged heels, created the moments of the most alluring novelty.' The excellence of technique combined with the originality of the production startled the critics. Thomas Beecham was elated. Diaghilev's production had 'sounded the death knell of the existing system of organised incapacity', he declared. Ballet would never be the same again.

The solemn day of the Coronation opened clammy and grey. Queen Mary woke in a state of apprehension, noting in her diary that the weather was 'damp but fine'. Her husband enhanced her description with his own observation: 'Overcast and cloudy', he wrote. Compared with the preceding days of June sunshine the weather was disappointing, and since there was a chance of seeing the proceedings later on film in the picture palaces it was thought that the cold and the threatened drizzle were sure to deter many onlookers. The organisers need not have worried. At 7.50 a.m. the crimson stands along the parade route, packed with thousands of resilient British royalists, suddenly turned black as thousands of umbrellas were simultaneously unfurled against the fine rain. Mary feared that her propensity to sea-sickness might be triggered by the unsprung sway of the coach that was to take her and George to and from the Abbey. She wondered if her husband's knock knees would spoil the elegance of his procession up the aisle.

Lady Huntingdon had been up since six that morning to be sure of being ready and in her seat in good time. Falling asleep on the journey to Westminster Abbey, she was jostled so violently in her own wildly-swinging carriage that her companion, the Countess of Fingall, found herself acting as impromptu lady's maid on arrival, re-settling the tiara on Lady Huntingdon's lacquered head. Some carriages paused for the horses to drink from the stone water troughs set deep into the pavements and generally used by the cab horses. Twelve thousand policemen lined the route. Around the Abbey itself the customary frantic mechanised buzz of the streets, the usual jostle for road space between horse-cabs, motor-cars, trams, bicycles and horse buses was missing. All of New Georgian London had come out on foot to watch the show.

The distinguished writer and Nobel prize-winner Rudyard Kipling, with an earning capacity of £30,000 a year the richest author in the English-speaking world, was annoyed that the dark green Rolls-Royce he had ordered, expecting it to be delivered in March, would not be ready for the Coronation: Barkers, the royal coach-builders to whom Rolls-Royce subcontracted their work, were committed to an urgent commission for the King and were behind with their orders. As a result the Kiplings had an early start in their old and slower Rolls, leaving Bateman's, their house in Sussex, at quarter to six that morning. They had been invited to have breakfast in the House of Commons, conveniently close to the Abbey, but to his annoyance Kipling became trapped in conversation over the toast and marmalade by George Buckle, editor of *The Times*, asking for the umpteenth time whether he would write a piece about the Coronation for the paper.

For Brian Calkin, the 13-year-old chorister from St Paul's Cathedral Choir School, who had sung at the unveiling of Queen Victoria's memorial the month before, this was the most exciting day of his life. His ambition was to become a professional singer when he grew up, and he had a solo part. He wore the medal that all the choirboys had been given that morning by the Keeper of the Privy Purse, accompanied by a card stating that it was a gift from the King himself 'in remembrance of their Majesties' Coronation'. In Brian's pocket was his personal ticket of entry to the Orchestra Gallery in the Abbey, signed by the Earl Marshal. To Brian's mild irritation, his name had been entered incorrectly as 'Bernard', but he knew the Earl Marshal had a lot on his mind and there was bound to be the occasional slip. Once inside the Abbey, the ceremony unfolded for Brian like the final scene from *Alice in Wonderland*, with the Heralds in their tabards resembling huge playing-cards, crimson against the grey Abbey. The choristers had been rehearsing for months. Brian's brother John was one of the scholars at Westminster School, and he envied them their exclusive and age-old privilege of shouting 'Vivat Rex Georgius! Vivat! Vivat! Vivat!' as the King arrived in the Cathedral.

As Brian watched the Abbey fill up, he was amazed by the exotic array of nationalities represented. Here were the Prince of Ethiopia, the turbans of the accompanying Abyssinian envoys shining like brilliant green enamel, and troops from across the Empire – from West and East Africa, the West Indies and the East Indies, from Ceylon and Malaya. In accordance with instructions issued by the Earl Marshal's office, peers' young sons wore black velvet knickerbockers, black silk stockings, steel buckles on their shoes and Glengarry caps of black velvet. Their sombre garb stood out, as no personal mourning was permitted in the Abbey that day.

The War Minister, Viscount Haldane, scuttled up the aisle, his peer's robes askew, resembling, according to Kipling, 'a Toby dog strayed from a Punch and Judy show'. Kipling, despite his earlier reservations, was taking notes. He thought Churchill, full of all his own self-importance and showiness, seemed 'like an obscene paperbacked French novel in the Bodleian'. The Queen arrived feeling a little bilious. The Master of Elibank thought she looked 'pale and strained. You felt she was a great lady but not a Queen.' Six thousand stools and chairs of fine mahogany bearing the royal coronet had been made especially for the ceremony, each one with the name of a guest inscribed on the back, but not everyone was guaranteed a good view. While Clemmie Churchill, nursing mother of a four-week-old baby, enjoyed her place in the Royal Box, Lady Ottoline Morrell, obliged as the wife of an MP to be there, swathed in white taffeta with a white mantilla covering her tiara-free head, found herself perched so high at the top of the Abbey that she was forced to squint to see anything at all. The Duke of Devonshire was relieved that so far things seemed to be going off smoothly, for at a rehearsal two weeks earlier, as he had subsequently confided to his diary, 'Nobody knew what to do. Good deal of confusion.'

After the long build-up the service eventually reached the solemn moment of crowning, and the young Prince of Wales approached his father, doffed his coronet and pledged his allegiance on bended knee before kissing him on the cheek. The watching congregation wavered between a smile and a tear. Several peers later confessed to the *Illustrated London News* that they restored their own coronets to their noble heads hoping that the butter in the emergency sandwiches concealed in the silk lining in grease-proof-paper packets had not begun to melt and seep.

As the Archbishop of Canterbury placed the crown on Queen Mary's head a single unified rustle was heard by everyone in the Abbey, even Ottoline in her cramped and distant lookout. It was the sound of the peeresses lifting their own tiaras to their heads. One of the guests, Vita Sackville-West, described the sight from her pew: 'a single gesture of exquisite beauty, their white arms rising with a sound like the rushing of birds' wings and a proud arching like the arching of the neck of a swan.' The effect was then slightly marred – in the opinion of several dowagers watching from above – by the many vulgar little mirrors produced from deep within the folds of the ladies' ceremonial robes. The younger women's 'furtive peeps' to check their appearance caused the dowagers to mutter that 'it was easy to see that the reign of Edward VII was over and the days of decent behaviour ended.'

In the end, the event was considered a triumph. Nevertheless, the Earl Marshal hoped there would be no more such productions, no more headache-inducing funerals or coronations, in the near future. Several hundred million people around the British Empire had saluted their new King. There were no reported arrests, and the cleaners who swept up the Abbey afterwards resisted the temptation to pocket three ropes of pearls, twenty brooches, half a dozen bracelets, twenty golden balls dislodged from coronets and three-quarters of a diamond necklace, in all a haul worth £20,000, most of which was eventually returned safely to its owners. Lady Ottoline returned home to Bedford Square, 'utterly exhausted by that puppet show', declaring further that 'It was hateful and I am more Republican than ever.' Three days later Queen Mary was writing her Sunday letter to her Aunt Augusta from the Royal Yacht at Portsmouth, where they had been watching the naval review the day before. 'You may imagine what an immense relief it is to us that the great and solemn ceremony of Thursday is well over for it was an awful ordeal for us both.'

The gay summer life of the capital continued. On Monday 26 June the Wimbledon tennis championships began, the 34th, with more than a hundred entries for the men's singles. The sunny days of earlier in the season had vanished and the weather ran true to form, providing the players with a cold and unsettled opening day. The *Daily Telegraph* reported wryly that 'there was seen the familiar spectacle of sodden courts and idling players.' No bookmaker had thought to establish himself at the tournament, but the *Telegraph* correspondent was prepared to risk a small sum on the impressive strokes of Monsieur A. H. Gobert, who had practised in the sunshine of his native France 'under conditions not prevailing in England.' To preserve the grass, tarpaulins were drawn up to make a shallow tent over the damp courts until the rain stopped, when 'the tent was lowered until it subsided onto the ground in stage billows like those which made Ariel sea-sick in *The Tempest*'. Unfortunately Monsieur Gobert was eliminated before reaching the final, and Antony Wilding of New Zealand won the trophy for the second year running.

On the evening of that same Monday, 26 June, the Russians were to dance for the King and Queen. Gladys Ripon arrived at the Opera House early, dressed in white brocade embroidered in diamanté, a giant pearl-tipped diamond tiara on her upswept hair. She was accompanied by her daughter Lady Juliet, in a gown of sea-green satin velour. Lady Diana Manners, another early arrival, watched the Marchioness move up and down the aisles 'with the zest and zeal of a girl', personally greeting people as they arrived, among them Winston Churchill, Lady Crewe in emerald silk, and the Duchess of Devonshire in white satin and lace. A hundred thousand roses had been used to decorate the tiers of boxes, but artificial flowers had been mixed with real so that the scent should not overwhelm the distinguished audience. The Queen, in pale pink satin, her bodice blazing with diamonds, took her seat next to the King in the Royal Box, decorated with a frieze of gold, white and mauve orchids for the occasion. The house lights remained undimmed as the programme began, and from the stage Karsavina had a good view of 'the wonderful stateliness in which Queen Mary wore her robes . . . and an Indian Rajah with pearls and emeralds woven into his beard.' The *Daily Mail*'s art critic observed that the opera glasses in the centre of the Royal Box were raised with some frequency, but Diaghilev was disturbed by the silence in the pauses between the dances. At the end, he heard a barely discernible noise he later described as the 'strangest of sounds', and realised that 'the public was gently clapping its kid-gloved hands'. He remained despondent.

But Diaghilev had misinterpreted the English reserve, and the level of his success soon became apparent. The reviewers scarcely had time to draw breath before the next performance, *Le Spectre de la Rose*. In this, a sleeping Karsavina was roused but not woken by Nijinsky arriving through the window of her small boudoir. After a *pas de deux*, Nijinsky embarked on a fifteen-minute solo, the longest in ballet, before leaving the sleeping girl, vanishing through the window by which he had entered. The dancer was dressed in a flesh-coloured silk tricot onto which Bakst had directly pinned dozens of pinky-red and purple silk petals – making Nijinsky wince in the process – and had insisted on being responsible for his own make-up. His face resembled 'a celestial insect, his eyebrows suggesting some beautiful beetle which one might expect to find closest to the heart of a rose.' He looked sensational.

But it was the dancing that stunned the audience as Nijinsky proceeded to make a mockery of the laws of gravity. As George Calderon of *The Times* wrote, 'He seems to be positively lighter than air, for his leaps have no sense of effort and you are inclined to doubt if he really touches the stage between them.' When asked, Nijinsky tried to make sense of his astonishing gift. Music had been part of his life since his baptism in the church in Warsaw that held Chopin's heart, but he attributed his gift for dancing to the time when he was six years old and his father had thrown him into the freezing waters of the Wisla River in Poland to teach him to swim. Feeling himself drowning, Nijinsky saw a strand of light through the murk and, conscious of a sudden physical strength, leaped upwards, defying the pressure of the water to save himself. As he grew older, he explained how he had made air his medium. 'It is very simple,' he said. 'You jump and just stop in the air for a moment.' At the end of the short ballet the audience shouted themselves hoarse, begging for an encore.

This single magical performance had the effect of breathing new life and enthusiasm into those who saw it. The privileged classes found their boredom alleviated and their own creative potential awakened. For Lady Diana 'the comets whizzed across the unfamiliar sky, the stars danced.' Mrs Hwfa Williams noticed that people started postponing their Saturday-to-Monday departure from town in order to go to the ballet, and remarked that 'what the French call Le Froid Londonien was swept away in a torrent of enthusiasm, a wave of excitement that seemed wholly foreign to our staid English audiences.' By the end of the week the Knightsbridge store Harvey Nichols had cleared their windows of the white, cream and lilac of summer fashion and filled them instead with hangings in Bakst purple and red. In the bedrooms of

Violet and Sonia Keppel, daughters of the old King's mistress, divans were piled high with Bakst blue pillows, the walls covered in 'eastern' murals. Leopard skins replaced carpets, light bulbs were dimmed, and Gladys Ripon's daughter Juliet lay on a sofa in her incense-laden room, 'a very tall willowy siren in Turkish trousers'. Karsavina sensed that Bakst had single-handedly 'wakened up the love of colour'. To socialite Osbert Sitwell it seemed that 'every chair cover, every lamp shade reflected the Russian Ballet.' The painter Duncan Grant took time off from the murals in the dining room at the Borough Polytechnic to see Le Spectre, declaring that 'the ballet made my hair stand on end.' Nijinsky made him 'believe that space belonged to us.' Meeting Bakst at Ottoline's house in Bedford Square, Duncan rejoiced that 'the impact of great painters in the theatre produced an immense excitement for the artists.'

On non-performance days, Diaghilev and Nijinsky were chauffeured down to Coombe in Lady Ripon's car to be introduced to her friends, who longed to meet them in person. The homosexuality that had scandalised a society confronted with the behaviour of Oscar Wilde only twenty years earlier was now hobnobbing with the enemy. At one of the lunch parties that included Bakst, Stravinsky and Diaghilev, Ottoline found herself sitting next to Nijinsky. She noticed how expressive his hands were, but also that he had a nervous habit of clutching his thumbs inside his other fingers. He was 'so different from all the smart people for he was such a pure artist, a drop of the essence of art.' She found him rather ugly, with his long muscular neck and 'pale Kalmuk face', but they managed to communicate despite his poor French and her non-existent Russian, and she was enchanted by him. He was rumoured to be dreadfully debauched, and to have accepted a belt of emeralds and diamonds from an admiring Indian prince, but Ottoline discovered a young man who disliked possessions and 'anything that hampered him or diverted him from his art.' He confided to her that he thought Le Spectre de la Rose 'trop joli', and was much more absorbed by the old Russian myths which he was beginning to explore in depth through Stravinsky's Le Sacre du Printemps, the profoundly innovative ballet

Diaghilev hoped to dare to bring to England the following year. That summer Ottoline often invited Nijinsky to tea at Bedford Square, where he would catch up Julian, her five-year-old daughter, and swing her ballerina-like through the air, or watch Duncan Grant and Adrian Stephen playing tennis on the Square's tennis court.

Lady Michelham, wearing several feet only of the nineteen yards of pearls in her possession, persuaded Pavlova and Nijinsky to dance on an elevated platform at her famous house, Strawberry Hill in Twickenham, once the home of Horace Walpole. Dinner that evening, according to Mrs Hwfa Williams, included one course 'made to represent lighthouses, surrounded with ortolans to represent seagulls, with waves and surf of white sauce breaking over them.' The generally indefatigable Mrs Williams confessed that the elaborate construction was so daunting that she dared not touch it, and left the table still ravenous.

For many intellectuals the performances of the Ballets Russes combined power, freedom, beauty and restraint. The civil servant Leonard Woolf went countless times to Covent Garden, declaring that he had 'never seen anything more perfect, nor more exciting on any stage.' Night after night he would go to the ballet and there meet his friends, 'the people whom one liked best in the world, moved and excited as one was oneself.' The poet Rupert Brooke went up to Drury Lane from Grantchester fifteen times during the ballet season. The actress Ellen Terry felt that the Russian ballet had restored the art of dance to its 'primal nobility'. The singer Nellie Melba, fifty years old that May and returning from Australia, found that in her absence a revolution had overtaken much that was so familiar to her. When she saw the curtain rise 'on a stage of marvellous colour, listened to the fierce fiery music, marvelled at the superb grouping and choreography of it all, I felt that I had discovered a new art.' Lytton Strachey, mesmerised as Diaghilev himself had been by Nijinsky's muscular limbs, sent the dancer an enormous basket of flowers.

Phyllis Bedells was 17, and the previous winter she had played the first twin in the West End production of J.M. Barrie's *Peter*

Pan; this year she had been engaged to dance at the Empire. There were no matinees at the ballet that first season, so she begged to be given the night off to see the Russian dancers – an unprecedented request, to which the director reluctantly agreed. She was able to afford only one seat, so her father escorted her to the Opera House, promising to return for her later. That night *Carnaval* was being performed, with Nijinsky and Karsavina. Phyllis was shocked to discover that people rich and spoiled enough to be able to afford tickets for the ballet night after night failed to show the dancers the respect they deserved. 'People who were sitting in neighbouring seats would keep chatting away in a blasé manner. I worked myself into a state of fury . . . several times, young as I was, I asked them to be quiet.' But when Nijinsky finally appeared she grew silent under the awe-inspiring impact of his dancing: 'I cannot write about Nijinsky. It is useless. Then he was at the height of his powers. I was breathless as I sat there in my seat and watched his dancing. As long as I live,' she told her father later, 'I shall not forget that night.'

6

Early July

An unending summer of the snakeless meadow.
Leonard Woolf, *Beginning Again*

The mingled country sounds of a bee, a mowing machine,
a mill and a sparrow. Peace!
Rupert Brooke, in a letter to Ka Cox

AFTER THE FRENZY of the Coronation weeks those lucky enough to have a choice were leaving London for the comparative quiet of the countryside. The King and Queen were about to embark on a tour of the United Kingdom; Winston Churchill planned to escape to build sandcastles on the coast at Broadstairs whenever the opportunity arose. Diana Manners was reunited with the Coterie in Leicestershire, and Gladys Ripon continued to entertain the Russian dancers on her lawn at Coombe Court in Surrey. If the Russian dancers had been feeling disoriented by their lack of familiarity with the English customs and way of life, another comparatively recent arrival in London was equally confused.

On 11 June Leonard Woolf, Jewish, aged 31 and considered by himself 'middle-aged', had returned to his family home in Putney after six and a half years spent becoming an 'anti-imperialist' in the Colonial Civil Service in Ceylon. He was slim and dark, with remarkably blue eyes, and the incipient tremble in his hands intensified as he became alarmed or uncomfortable; when he was writing or thinking he scarcely trembled at all. The din that engulfed him as he was driven out of Charing Cross station both dismayed and depressed him. London was of course recognisable, but from the perspective of the recent familiarity of the sights and sounds and smells of Asia, it was only a half-remembered, half-convincing reality. During his absence abroad the familiar two-wheeled horse-drawn hansom cab had all but disappeared, and as he made his way down the Fulham Road through the 'mechanised, bricked-up sunshine of this London summer' the line between familiarity and newness blurred still further. Arriving at the house in Colinette Road off the Upper Richmond Road, where the yardsticks of his childhood – the old pear tree in the garden and the sideboard in the sitting room – were in their accustomed places, unaltered despite being twenty years older, he felt bewildered. As soon as he decently could without upsetting his mother, he escaped to Cambridge to stay with his old friend Lytton Strachey.

As the summer screen of nettles and goose-grass began to climb and thicken against Cambridgeshire village walls, the old friends took to the punts. Floating down the river backs among the drooping willows, past Persian-carpeted banks thick with amethyst clover, scarlet poppies, yellow dandelions and blue forget-me-nots, they passed boats full of beautiful girls whose undergraduate suitors held parasols to shade their lovely heads. Leonard's loyalty to this place was 'more intimate, profound, unalloyed' than any of his other loyalties, and here he found continuity. Here were his friends from The Society, here was the Great Court of Trinity, here the bowling green, here the resonance of the novels of Thomas Hardy, here 'all the eternal truths and values of my youth – going on just as I had left them seven years ago.' 'The Society', a secret club of twelve members known otherwise as The Apostles, founded in 1820, comprised the twelve cleverest students in Cambridge. A graduating member became known as an Angel, and the only rule was that there were to be no rules. Tennyson and Hallam had formed their friendship at meetings of The Apostles, and during and after Leonard's years at Trinity G.E. Moore, Lytton Strachey, Maynard Keynes, E.M. Forster and, most recently, Rupert Brooke had been members. The club menu famously included sardines, always referred to as whales. For such aesthetes, food was not a priority.

On Saturday 17 June Leonard dined with Lytton and a 23-year-old poet at work on his first book. When introduced to Rupert Brooke, Leonard's stunned reaction was to think him 'Exactly what Adonis must have looked like in the eyes of Aphrodite.' Lytton, in contrast, had begun to grow a reddish-brown beard, making him resemble (he feared) 'a French decadent poet'. He had been suffering from mumps in May, and as the swelling subsided had thought a beard might enhance his now depressingly sunken face. He wrote defensively to his mother that 'Its colour is much admired and it is generally considered extremely effective, though some ill bred persons have been observed to laugh.' An unknown woman who enquired whether he kept the hairy extension above or beneath the bedclothes at night was irritably invited to come and see for herself.

On Monday 3 July Leonard returned to London and went to dinner in Gordon Square, Bloomsbury at the house of Clive and Vanessa Bell, now married, with whom he had last dined in 1904. He had seen Adonis in Rupert Brooke's godlike features, and now in Vanessa's appearance he detected further classical divinity, 'a mixture of Athene, Artemis and Aphrodite.' Other guests joined them after dinner, among them Vanessa's sister Virginia, 'an intense almost ethereal beauty', the painter Duncan Grant, and Walter Lamb, a Classics don and former suitor of Virginia's.

That night Leonard felt himself to be in the middle of 'a profound revolution'. He had spent the evening observing the way this group of friends behaved with one another, and found it all very exhilarating – the surprising and liberal use of Christian names, tossed among each other, the previously unimaginable greeting by kissing, the intimacy and frankness of conversation between these men and women, the daring to call 'a sexual spade a spade'. After the initial shock of the unfamiliarity of London itself he had been reassured by the sense of continuity he had found in Cambridge but, paradoxically, he was not alarmed by the new social code he found in Gordon Square. He realised it was possible to accommodate the old and the new into one life, and that there was 'no reason why if you like cats and claret . . . you should not like dogs and burgundy'.

Dramatic changes and developments more sinister in nature were evident to anxious members of the Cabinet and its Shadow. On 1 July the new German warship *Panther*, at the command of the Kaiser – recent guest of honour at the Coronation of his cousin – had left Germany on its way to Agadir on the west coast of Morocco with the ostensible purpose of protecting German expatriates from trouble in an unsettled, French-occupied part of Africa. The Foreign Secretary Sir Edward Grey and Winston Churchill, the Home Secretary, suspected the Kaiser's motives, fearing that an increased German presence in Morocco would prove to be an excuse for territorial aggression, conveniently undertaken in a country where French military power was weak and at a time when their English allies were too busy with domestic problems to pay attention. On 5 July, the day on which Edward Grey warned the German Ambassador in London that the British Government was not indifferent to the arrival of the gunship, and Arthur Balfour promised that the Opposition would support the Government in any action taken against Germany, an aeroplane flew for the first time over the City of London.

Mr Pringle was in the middle of discussing the National Insurance Bill in the Commons and Lord Salisbury was on his feet ready to attack the Parliament Bill in the Lords when a buzzing noise – 'like a rattle twirled by a young giant', according to an eye-witness reporter for the *Daily Mail* – filled the chambers and all oratory was halted. Members of the two Houses deserted their benches and rushed outside to the long terrace overlooking the Thames. Ignoring the strict rules of the Aero Club, Mr Graham Gilmour had begun his journey by making a circuit of St Paul's

Cathedral in a Bristol bi-plane. Between six and seven in the evening, at a skimming height of only 200 feet, his plane approached Parliament Square. The gentlemen on the terrace were just in time to catch sight of Mr Gilmour's innovative airborne display. On Blackfriars Bridge a group of Boy Scouts looked skywards, roaring out in excited greeting as the aeroplane flew past.

The oppressive weather was becoming increasingly hard to tolerate. On Saturday 8 July stuffy theatres reported matinee attendances well below average, while four people were admitted to St Bart's Hospital and another four to Guy's, suffering from heatstroke. William Frome, a labourer from a farm near Alton in Hampshire, having arrived in Covent Garden on his donkey-cart with the weekly delivery of carrots and potatoes, was overcome with faintness and fell off his cart, injuring his back badly. To the young novelist D. H. Lawrence, from the Midlands, London seemed like 'some hoary massive underworld, a hoary ponderous inferno. The traffic flows through the rigid grey streets like the rivers of hell through the banks of rocky ash.'

On 7 July the newly crowned Royal couple left London for their tour of Ireland, Wales and Scotland. The Royal party was by no means immune to the high temperatures that accompanied them, and special cooling arrangements had to be made, as the Duchess of Devonshire, Mistress of the Robes, described in a letter to her husband after arriving at Dublin by sea: 'The yacht was too delicious after the heat in the train, though even that was quite bearable with fans and lumps of ice.'

Leonard, setting out on a rural progress of his own, was looking forward to going to Somerset to meet another old friend from his Cambridge days. Here was a part of England that seemed on the surface to have remained unchanged, not merely during Leonard's own absence of a few years but since the days of Chaucer. Leaving 'the incessant whirl' of London to travel to the deep quiet of the south-west of England seemed to him 'like passing straight from a tornado into a calm, or from a saturnalia into a monastery.' A Trinity contemporary, the Reverend the Honourable Leopold Colin Henry Douglas Campbell-Douglas, had become Vicar of Frome, a Somerset market town of less than ten thousand people. The son of Lord Blythswood, this High Anglican parson with a background of Eton, Cambridge and the Scots Guards satisfied all the little snobberies of the social aspirants of Frome. Leopold was neither particularly stimulating in speech nor lacking in class prejudice, and his rather affected and absurd sermons were unintelligible to most of the parishioners. But Leonard had discovered a 'spontaneous gaiety and benevolence in his nature and an unusual mental curiosity' that had attracted him enough as an undergraduate to make of Leopold a long-term friend. The lazy days were spent sitting in the vicarage garden talking of old times, or walking around the unaltered eighteenth-century crescents and streets of the nearby city of Bath before trotting back to the vicarage in the parson's gig. Once home they would tuck into familiar (if inappropriate for temperatures of 86°F in the shade) English meals of roast lamb, peas and beans from the garden. The slow rhythm of these few peaceful days held a great appeal for Leonard, and he found them a further soothing contrast to the startling impressions of his homecoming.

The straightforward and even monotonous pattern of Leopold's life was not unusual for a country parson in 1911. Another man of the cloth known to Leonard, The Reverend W. W. Thomas, the Rector of Southease in Sussex, led an unchallenging existence in his sleepy parish of eighty people. After completing his clerical duties in the small church with its pretty twelfth-century circular tower which sat across the lane from his splendid seventeenth-century rectory, he would spend most of the day in his study, gazing through the window at the uninterrupted view of goods trains rumbling across the water meadows along the Lewes-to-Newhaven line. Villagers knew he had been amply rewarded when he announced that a record number of carriages had passed by that day. Yet another Sussex vicar of Leonard's acquaintance, the Reverend J. B. Hawkesford, found the effort of giving his own sermons so exhausting that he chose an especially long hymn to follow his Sunday homily, and while the choir embarked on the first of numerous verses would slip out of the side door to lean against a gravestone and enjoy a restorative cigarette. His wife longed to leave both the countryside *and* the Vicar forever, and move in with her cousin living in a smart London flat overlooking the Queen's Tennis Court in West Kensington. She dreamed of spending her summers watching the tournaments, her winters the Oxford and Cambridge football matches which took place on the scuffed courts.

Unknown to Leonard, an invitation to spend a few days in Devon after his return from Somerset extended a week or so earlier by Lytton Strachey was in danger of being rescinded. Lytton had rented Becky House in the beautiful and remote Dart Valley, a few hundred yards from the Becky waterfall. The moor was home to goats, lambs, ponies and rabbits as well as otter, mink, badgers, foxes, weasels and stoats, but these apart the isolated house provided Lytton with much-wanted seclusion, an escape from the social activities of London and Cambridge and a place to write his new book, uninterrupted. The impending arrival of Leonard with his 'long drawn weather-beaten face' and Lytton's other invitee, the philosopher G. E. Moore, was giving him cold feet. Lytton was working on *Landmarks in French Literature*, and not looking forward to the demands of guests who would take him away from his work. Panicking, he wrote to his friend the painter Henry Lamb, a member of Roger Fry and Duncan Grant's Camden Town Group, begging him to come instead. He also wrote to warn Leonard that he might no longer wish to come, for he feared he and Lamb would not get on. 'My heart quails at the thought of their conversation . . . the curiosity of existence seems to vanish with them,' Lytton wrote to Lamb, who having at first accepted then cried off at the last minute. Leonard and Moore arrived on Dartmoor oblivious of the fact that their host was wishing they would both go away.

Secretly, Leonard himself was not sure if he wanted to be in Devon: the intellectual leap from Leopold's parishioners to the conversational demands of the authors of *Eminent Victorians* and *Principia Ethica* he felt would be as dramatic as 'stepping from the pages of *The Vicar of Wakefield* to those of Voltaire and Diderot'. He was terrified that his own contribution to the life of the mind would not reach the required standard. Intimidated, and wary of revealing his own intellectual shortcomings during conversations that he found 'astringent', Leonard lived constantly under the ever-threatening cloud of a question he dare not ask his erudite companions: 'What do you mean by that?' The two intellectual giants would spend mornings sitting in the garden working on their respective books, wearing matching panama hats. Both claimed to be suffering from literary constipation. Lytton would sit on the lawn, a tangle of arms and legs, 'his toes . . . corkscrewed . . . up and round to within a foot of his nose'. His hat pulled down firmly against the sun, he would groan over the blank sheet that Leonard never doubted would eventually become part of a great work on French literature. Moore, in a nearby deckchair, wet with the sweat of mental industry, would groan from under *his* hat about *his* lack of inspiration. In the afternoon the house party would go for very leisurely walks on Dartmoor – Lytton, who set the pace, had never been known to hurry. Reaching a rocky pond, Lytton would refuse to get into the water, having made a lifelong pledge not to get wet in the open air; Moore would dive without hesitation into freezing black pools hidden between rocks, shaming Leonard into following his example – though after the delicious remembered warmth of the Indian Ocean the temperature made Leonard shudder. In the evenings Moore would sing Schubert songs and play Beethoven sonatas on the Becky House piano with such passion that he would rise from the stool yet again basted in sweat, this time from the emotion of his own magnificent playing. Lytton revised his opinion of his old friends, finding them after all 'Oh! Quite extraordinarily nice.' In his new, generous-spirited mood he reported in a letter to Lamb: 'My health is a great success, fatness increasing and peevishness at breakfast almost unknown.'

★

Across the country, in Grantchester near Cambridge, Rupert Brooke was renting a house on the banks of the river Granta. Leonard was not the only one to be taken aback by Rupert's astonishing beauty. Frances Cornford, an older woman friend, described 'the clear line of his chin and long broad-based neck on broad shoulders' as 'so entirely beautiful that he seemed like a symbol of youth for all time.' That summer the poet's favourite things included lust (a word he had chosen for the title of one of the poems he was currently writing), love, Keats, the weather, truth, guts, marrons glacés, and his girlfriend Ka Cox. He might have added swimming, the Russian Ballet (after watching them dance fifteen times), and Noel Olivier, a 17-year-old student at Bedales School to whom he was secretly engaged, despite his love for Ka Cox.

The vicarage in Grantchester – 'a deserted, lonely, dank, ruined, overgrown, gloomy, lovely house: with a garden to match' – was a long red-brick ramshackle building, three storeys high. For thirty shillings a week Rupert rented three rooms, including his bedroom, which was reached through an old children's safety gate. The sitting room had a glass door with yellow panes which gave the illusion that sunshine was permanently flooding the nearby-box-tree-darkened room. There was a sagging canopied veranda at the back, and the romantically disordered garden was overgrown with huge chestnut trees and filled with unkempt and rambling bushes covered in the delicate wild flowers of, in Rupert's words, 'England's unofficial rose'. The heavy scent of Madonna lilies nearby displeased Rupert, making him fear that 'the Angel Gabriel might pop out from behind them at any moment and announce something dreadful.' The lawn stretched down to a tangle of long grass abutting the briar-filled banks of the Granta, described by him in verse:

> Oh! There the chestnuts, summer through,
> Beside the river make for you
> A tunnel of green gloom and sleep
> Deeply above; and green and deep

> The stream mysterious glides beneath,
> Green as a dream and deep as death.

In the corner of the garden, beehives belonging to the landlord Mr Neeve reverberated with the high-summer activity of their inmates and Mr Neeve, 'with an accent above his class who sits out near the beehives with a handkerchief over his head and reads advanced newspapers', made sure there was always plenty of honey for afternoon tea. His wife Florence was also solicitous of the young lodger, and would leave a slice of home-made apple pie in the larder for when Rupert returned late at night and ravenous from the ballet. Everywhere in the garden the heavy, clammy scent of the river hung in the air.

> The thrilling-sweet and rotten
> Unforgettable, unforgotten
> River-smell.

Through the five-barred gate to the road, permanently hooked open to the gravel drive, stood the village church, 'fusty with the ghosts of mouldering clergyman', where the unreliable church clock, a local joke, chimed at odd hours, and the driver of an idle hansom cab seemed to be permanently lounging against the church wall. Grantchester was originally a Roman settlement, and from it the town of Cambridge had grown. Its beauty – it was 'a fine place to write my poetry' – lured many of Rupert's friends there that summer. The lawn of The Old Vicarage was always littered with Rupert's notebooks containing the poems he was assembling for his first collection, due to be published in the winter of 1911. He was also writing a thesis on the Elizabethan dramatist John Webster that he hoped would qualify him for election as a Fellow of his old college, King's. He found inspiration in the deep, unhurried countryside. 'There is no wind and no sun,' he wrote to Ka Cox in early July, 'only a sort of warm haze and through it the mingled country sounds of a bee, a mowing machine, a mill and a sparrow. Peace!'

In the poem *Dining Room Tea*, written that August, Rupert described how 'Proud in their careless transience moved/The changing faces that I loved.' Virginia Stephen was one of his many house-guests, a childhood friend who with her sister Vanessa had played with him on the beach at St Ives. Virginia briefly wondered during the summer of 1911 whether she might be a little in love with Rupert herself. His feet, she wrote, were 'permanently bare; he disdained tobacco and butcher's meat, and he lived all day and perhaps slept all night in the open air.' Sometimes when stuck for the right word he would call across the lawn to Virginia. Once he asked her for the brightest thing she could think of. 'A leaf with the light on it,' she called back, thus filling in the blank space in a line in the poem *Town and Country.* In the great heat of July they were always swimming, rather more robustly than Lytton Strachey at Becky House, with his hesitant paddling. David Garnett, Virginia Stephen, Ka Cox and Churchill's sociable private secretary Edward Marsh were among those who cooled themselves in Byron's romantic pool that summer. Midnight was a favourite time to walk out into the white dusty-with-heat lane, down to the meadow and over the wall of the mill from which Chaucer's *Reeve's Tale* took its inspiration. The powerful scents of wild peppermint and mud rising from the mill pool assailed the bathers as they jumped naked into the water. Rupert had a party trick that depended on cold water and an appreciative audience. Visible by the light of the moon, he began with a rather disappointing half-dive – because of 'the moment of doubt before one struck the water' he had never acquired the courage to stretch out fully. After hitting the water, belly flattened with a splosh, he would rise triumphant from the blackness flaunting an unapologetic and unmistakable erection. To David Garnett these summer moments with 'the smell of new mown hay, of the river and weeds, the curious polished smoothness that fresh water leaves on the skin' brought an emotional satisfaction in which 'all heartaches were purged and healed'.

The medieval roofs of King's College were just visible across the water meadows, close enough for Rupert to canoe back to The Old Vicarage at midnight after dining in the town. One hot day the Cambridge philosophy don Goldsworthy Lowes Dickinson succumbed to the temptation of the cool water walking along the riverbank on his way to Sunday lunch at The Old Vicarage. Leaving all his clothes and his spectacles on the grass he jumped in, and swam to the opposite side. Suddenly a punt appeared round a bend in the river, packed with beautiful girls, rapidly approaching the exact spot where Goldie had left his clothes. Hiding in a reed bed, he decided to wait till they had passed before swimming back to retrieve his things. To his horror, the gay and noisy young people tied up their punt and proceeded to unpack a most elaborate and time-consuming picnic. Slowly the distin-guished philosopher, trapped and sightless, sank further into the smelly depths of the river, black mud oozing round his naked limbs. Only hours later did the punt move off with its garrulous cargo, enabling Goldie, stinking and filthy, to make his way at last to The Old Vicarage and the worried party waiting there.

In a different corner of the south of England another emerging poet, Siegfried Sassoon, who had been a year ahead of Rupert at Cambridge, was living with his mother, a painter sufficiently dis-tinguished to have exhibited at the Royal Academy, in the house where he had been born and grown up; his father had left home when he was five, and died when he was nine. Weirleigh, in the Weald of Kent, was a red-brick Victorian Gothic house with a sixty-foot spire, of considerable hideousness to Sassoon's eye, and the foxhunting of the winter months had been replaced by cricket, his favourite summer activity. On the village green at Brenchley fat men, their huge moustaches still dripping from the contents of a tankard swallowed in the back of the pavilion, took their wickets with slow yet deceptively lethal bowling. Sassoon was 25, tall and fit, big-eared but handsome, and a member of the Tunbridge Wells Blue Mantles Club. He would travel the county for a match, and his average that summer over 51 innings, ten of them not out, was 19 ('quite a creditable record for a poet'). The fattest member of the team was Mr Baldwin a wheel-wright; Walter Humphreys was the most successful member of the side, in a pink flannel shirt with a sneaky home-made flapping sleeve which distracted the batsman's concentration just as he should have been anticipating the break of the ball. The civilised sport of bat and ball, enjoyed by gentleman and farmers alike, was a symbol for Siegfried of 'Good Old England holding its own against the modern pandemonium'. Yet the local pandemonium was also considerable. The village cricket match always coincided with the Village Flower Show, and in the competitors' tent the scent of the sweet peas fought disagreeably with that of the prize onions. Outside, the clashing cymbals of the village brass band struggled for attention against the strident din of steam-organ music blasting out of the gold-and-red carousel, the shriek of the children circling while on top of the painted wooden horses adding to the racket.

Sassoon had turned down an invitation to a London party to celebrate the Coronation in favour of staying in Kent to play cricket, only for the local match to be scuppered by rain. It was disappointing, but since then there had been plenty of lovely days as July settled into its own warm, comfortable routine. The geese walked slowly in single file across the village green, largely untroubled by the world except for the sound of the occasional motor-car bumping along the dusty roads. For Sassoon 1911 was becoming 'one of those specially remembered summers, from which one evolves a consistent impression of commingled happiness.' It was, in fact, apparently perfect. 'Sitting under the Irish yew,' he wrote, 'we seemed to have forgotten that there was such a thing as the future.' Nothing had changed since his childhood. The routine of his days was well established. Walking at dawn in a garden filled with tea roses, tree peonies and lavender, he would hear the distant sound of the early morning milk train leaving Paddock Wood station where the stationmaster wore a top hat and a baggy black frock coat to greet the arriving London trains. He would hear the sound of pigeons cooing monotonously in their dovecot, awake too early with the rising sun and already bored. He would watch the old white pony pull the mowing machine up and down the lawn, as he always had. The manservant never failed to knock on the door with a jug of boiling water to pour into the hip-bath. Iced coffee and claret cup were served in the intervals between games of tennis. Ladies came over for the day from Tunbridge Wells in their best bonnets to visit Sassoon's mother, travelling in an open barouche, a journey of nine miles that sometimes took an hour because the kindly coachman preferred to let the horses take the hills at a walk.

Preoccupied as he was by sport and by poetry, Sassoon welcomed the timelessness and dependability of the returning seasons, and the pace of life they dictated. He said later that his poetic consciousness had been stirred when he was five and, convalescing from pneumonia in the garden at Weirleigh, had became aware of the restorative effect of that peaceful place. In this perfect summer, while Rupert Brooke was trading words with Virginia Stephen in Cambridgeshire, Sassoon was bent in thought over the Brenchley tennis court, clutching a dandelion root between finger and thumb, a broken kitchen knife in the other hand. His elderly friend and champion Helen Wirgman, known to everyone who loved her as Wirgie, was staying at Weirleigh for her annual summer visit, and stood watching him. 'The way you wriggled that root up', she remarked, 'makes me think that you ought to become rather a good workman with words.' A slip on a polished floor and a cracked rib caused Wirgie to cancel a planned extended visit to St Ives, and during the next few weeks she remained in Kent, encouraging her young friend.

Wirgie's enthusiasm for his writing and John Masefield's poem *The Everlasting Mercy* on the shelf inspired Sassoon to write an 'extravagantly unoriginal' pastiche, which he sent to Edmund Gosse, literary critic and Librarian to the House of Lords, whose own collected poems were being published that year. Gosse was married to one of his mother's great friends, and Sassoon had met him earlier that summer at his house in Regent's Park. Emboldened to write after the warmth of Gosse's reception then, Sassoon was delighted when he wrote back offering advice and encouragement.

Another guest joined the Weirleigh party that week. Sassoon had met Nevill Forbes, a former pupil of his governess, several years before, and they had liked each other. Nevill played the piano beautifully, but it was the way he rubbed his glasses and blew out the candles and smiled after a performance that attracted Sassoon's attention that summer. He had not the self-confidence to ask Forbes himself or Wirgie to sympathise with him about his emerging suspicion that he might be a homosexual – a suspicion yet to be put to a practical test. Instead, in between cricket matches and tending the tennis court, Sassoon wrote to Edward Carpenter, a one-time musical academic and ordained curate at Cambridge and now a writer who stirred up controversy with his outspokenness over his own publicly admitted homosexuality. It was only 16 years since the prosecution and imprisonment of Oscar Wilde for his illegal homosexual relationship with Lord Alfred Douglas; homosexuality was still illegal but, remarkably, Carpenter avoided the law. The police several times investigated his books on the grounds of their suspect moral content, but Carpenter successfully avoided a prison sentence – perhaps his isolation in the Derbyshire countryside helped.

Sassoon had heard of Carpenter from Forbes. He introduced himself by sending Carpenter two photographs of himself and copies of his two privately-printed books of poetry. Praising Carpenter's new book *Intermediate Sex*, Sassoon confided in another person for the first time his own 'intense attraction' to men and his 'antipathy for women'. Carpenter replied immediately, returning one of the photographs and inviting Sassoon to stay with him in Derbyshire. But Sassoon's courage failed him, and he remained at home in Kent.

The emotional disruption that Sassoon felt in publicly confessing his sexual inclinations was alleviated by the almost spiritual stability he enjoyed in the seasonal rhythm of his rural life. But John, son of Tom Richardson, coachman and groom to the Sassoon family and the inspiration behind Sassoon's passion for foxhunting, saw rural idealisation from a different perspective.

John Richardson felt that the romanticising and poetising of 'red tiled villages with ancient grey stone churches; the outlying farms with their oast houses and barns' had become a rich man's smoke screen against the true hardships of rural life. Sassoon saw the wives of the farm workers knitting and chatting in contented friendship during long, lazy, Saturday afternoons as they prepared the cricket tea; John knew that those afternoons were among the few moments the women had to themselves all week. He knew that 'drudgery and hardship lurked beneath the charm of rural beauty in our part of Kent with its wooded hills, its apple, cherry, and plum orchards.' The inhabitants of the small farm lodgings were known to the gentry as 'cottagers', but 'cottage' was a euphemism for something little more than a hovel, with straw laid over a bare earth floor and no sanitation except for a foul-smelling hut at the bottom of the garden.

Disease and dissatisfaction afflicted the rural poor. A country doctor would arrive to treat the most prevalent illnesses, a surprising sight in his frock coat, with his stethoscope tucked beneath his top hat. Diphtheria and whooping cough were common, typhoid now fairly rare; cancer of the lung was too baffling to be treated effectively. It was well known that pneumonia had become serious when the patient's fingers began to pluck at the bedclothes that covered them. A doctor and midwife visiting a shy, suspicious woman about to give birth at her gypsy encampment were forced to help with the delivery beneath a tarpaulin barely two feet above the ground. Unfortunately wasps had decided to nest beneath the canvas, and the medics emerged from the darkness holding the baby, but covered in stings.

Had those eighteenth- and nineteenth-century defenders and celebrators of English country life Gilbert White and William Cobbett (who once threw a village feast to celebrate the failure of a new local bank) returned to England in 1911 they would have been horrified. Cobbett's fear of the erosion of rural traditions by the increasing industrialisation of life was becoming a reality. Younger farm workers were tempted to head for the cities, where they found better-paid jobs in the mills, factories and shops, but the older generation was as rooted as the new was on the move. At Bateman's, the small farm in East Sussex belonging to the writer Rudyard Kipling, one of the cattlemen 'was on terms of terrifying familiarity with the herd-bull, whom he would slap on the nose to make him walk disposedly before us when visitors came.' The cattleman's son had no interest in the land, grew up to work in a grocer's shop, and wore a smart black coat to church on Sundays while his father spent the day in the cowsheds milking the herd. The head of the carpentry shop at Knole near Sevenoaks in Kent was in despair when his son announced that he did not intend to carry on in the family woodworking tradition. In tears, the older man explained to Vita Sackville-West: his son wanted 'to go into the motor trade. What is engines? What's screwing up a nut beside handling a nice piece of wood?' Unable to understand the state of mind of the coming generation, the carpenter concluded that his son was 'giving up a sure job for a shadow. It seems to me that everything is breaking up.' Kipling's great friend Rider Haggard, novelist and writer about countryside matters, looked with some scorn on the cowman's son's choice. 'Nature has little meaning for most of them, and no charms; but they love a gas lamp,' he scoffed. 'Nature in my opinion only appeals to the truly educated.'

The advance of expensive mechanised farm tools, including milking and shearing equipment, made many jobs on the farm redundant. The hereditary skills of thatching and ditching were dying out. The advent of refrigerated ships meant that meat need no longer come exclusively from Britain. The importation of competitively priced beef and mutton from South America, Australia and New Zealand and of corn from North America all contributed to the agricultural slump. Farm rents had crashed over the last thirty years, and in the preceding two decades a steady 45,000 acres a year had been taken out of arable cultivation and either become rough grazing or been put to some non-agricultural use, such as hunting grounds for the rich. Chicken-rearing was so unsuccessful that one farmer offered £50 – the equivalent of a year's wage for a farm labourer – to anyone who could show an annual profit of that amount. He did not have to part with his money. A loss of confidence in the old ways was becoming widespread. New crops such as cucumbers and grapes grown under glass were being developed by wealthier 'prospecting' landlords, and in the Vale of Evesham asparagus was found to thrive in the stiff clay. But most landlords were unable to keep up with the cost of repairs to tenants' accommodation, and the squalor of cottages with broken window-panes and leaking roofs was all too familiar to John Richardson.

In the summer of 1911 a schoolmaster from Farnham in Surrey named George Sturt was writing a book, *Change in the Village*, under the pseudonym George Bourne. It was based on conversations with his gardener, Bettesworth, which Sturt felt perfectly illustrated the problems the countryside was experiencing in adapting to the advances of the new century. Innate suspicion combined with inertia in the older generation inhibited change and caused deep distress. Many could not understand the need to alter a way of life that had worked well enough for centuries. Farnham was a place where the names of different varieties of potato – the red-nosed kidney, the magnum bonum – were more famous and regarded with more reverence than the names of any politicians. The heath-land provided robust turf from which to cut sods for thatching, delicious warm smokey flavoured bread was baked in the cottage ovens, the bees in their hives produced plenty of honey, and the small plot of hops at the bottom of the garden provided all the beer a man could drink. No one minded too much about personal hygiene, or that the men smelt of their cows, and there was usually enough water left in the well for washing. If it rained, it was 'good for the ducks'; if a pig fell sick, it was an opportunity for a big feast. The work was hard and relentless but, as Sturt realised, 'patience and industry dignified the hardship'. Money was barely relevant, since goods were frequently paid for in kind, and expenses were minimal as in general people were 'wanting no holiday, independent of books and newspapers, indifferent to anything that happened farther off than the neighbouring town.' Above all, George Sturt concluded that the experience of living 'dignified lives of simple and self support-ing contentment' meant that Bettesworth's generation never knew what it was to feel unfulfilled. The average countryman found his satisfaction 'in the cow stall, or garden, or cottage, or in the fields or on the heaths,' and to him these were 'all absorbing; and as he hurried to thatch his rick before the rain came or to get his turfs home by nightfall, the ideas which thronged his doings crowded out ideas of any other sort.'

Change was threatening this rooted contentment. The com-mon heath and the land on which the donkeys used to graze had become tennis courts for the rich town folk who had their week-end cottages in the village. The fall in farm incomes created a mood of anxiety, and the pressures were beginning to show. In July 1911 George Sturt was woken in the middle of the night with a jolt to the sound of a woman's scream followed by a volley of oaths in a deep voice, ringing out across the village – reminding him that drunkenness was just one sign that life was sometimes only tolerable if it was anaesthetised. Physical violence also pro-vided a release of feelings. However resilient, human nature was not in the end impervious to hardship.

It was common for suspicion to be directed against those who wanted to help. Strangers in a village were stared at with undis-guised hostility or given 'the rapid sideways cautious glance' that Leonard Woolf, with his Ceylon-darkened skin, habitually attracted. Strangers brought their strange city ways with them, and while publicans might welcome the extra income from bicyclists and out-of-towners, not everyone was pleased by their arrival. In E. M. Forster's novel *Howards End* the woodcutter's son voices his distaste for the city people's behaviour at Mrs Wilcox's country funeral: 'They didn't ought to have coloured flowers at buryings.' George Sturt was aware of Bettesworth's resentment at being used as copy for his book; in the same way, Churchill's sudden philan-thropic beam of light had appalled the Dartmoor shepherd.

Occasionally pride was swallowed and an appeal for help was made. Leonard Woolf had a housekeeper, Mrs Funell, who kept a white apron behind her door to whip on in case the gentry called unexpectedly, lest they might not think her clean; she had never been further than the local town, just four miles from her home. One day she came to him with 'a dark fierce but worried look on her broad lined handsome face.' Having to confess that her young unmarried daughter was about to give birth and ask to borrow a basin and some towels from her employer was a profound humiliation for her, a country shame as deeply felt as any depicted in Thomas Hardy's *Tess of the d'Urbervilles* or the American Nathaniel Hawthorne's earlier book, *The Scarlet Letter.*

For poets and painters and thinkers and novelists, the countryside had become an idealised place of ready inspiration, an alternative to the revved-up atmosphere of the cities. While ready to embrace the stimulating arrival of the ballet, the car, the underground, the aeroplane, the cinema and all the other advances offered by life in the city, artists were loth to let go of the romantic sensibility they found in the countryside. Even the Home Secretary had a rose-tinted view of rural life, derived from his nurse Elizabeth Everest, who had spent her childhood in the Weald of Kent. 'No county could compare with Kent,' Mrs Everest told Churchill, her nostalgic love inspiring his own profound affection for the county. The age-old pessimism and hand wringing that was the country way was seen patronisingly as 'charming'. A liberating 'spontaneity' was to be found outside the towns. There was a movement to renew the charm of down-at-heel villages by injecting hokey-folkiness. The widow of an Eton bursar founded a village singing group, pleased to think she had helped put an end to boredom and decadence. Kenneth Grahame, author of the 1908 children's book *The Wind in the Willows*, saw through this manufactured vitality. He attended her production of *George and the Dragon*, which seemed to him 'to consist of little more than an importing of cheap songs from the London Music Halls.'

★

The writer Rudyard Kipling promoted two views: cherishing the values of the past, he also welcomed the exciting opportunities of the new. It was in 1902 that he moved into Bateman's, a fine seventeenth-century house sitting 'like a beautiful cup on a saucer' in the heart of the valley of the river Dudwell near Burwash, just over the county border from Sassoon's Kentish home. Kipling found Bateman's 'a good and peaceable place', a balm for the misery he had suffered since his daughter's sudden death three years earlier. Josephine, for whom the *Just So Stories* had been written, had contracted pneumonia at the age of seven and had not recovered. The pain of the tragedy never left him.

The house, reached from 'an enlarged rabbit hole of a lane', had been built by a local ironmaster when the Sussex Weald, rich in charcoal, had been a centre for the ancient English iron industry. Several dozen generations had worked that soil and been buried beneath it, and Kipling immersed himself in its ancient history. The deep-rooted certainty of the past soothed his troubled present, and at the same time provided him with imaginative richness for his writing. In the poem *The Way through the Woods* he celebrated the way the presence of the past in an ancient landscape is retrievable deep within the trees:

> Of a summer evening late,
> When the night-air cools on the trout-ringed pools
> Where the Otter whistles his mate.
> (They fear not men in the woods
> Because they see so few.)
> You will hear the beat of a horse's feet
> And the swish of a skirt in the dew.

In the stories he continued to write for his other two children, John and Elsie – *Puck of Pook's Hill*, and the later *Rewards and Fairies* – he demonstrated what T. S. Eliot called 'the contemporaneity of the past.' After long absences abroad, particularly in India, Africa and America, he revelled in having exchanged the geographical breadth of the Empire for the historical depth of England. In some ways he resembled Sassoon, for his experiences in other countries made him something of an outsider, just as Sassoon's sexual feelings (and his family's wealth) made him feel different from others. This 'outsiderishness' seemed to give both writers, as it did Leonard Woolf, an imaginative objectivity which, fuelling the creative process, led them to write about a lost, decent England.

Unlike Thomas Hardy, who lamented the decay and passing of the Dorset of his childhood, Kipling was determined to celebrate and preserve history for the present. In the story 'Cold Iron' the earth god, Puck, tells the children that he has seen slaves sold at Lewes Market with rings in their noses; similarly, Kipling's own children were accustomed to seeing squealing be-ringed pigs displayed for sale there in 1911. The stories are filled with descriptions of lead windows in Chichester Cathedral, tales of the local mill-wright, details of the art of wood-carving – all bringing the deep past of the countryside magically alive.

Kipling could be judgemental about all strata of society. Passionately protective as they were of their private life, in 1910 he and his wife Carrie had nevertheless agreed that they would open their beautiful garden (created in 1907 and paid for with the £7,700 Nobel Prize money awarded him that year) to the public; but in the July of 1911 he refused to repeat the event, for he was still smarting from the experience of having thousands of curious members of the public invade his precious place. Their tramplings had left Carrie 'devastated'.

Kipling was as intolerant of the 'stuffy' land-owning classes as he was impatient with and contemptuous of the complacent middle classes who had no feeling for the roots of the country. He thought his fellow countrymen 'a rummy breed'. He dismissed the genteel seaside town of Torquay as '[such] a place as I do desire to upset by dancing through it with nothing on but my spectacles. Villas, clipped hedges, and shaven lawns; fat old ladies with respirators and obese landaus. The Almighty is a discursive and frivolous trifler compared with some of them. But the land is undeniably lovely.'

The land might be lovely, but Kipling was critical of the commercialism of tenant farmers, of the way they pushed the fields to their limits for profit, without considering the future health of the land. At the same time, he had little sympathy for the underpaid agricultural workers of his own village of Burwash, whose suppressed riots of eighty years earlier he never mentioned in his writing. He concluded that modern farming was 'a mixture of farce, fraud and philanthropy that stole the heart out of the land', but at Bateman's he had his own microcosm of the perfect farm, including a herd of splendidly alliterative Guernsey cows: Bateman's Baby, Bateman's Bunting, Bateman's Blizzard and Bateman's Butterpat all won prizes at the local Tunbridge Wells cattle shows. He also kept red Sussex beef cattle, bees, geese, chickens, and a collection of small, snuffling black pigs. This perfect farm cost and lost Kipling a great deal of money, but it fulfilled a fantasy for him in the same way that his books fulfilled fantasies for children.

The arrival of the motor-car was unmissable evidence of science encroaching on the country lanes, and here Kipling differed from his contemporary E. M. Forster, who described how the 'throbbing stinking car' threw up dust in the summer heat that drifted through open windows and into people's lungs after veiling the hedgerows, and the roses and raspberry bushes in the cottage gardens, with a sifting of white powder. Forster was under no illusions. 'The little houses that I am used to will be swept away, the fields will stink of petrol and the airships will shatter the stars.' But Kipling, complex as ever, was passionate about the new 'horseless carriage'. Having owned one of the first steam cars and then several early Lanchesters, after the Coronation in 1911 he took delivery of a new Rolls-Royce. 'A day in the car in an English county', he wrote, 'is a day in some fairy museum where all the exhibits are alive and real.'

As the summer temperatures remained steady – at a steamy 85 °F on Thursday 13 July, with thirteen hours of unbroken sunshine –

farmers responded to an urgency to complete the harvesting as soon as possible because the wheat was in danger of becoming so badly burnt as to make it unusable. Tripping over their long skirts and weighed down by their working boots, women left their household duties and went out to the scorched fields to help their husbands. There was little water for irrigation; wells all over the country were drying up, and the forecast offered no hope of rain.

That sweltering 13 July the travelling Royal pageant was in Wales, where an enthusiastic crowd of ten thousand awaited the centuries-old ceremony of the Investiture of the Prince of Wales. An eyewitness described the transformation of the precincts of the vast grey ruin of Caernarfon Castle into something resembling 'a medieval tilting ground'. To the surprised pleasure of the Royal family, David Lloyd George, Welsh-speaking radical Chancellor of the Exchequer, had momentarily set aside his widely-known disdain for inherited wealth and privilege in favour of the national pride the ceremony would bring to his people. In a break with tradition the Prince was to address the people of his Principality in their own language, and Lloyd George had volunteered to coach the chubby-faced 17-year-old. For all his current eminence, the language of his own childhood was still second nature to the Chancellor. Lady Ottoline Morrell sat next to him at a lunch after which he was to speak about the Land Tax, and noticed with pleasure that the remarks he was scribbling down during the pudding course were unintelligible to her: they were in Welsh.

Perhaps to avoid any appearance of unsightly perspiration that 'sweltering summer day', the Prince of Wales had parted his hair over to one side. He confided later that he was 'half fainting of heat and nervousness' as he haltingly spoke the words 'Mor o gan yw Cymru I gyd', declaring all Wales to be a sea of song, and the Chancellor beamed at his protégé and pronounced that Welshmen throughout the land would always love him for that. Then it was the turn of the Home Secretary, who without stumbling once – he later confessed to the Prince that he had been practising on the golf course – proclaimed the long list of titles with which the Prince had just been invested. The Queen's Mistress of the Wardrobe, the Duchess of Devonshire, had written to her husband on 11 July, before the Investiture, that the Prince 'still seems very young for his age. It is most difficult to treat him as a boy of seventeen.' His mother thought he had looked 'charming in his purple and miniver cloak and gold circlet,' and praised him to her Aunt Augusta: 'he is quite a contented person and never rushes about after amusement.' The *Tatler* magazine thought he looked 'terrified and small'.

The Prince himself considered his clothes for the Investiture (they included tight white satin breeches) a 'fantastic costume', and was appalled to think that his naval cadet friends would be bound to see pictures of him the next day: they would rib him mercilessly. The night before the ceremony, his objections caused a 'family blow-up', but his mother's calming influence persuaded him to appear in his 'preposterous rig'. But if the Prince was that day condemned to wear archaic and impractical clothes, he still managed to show that it was possible to break some traditions, even those that were centuries-old. His willingness to speak the language of the people whose declared Prince he now was demonstrated a new flexibility, new possibilities for modern expectations of a twentieth-century monarchy. If Royalty could accept change, perhaps their subjects, even those in the House of Lords, could manage it too.

7

Late July

A servant must be absolutely perfect in form, disposition and action.

Eric Horne, What the Butler Winked At

ON 17 JULY most of the country was perspiring in eighty-degree temperatures. It became too hot to work after midday, so the managers of the cotton mills and stone quarries in Clitheroe decided to shut down in the middle of the afternoon. To compensate for lost hours, the quarrymen's day would now begin at first light, 4.30 a.m. The managers were delighted that the Daylight Savings Bill had not yet been made law, so they were able to take advantage of the early dawn. On the same day, a man walking six miles along the road between Romford and Brentwood in Essex was spotted hatless and shoeless about half-way along his route, at Harold Wood. He then threw his coat (still containing his wallet) and waistcoat over a hedge, and by the time he reached Brentwood two hours later he was stark naked. Incoherent from the heat, he was carried to the local police station, where he was certified insane by a local doctor and admitted immediately to the Brentwood asylum for lunatics. The weather was having its effect on the ordinary Englishman. *The Times* began to run a regular column under the heading 'Deaths From Heat'. And the weathermen forecast that temperatures would continue to rise.

The July temperatures did not make a butler's work very easy. Eric Horne had from time to time tried his hand at other jobs, but had now spent more than forty years in domestic service. He was married – not an ideal arrangement for a butler, who was expected to work single-mindedly for the family who employed him. His duties allowed him only one day a week off, and when Mrs Horne caught an infection that left her blind in both eyes, Eric began to consider whether he should spend more time at home.

Eric kept a secret diary. Not quite the faithful servant he was assumed to be by the deluded individuals who employed him, Eric's was an increasingly cynical view of the changing world. Some of the noblemen and women he worked for had what seemed to him 'a kink in the brain'. To protect his own economic welfare he maintained a convincing semblance of respect for his employers, all the while planning that one day the world would hear about the reality of a life spent in domestic service. In the pages of his journal – in which, for security reasons, he consistently changed names, dates, and even aspects of his own identity – he was building the archive of memory he planned to use as the basis for a best-selling book, a pension for his retirement. Eric bridged the gap between the servers and the served. The evolving memoir, written in his idiosyncratic and uncorrected style, recorded what life was like not only in his pantry below-stairs but in the drawing rooms and bedrooms above. It was incriminating and explosive stuff. Eric knew too much; in fact, he knew the truth.

At only five foot nine, Eric was a full three inches below the ideal height for a butler, and he might have struggled to reach the pinnacle of his profession (Blenheim would not even look at a footman under six foot). Of course, height was not the only physical or mental quality demanded of a butler. Eric clarified: a butler should also be 'perfect in form disposition and action.' He would not make the grade if he was 'knock-kneed, flat-footed, humpbacked, or idiotic, neither do they like the bald headed ones, they must be properly thatched.' Nor must a butler have 'sweaty smelly skin or feet.' The interview for a prospective butler could be so rigorous that Eric sometimes thought 'it was an angel they were looking for not just a human being with a pair of hands.' Eric had his own tip for a young man hoping to land a good job. 'Now, James,' Eric would tell him, 'hold up your head and look as if you had £10,000 a year and a deer park.' At Hackwood, Lord Curzon conducted all staff interviews and made all staff appointments himself. He was rigorous in his inspection of a footman's hands – for waiting at table ungloved – and insisted on a daily check of fingernails and uniforms. An old lady in Eaton Square demanded matching footmen, and would ask prospective appointees to walk up and down to see if she approved of their action, as if she were considering buying a pair of carriage horses.

But Eric was lucky enough to have been brought up by a mother who was a self-educated woman and encouraged her son to read – he was soon hooked on the novels of Walter Scott. She had also taught him to play the violin, and during his years in service he was always in demand for musical contributions to parties both above and below-stairs, keeping people 'hopping for hours to lancers waltzes polkas and quadrilles.' He also became rather a good photographer, and at the end of a Saturday-to-Monday was often asked to take a group photograph on the steps of the hosts' house to record the happy occasion for posterity. Even the grandest ladies kept scrap-books to commemorate their visits to stately houses. A decorative lozenge containing the embossed address was cut from a sheet of house stationery and pasted at the top of the page, and beneath would go a clipping from a guide book, perhaps a page from *Country Life*, and one of Eric's photographs. For a better shot Eric would commandeer a farm wagon and climb on top to improve the perspective. Usually 'it turned out to be a good picture, with the mansion in the background. I worked a few clouds in the sky. I quickly got orders for a hundred copies . . . the gentry were mightily pleased.' These small talents that marked him out from ordinary servants were happy compensation for his deficiency in height. But he remained concerned about the future, and wrote in his diary of the regret he felt that 'the old wages and traditions of gentleman's service should die with the old places where so many high jinks and junketings have been carried on.'

By 1911 Eric had seen it all. In his time he had worked in some of the grandest houses in England, and had now reached the stage when 'nothing short of being in the family of a Marquess would suit me.' Eric knew his worth. He was piercingly observant about the time-filling occupations to which many of the gentry were reduced in their boredom – they were 'constantly re-arranging the furniture' – while he was also blisteringly sceptical about the *nouveaux riches*, whom he considered 'a poor substitute for the real thing'. Every social occasion and noteworthy incident was recorded, under such sub-headings as 'The Marquess and the port', 'The Earl falls in the Moat', 'Footman with religious mania; Free supper for Converts', 'The Mistrustful Heir', 'Betting in the servants' hall' and 'The Gardener who courted the Cook'. The grand parties held during the London season, country-house cricket matches, Scottish shoots and the opening meets of local hunts were all meticulously written down.

Some of the habits of the nobility baffled Eric. The desire, when in Scotland, to be woken by pipers he considered insane – bagpipes were pleasant enough at a distance, but 'inside a house at close range, I think it rotten, when the notes have not enough space to disentangle themselves from each other. I suppose one has to be cultured up to a taste for it.' He gradually became immune to the appalling language used by the toffs, but found Sir Henry Cayenne (a squire 'as hot as they make them') a little much. Out shooting, Sir Henry would shout at his fellow guns using what Eric described as 'not ordinary swearing but stringing *nothing but* swear words together. How he thought of all the words I can't make out.' Then there was the dithering gentleman who, on Sundays, liked to try on every one of his 60 suits before deciding on the perfect one for church. Every rejected and crumpled jacket and pair of trousers had to be dusted and folded and put away by Eric when he returned from his day off on Monday. That same indecisive gentleman would lug four or five coats with him on a country walk, chucking each unsatisfactory garment onto the ground as he strode along, leaving Eric (running behind) to retrieve them.

Eric had opinions about everything, from the proposed National Insurance benefits, which he condemned as a 'farce', to drunkenness or being 'tishy', which he tolerated though himself a teetotaller, or 'tote'. Reasons other than the demands of his family accounted for his growing disenchantment with his career. Essentially, he felt that 'Old England is cracking up'. Young people were reluctant to follow their parents into service, attracted like their country cousins to jobs in the factories by the temptation of time off for themselves, and better wages. If they resisted the lure of the factories, there were opportunities in the new hotels that were constantly opening, or in jobs abroad. The result was a scarcity of servants prepared to do the more menial jobs. Even the grandest houses were feeling the pinch. A shortage of housemaids at Knole in Kent had resulted in the laundry being sent out to the local town of Sevenoaks. At Woburn the Bedfordshire village baker was asked to supply the bread for the servants' kitchen, and at Longleat there was surprise in the servants' hall when the female staff were asked to wear print dresses bought off the peg at Harvey Nichols, rather than made on the premises by the Bedford seamstresses. There was a dramatic exodus of upholsterers and sewing staff from private houses. Many found work in clothing factories in which in 1911, a quarter of the female population of Leeds were employed. At Holkham one faithful retainer managed to hold on to his job by using up 'some of the old'; this included cutting up bits of priceless tapestry to patch the stair-carpet.

In some ways Eric hated change. A few years earlier, dissatisfied with the new class of moneyed employers, 'the profiteers' ('you cannot make a silk purse out of a soused mackerel'), he had joined the railways as a porter. But he found the work dispiriting, and on one occasion was nearly trapped between the buffers, and after recovering from the shock, returned to domestic service, and tried to adapt. Another attempt at a career change also failed when his efforts to secure an official Scotland Yard taxi licence nearly robbed him of the chance of employment altogether. To demonstrate his comprehensive knowledge of the eight square miles of London, a taxi driver was required to know not only street names but the whereabouts of clubs, hotels, railway and tube stations, theatres, music halls, hospitals, police stations, mortuaries, cemeteries, prisons, docks, wharves, banks, museums, and all the principal buildings. The cost of lessons for this demanding feat of memory was £7, or roughly the equivalent for a journey to America in steerage on one of the transatlantic liners. Eric's brother had warned him that there would be additional questions concerning the colour of certain buildings, and even the different materials used for roads – some London streets were still made from packed earth beneath wooden slats, whereas others, like the Embankment, had been asphalted over. In preparation for the theory exam Eric walked the streets day and night over a three-month period; he was one of only 10 per cent who passed. The practical test was not such a challenge, although he thought it most unfair that he was required to reverse round a corner and through an arch, while the horse-taxi drivers just had to turn their vehicle in a circle. But the experience left him exhausted. Accustomed to working indoors, he soon came down with shingles and pleurisy, and for a time was dangerously ill. When he eventually got well he returned, disillusioned, to his old life.

The summer shooting season in Scotland was still a month away, and Eric was not looking forward to the arrival of the foreigners who came for the August grouse slaughter. A Frenchman the year before had behaved in a shocking manner when confusing the 'black faced shaggy looking beasts with curly horns on the Scottish moors' for alien animals. 'Of ze grouse birds I got none,' he announced apologetically to Eric, but added proudly, 'of ze *moutons sauvages* I 'ave twelve already.' The Coronation and all the extra preparations it involved – for travel and dress and entertainment – had been a big strain on the staff, and there were other things to worry about as well.

Those 'in service' made up 16 per cent of the labour force, the largest single group in the country. Eric was one among thousands who felt resentful that the servant's voice was rarely heard. 'It requires the temper of an angel to take the insults of some of the gentry,' he would say to the first footman, bristling. The gentry were always overstepping the mark, making demands beyond the call of duty. Lady Ruthven, an insomniac with a soft spot for romantic fiction, insisted that her husband's valet read racy French novels aloud to her until well into the night. He had a particularly good French accent which she found comfortingly soporific, reassuring her anxious women friends that he did not actually understand a word of what he was reading, so there was no danger of him being corrupted. In 1911 servants were indispensable to the rich. In the Borough of Westminster there were twelve male servants for every hundred male residents. Miss Ernestine Mills, author of a recent book, *The Domestic Problem*, could not envisage the survival of the upper or middle, or even some of the lower classes, without servants, and she thought the chances were slight that a new publication, *Life without Servants*, would enjoy commercial success. A more appropriate title, Miss Mills suggested helpfully, might have been '*Life with your own very capable wife as cook, your amiable energetic daughter as housemaid and your sympathetic gardener as stoker to your up-to-date system of heating*'.

At Chatsworth in Derbyshire some 260 people worked on the estate; there were two full-time rabbit catchers, 44 woodmen, 55 under-gardeners, and a resident fireman. This figure was added to when the Duke and Duchess were in residence, bringing with them their 'travelling' staff who included a considerable number of personal footmen and maids. Arriving for a hunting weekend at Blenheim, Churchill's friend F. E. Smith would bring with him not only three grooms to look after his own two hunters, his wife's two hunters and his children's ponies, but also two nurses, a maid and a valet. In the house, 40 indoor staff prepared for guests, and there were five electricians and a couple of full-time florists. The night-watchman patrolled the Palace with his especially trained Airedale police dog, and throughout the summer a professional cricketer was available to give guidance and instruction. Gerald Horn, who worked as hall boy at Blenheim, described the ritual of the several footmen preparing their hair before appearing for public duties. 'They powdered every day, washing the hair with soap, combing it out, setting it in waves and then applying the powder. The hair was never dried but was left to set hard like cement. The powder the footmen mixed themselves, buying violet powder that was then blended with flour. For this they were allowed two guineas a year.'

The number of servants registered on the National Census in 1911 was a fifth lower than in 1891. Apart from the new generation's unwillingness to continue in service, scientific advances had made many jobs obsolete. Electricity was a mixed blessing. No longer did the 'odd' man at Hardwick have to trim and fill 14 lamps for each of the larger rooms every day, and carry them to the rooms before dusk. He no longer had a job. The wooden case that once hung in the servants' hall of every large house, with a bell for each room, each with its own idiosyncratic tone or jangle, had been replaced by an unpopular electric version that required checking every time it rang since all the rings now sounded the same. After the arrival of plumbed-in baths the 'water men' of Diana Manners's childhood were no longer to be seen in the dark underground corridors at Belvoir. She missed the 'unearthly water giants, the biggest people I have ever seen' who used to carry vast cans of water to the upstairs part of the house, suspended from a giant yoke balanced across their great shoulders. Dressed in brown with green baize aprons, they never spoke more than the two words needed to announce their arrival from beneath the ground: 'Water man'. The gong man who walked the corridors at Belvoir brandishing his knobbed and padded stick, the coalman who had to knock on doors with his knee because his hands were too dirty and the upholsterer in his room that was a 'confusion of curtains and covers, fringes, buttons, rags and carpets, bolsters, scraps and huge curved needles' – all had vanished.

Those who owned the great houses of England were rattled by their staff's new unpredictability and insubordination, and by the blurring of the boundaries between servers and served. A spirit of rebellion that reflected the feelings of many discontented people in England rippled through the ranks of domestic servants that summer. The young novelist Virginia Stephen had become aware of the changes below-stairs. 'The Victorian cook lived like a leviathan in the lower depths, formidable, silent, obscure, inscrutable; the Georgian cook is a creature of sunshine and fresh air; in and out of the drawing room, now to borrow *The Daily Herald*, now to ask advice about a hat. All human relations have shifted – those between masters and servants, husbands and wives, parents and children. And when human relations change there is at the same time a change in religion, conduct, politics and literature.' She may have exaggerated, but until Edward VII's death a rigorous adherence to the rules had gone largely unquestioned.

Below stairs romance could be frustratingly difficult. Blenheim footman Gerald Horn had fallen for the sweet charms of Nellie the head kitchen maid. They would leave each other notes under the mat in the lamp room, arranging a rendevous in the larder at 4 a.m. Planning a walk in the woods one pre-dawn morning they escaped through the larder window, but Nellie, in her best blue dress, slipped on a plank that had been laid over a ditch below the window. 'I had a devil of a tug o'war with the mud before it would let her go,' confessed a bedraggled and still romantically frustrated Gerald. The penalties for misbehaviour could be extreme: wages might be docked for an accidentally broken plate, possessions confiscated or wages withheld if a servant expressed unhappiness at harsh treatment; a maid might have her hair cut against her will. Young girls from the workhouse were recruited for the most menial tasks, popular for the low wages they commanded. One teen-aged girl who arrived for work weighing 76 pounds was returned to the workhouse a year later weighing just 62 pounds, and with no sign of the two shillings a week wage (a poor Londoner might pay rent of five shillings) she had been promised. It was hardly surprising if servants in 1911 were beginning to object to their employers' failure to treat them like people.

The summer heat was making Eric's work more difficult: no fires had been lit for weeks, and to heat the kettle for tea he was driven to using a hot plate belonging to the rather irascible Italian cook. To Eric's horror the Italian was so angry at this that he attacked Eric with a long knife. This new passion for foreign servants was something Eric found threatening: 'Gentry are very partial to them and will chatter to them, whereas if it is a British servant it is *"go on and get on with your work you dirty dog"* sort of air.' He knew of one MP who employed a German housekeeper, a French chef, a German under-housemaid, a Swiss under-housemaid and a French lady's-maid, all under the same roof. At least Eric's employers did speak to him – unlike the old Duke of Portland, who had such a phobia about being seen by anyone at all that in the 1890s he had a series of underground tunnels built so that he could move undetected from room to room. When he travelled to London, black blinds covered his carriage windows, and the carriage was then loaded into a railway truck with the fearful Duke hidden inside it. The Duke of Bedford's antipathy to servants and particularly women prompted Lady Troubridge to believe that he had 'some great hidden pride in his own rank and station in life, some consciousness that he was set apart from the rest of the world by it.'

One of the most unpopular developments of recent years was the addition of chauffeurs to the staff payroll. The first drivers, like the first car manufacturers, had been French, so all were thenceforward known disparagingly by their British co-workers as 'shuvvers'. Faced with a specimen of this new breed, senior male indoor servants indicated their contempt by the agreed sign of hooking their thumbs into the armholes of their waistcoats.

At Chatsworth, two large sections at the back of the stable block next to the plumber's shop and the small area previously reserved for carthorses had been converted into 'motor house' areas. The 33 mechanics employed adopted an attitude of superiority designed to undermine the pre-eminence of the butler in the staff hierarchy. It was muttered that the shuvver 'preferred to think of himself as a gifted artisan rather than a servant'. Many were recruited from car factories – coachmen and grooms generally despised the new calling; ignorant of the refinements required of indoor servants, they brought the smell of petrol with them into the house, in the same way that a farmer carries with him the unmistakable stench of cows. Their arrogance extended to a refusal to muck-in at other jobs, apparently believing, Eric concluded, that combined posts like chauffeur-valet or chauffeur-gardener should be left for 'the Chinese or other amiable aliens'. Their rudeness and their tendency to ignore the advice of *The Chauffeur's Companion* (published in 1909, it cautioned 'let not the chauffeur be offended if his master is not inclined to listen to his conversation and tells him so') meant they did not hold their jobs long, and turnover was rapid.

As if Eric did not have enough to contend with below-stairs, he found the deterioration in the standards of behaviour prevailing on the floors above the servants' hall increasingly disturbing. The passion for gambling had intensified. There had always been a great deal of cheating at cards, husband and wife in league, raising a left eyebrow to indicate a hand that held a heart, rubbing the left-hand side of the nose for a diamond. But by the summer of 1911, Eric noticed, the toffs were beginning to play for 'really big money'. It was not uncommon for sums approaching £10,000 – enough to buy a decent-sized Georgian manor house with its own deer park – to be wagered in one night, and as he watched the frenzied craze for baccarat and chemmy (chemin-de-fer) Eric felt they were playing 'as if they were working up for a disaster'. Some of these gambling evenings were run as illegal clubs: 'Ladies and Gentlemen well known in Society' would rent a big house in the West End, paid for by creaming off a percentage of the winnings; Eric would be taken along by his employer, with instructions to get everyone 'as fuddled as possible for the more fuddled they were the more reckless they were likely to be.' There were scenes of terrible distress when ladies lost everything, but they could often be cheered with a 'stiff little dose of brandy' and a reassurance that an

IOU would be quite acceptable. One gentleman who could not be cheered up ran to escape his creditors by hiding in the conservatory, and then tried to shoot himself. Unfortunately he had drunk so much that he misfired, survived, and was taken to hospital with a bullet in his ribs, the debtor's chit still in his otherwise empty wallet. Another unfortunate, a young lady who had been alerted that the gambling salon was about to be raided escaped by slithering down a drain-pipe and straight into the arms of the police. Her father was 'in a pretty good rage', Eric heard, when he had to bail her out of the Bow Street cells the next morning, still wearing her by then bedraggled evening dress.

If the behaviour of the adult gentry did not earn a butler's respect, nor did the next generation offer much hope. According to Eric, the children of one family he worked for had a habit of smuggling the family silver along to the pawnshop. Discovering that the knives and forks and ivory billiard balls in his custody were missing from their rightful places, Eric was obliged to ask the son and heir to turn out his pockets, from which fluttered the pawn-broker's tickets. Some wise owners identified their silver with the words 'stolen from . . .' and the name of the house stamped on each piece. It was also possible to threaten the pawnbroker with an action for illegal dealing with underage clients, but pawn-broking was a cunning profession and crooked dealers knew a butler was often reluctant to pursue the matter for fear that a forged pawn ticket might be produced with his own name written on it by the pawnbroker himself.

Butlers and other 'upstairs' servants were expected to pretend not to notice inappropriate high jinks, and were advised to have neither eyes, nor ears nor understanding for anything an employer might wish to conceal from them. 'There is nothing will sooner make you feared distrusted and ruined,' Eric commented wisely. He frequently stumbled upon sights 'not fit for curates', but was expected to forget the married lady taking a bath in an unmarried gentleman's room, and the couple he surprised behind the study sofa. 'Every day there is evidence', he noted in his diary with some satisfaction, 'of anyone's wife but his own. And anyone's husband but their own.'

But maintaining the strictest discretion proved impossible for some, especially where a cash reward for spilt beans was involved. Lady Colin Campbell's distress during the divorce proceedings against her was compounded by the fact that several of her senior servants appeared as chief witnesses for her husband, their through-the-keyhole evidence providing invaluable material for his case against her. There were indications that servants were no longer content to accept bad treatment from their employers as a return for loyal silence: they wanted to get their own back. George Cornwallis-West's butler once admitted to him that the greatest amusement a servant could hope for was the piecing together of torn-up letters retrieved from the upstairs waste-paper baskets. 'Far more entertaining than jigsaw puzzles,' he confided.

In the early summer of 1911 a lucrative trade between English private servants and American newspapers was exposed in the pages of *The Times*. A butler unhappy in his job who had placed an advertisement in the *Morning Post* seeking a new position was surprised a few weeks later to receive a letter from an American lady journalist offering him tempting sums of money for juicy inside stories about leading members of Society. Her American readers were fascinated, she said, by the goings-on in the English aristocracy, particularly those involving marital upset, financial ruin, or any whiff of illegitimacy. The lady, 'Harriet' (her full name was not revealed by *The Times*, to avoid giving her undeserved publicity), went further, inviting the butler to write her long gossipy letters packed with any anecdotes he could wheedle out of the domestic staff who worked for Lord Howard de Walden, an exuberant peer, Lady Gerard, who was involved in a delicious slander case, and Mrs George Keppel (former mistress of the late King); she was also interested in stories from well-placed employees at the Turf Club, White's, Claridges, the Savoy and the Waldorf. 'Harriet' promised to pay 'liberally and settle each month', on the understanding that the informant was entering into an ongoing arrangement.

The Times was outraged by the discovery, calling the practice 'a disgusting invasion of the sanctities of private life', and a correspondent wrote to the newspaper claiming that it shed 'a lurid light upon the tastes, ideals, standards of life which flourish in a modern democracy.' A literary agent, Mr Curtis Brown, wrote to *The Times* to counter this attack on the servant class, revealing that he had been offered some stories gathered by a William Pierrepoint, an American who had set himself up as 'enquiry Agent to the Nobility and Gentry entrusted with confidential enquiries and delicate negotiations all over the world'. Mr Pierrepoint had gathered his material from 'quite an array of girlfriends in the best of the English County sets', providing proof that tittle-tattle was likely to seep out from both sides of the baize door. The *Evening Standard* was more sanguine about the ways of the world, arguing that this sort of 'kitchen journalism' had gone on for years, and that if dinner-party guests were not so garrulous, the servants standing behind their chairs would not be able to gather material to pass on. Yet another *Times* contributor quoted Juvenal to demonstrate that human nature had not changed for many centuries:

> If the servants shut their mouths, the very beasts, the dogs, the posts, the marble pillars will speak out. Shut up the windows, draw the curtains close, bar the doors, put out all the lights, let all be hush, let no soul lie near, what the rich man does in the morning at three will be the talk of the next tavern before day; there you will hear the lies raised by the steward, the master book, the butler of the family.

By 20 July there had been twenty consecutive days without rain, and Richard Stratton, an elderly farmer in Monmouth, reported gathering his earliest harvest since 1865. Schoolgirl Amy Reeves, aged ten, took off her boots and stockings and left them on the grass beside a shallow pond at Longcross near Chertsey. She was discovered drowned later that afternoon, her head caught in the weeds beneath the water. Two days later fires began to break out spontaneously along the railway tracks at Ascot, Bagshot and

Bracknell, and the gorse on Greenham Common in Newbury caught light. In London the sky seemed unusually clear, and in King's Lynn a temperature of 92°F broke all previous records for that part of the country. Motorised fire-engines tested their water jets for the first time on St Paul's Cathedral. The water reached the 365-foot-high dome, well above the cross.

The 'Harriet' story rumbled on over the next few weeks to mixed reactions of outrage and amusement, and took an entertaining new turn when on 21 July a law suit was brought against Amalgamated Newspapers by Miss Irene Chester, a Manchester tobacconist and moneylender. She was suing the company for identifying her with a character of the same name in a novel by Mr Douglas Welshe, *The Scandal Mongers*. 'I want you to provide us with all the scandalous titbits you can pick up,' said Miss Chester of the novel to another character, Miss Rachel Fleming, to whom she had lent a few pounds. 'I will pay you well for them and so long as you continue to act as one of my secret correspondents, I will allow your loan to run out.' Mr Welshe, speaking as a witness for the defence, said he had never heard of a real Miss Chester or Miss Fleming, and that they were both the product of his creative mind. Miss Chester of Manchester was the next day awarded £75 in damages.

However, 'Harriet' may well have influenced Miss Louisa Mary Heritage, who claimed to run a charitable agency for out-of-work servants. She admitted in the magistrate's court that there was no such agency and that she had been taking contributions on a false basis from Mrs Walter of Bryanston Square, Mrs Henry Bentinck of 53 Grosvenor Street, and Mrs Helen Fletcher of 10 Grosvenor Place, as well as a sovereign a year for eight years from Mrs Leopold de Rothschild. Miss Heritage said she had the blessing of the vicar of St Paul's, Knightsbridge, and had amassed £300 for her fictitious staff. Miss Heritage lost her fortune, and was invited to spend the next six months in gaol.

Eric and others like him in senior positions in a servant-rich household objected not just to being taken for granted but to the expectation that they would not complain about it. There was also another less immediately evident reason for their discontent: they were distressed because the old ways of doing things had in some respects changed too much. There had been security in the familiarity of a routine that had remained the same for generations. The butler in his smart dark trousers and immaculate dark tail-coat was often so grand a figure that he might have been confused with the master of the house himself. A butler referred to the servants of house guests by their employers' names: their identities effectively merged. The grandest butler wore a top hat to walk down the street. He knew his place, and it was at the top. 'Under and upper servants are as likely to converse with one another as Kings and Queens are to the sentries in the boxes,' Eric explained. 'They have caught a disease from their employers, snobbery, damn snobbery.'

When a butler was not working upstairs he was to be found downstairs in one of at least two rooms set aside for his own special duties. The servants' hall formed the nucleus of 'downstairs' social life, but various servants, including the butler, the housekeeper, the cook and the footmen, had rooms allocated for their particular use. At Chatsworth the vast stone underground floor where the servants spent their time preparing to meet the needs of those upstairs comprised 30 different rooms of varying sizes. It resembled a department store. There were specific rooms for plucking game, peeling vegetables, brushing gentlemen's coats, and washing up. There was a confectionery room, an electrician's room, an ice safe, and a meat larder as large as a butcher's shop. The Housekeeper's Room was separated from the Servants' Hall by the Steward's Room, and on the other side of the passage was the Butler's Room and his adjoining pantry.

The butler's pantry was Eric's private domain, and contained the house silver. Some butlers were known to sleep 'on guard', across their pantry door. Keeping the silver clean was a source of pride, but the jeweller's rouge mixed with ammonia that must be applied with the fingers to produce the most sought-after shine was so corrosive that at first it blistered the skin, which eventually hardened up into 'plate hands', the badge of honour of an industrious butler. Butlers were also in charge of the cellar, and Eric would refine the sherry wines, ferment sack, mead and shrub, and produce ginger beer and perry, as well as cherry, apricot and orange brandy. In large households the butler was the choreographer of the dining table, working in conjunction with the gardener for the flowers and the cook for the menu. Eric had seen the sort of disasters that could occur at the table when the butler was inattentive: peas inadvertently spilled into a décolletage, an elderly lady's ear trumpet, laid beside her plate when not in use, mistakenly filled with mashed potato.

A first-class butler possessed a fund of special information. He knew that a finger rubbed first on soap and then round the top of a bottle of champagne would stop the wine frothing. He could quote pages from the current *Bradshaw*, the bible of train times, his knowledge of which was as profound as the vicar's was of the Prayer Book. Lady Cynthia Asquith knew she was in the presence of a superior servant if he was both 'puma footed' and 'of impalpable presence and uncatchable eye'. The butlers most highly treasured were those who managed to retain their distance, scepticism and sense of humour but were at the same time capable of revealing a fellow humanity where it was needed. Some found a way of being firm yet not severe, kind yet not familiar. Henry Moat, butler to Sir George Sitwell, remained undaunted by his mistress's querulous enquiries about the malfunctioning servants' bell, which was always going off by mistake. 'Sign of death, my lady,' he would murmur as he offered her a dish of glazed salmon mousse.

As sceptical a character as Eric, Henry complained that Sir George spent nearly as much time in a horizontal position as Lady Ida. 'Tired of laying in bed, he would get up to have a rest,' Henry explained to his confidante the housekeeper, 'and after he had rested get back into bed again like a martyr.' He was critical of Sir George's thriftiness, not amused when travelling and staying in hotels at being sent out in search of eggs which he was then expected to whip up into a money-saving omelette in the hotel side-kitchen. But Henry's prevailing good humour was evident. He had a passion for singing hymns with all the operatic drama of a Caruso. His voice Sir George's daughter Edith described as 'some foghorn endowed with splendour', and it irritated the entire household, particularly the women, who detected a pagan enjoyment in his doom-laden delivery of 'For those in peril on the sea'.

Young Edith saw the 16-stone butler who swung his arms so vigorously when walking – 'as if he was in a state procession' – as 'an enormous purple man like a benevolent hippopotamus.' And when Master Osbert Sitwell was found to be anxious about his first day at boarding school, Henry accompanied him on the train, telling him long and funny stories all the way to 'divert me on the way to the scaffold'. Osbert never forgot his kindness: 'treating me thus as someone whose good opinion he wanted and whom he liked to amuse, he restored . . . my self esteem.' During the term Henry wrote to the homesick boy:

> Oh Tall and merciful Mr Osbert,
>
> I hope you have not erred nor stayed from your way like a lost lamb. Nor has followed the devices and desires of your own heart (where chocolate and fruit is concerned) nor offended against the laws of the Railway company, nor has done those things which you ought not to have done or left undone those things you ought to have done but hope you arrived at Snettisham in peace and I trust your stay at Ken Hill will be joyful and when you depart that place you may safely come to your home and eternal joy and lemonade.
>
> Trusting you are in the pink of condition, Sir George is A1.
>
> > Yours obediently,
> > Henry Moat

And it was not only children who benefited from the sympathy and wisdom of servants. Edith Lytton, wholly ignorant of the facts of life, managed to persuade her older and wiser lady's maid to enlighten her a few days before her wedding, although it was not easy. 'I pretended to know more than I did,' she explained, 'to draw them out. A cousin and I made a bargain to find out all we could and report our discoveries to each other.'

Loyalty in servants was often rewarded with perquisites or 'perks'. At Worth, a house belonging to the Montefiore family, the servants had their own billiards table, ballroom, theatre and piano, and had the reputation of being 'arrogant and presumptuous in proportion'. The Earl of Lonsdale took his 24-strong-band of musicians abroad with him, an unusual and enviable opportunity for travel. From Royalty downwards the great families gave parties for their staff, and sometimes attended themselves. Conversation could be a little sticky. In J.M. Barrie's play *The Admirable Crichton* the master of the house, searching desperately for a suitable conversational topic, asks the housemaid, 'What sort of weather have you been having in the kitchen?' Eric played his violin (and sometimes the second fiddle, which he enjoyed less) at many servants' parties, and made sure the programme of dances mirrored exactly the lancers, quadrilles, waltzes and polkas favoured at Buckingham Palace. At Longleat dances were held regularly on Tuesdays and Thursdays, and the housekeeper acted as chaperone, keeping an eye on the housemaids to make sure they did not flirt too much.

Access to alcohol was the best perk of all. At Chatsworth and Longleat there was always a jug of beer and a plate of cheese on a table in the servants' hall for the benefit of below-stairs visitors. The ready availability of alcohol was often abused. In a *Punch* cartoon of 19 July a guest at a country house is pictured in the cellar with the butler, in front of a keg twice the size of both men. The guest remarks to the 'affable and possibly slightly inebriated' butler, 'Ah Ha! So you've been laying down the fashionable drink I see. The doctors are all mad about it.' To which the 'Affable Butler' replies, 'Yezzir, less hacid they say in good malt whiskey than in any other form of alco'ol. I've took to it to myself. In fact I may say I've quite given up champagne, clarets, burgundies and 'ocks.'

Butlers were not the only servants 'in the habit of taking a drop too much', and one afternoon Eric was much amused by the sight of the fat cook shouting at the top of her voice and 'dancing up and down in the passage in her nightgown blind drunk.' She set all the call-bells ringing at once, and the mistress of the house had no choice but to sack her, although as Eric knew, the loss of her pastries was mourned for years afterwards. At Woburn beer was used in making the wooden floors shine, and a footman would be dismissed on the spot for stealing a drink from the bucket instead of washing the floor. After Hwfa Williams, husband of the irrepressible socialite Mrs Hwfa Williams, was accidentally shot and wounded in the Mall by 'an overworked telegraph clerk whose brain had given way under the strain', the arrival of four hundred visitors calling to commiserate was too much for the butler. He began taking little nips from the brandy bottle and answered the door singing ('rather well', according to Mrs Hwfa) one of Nellie Melba's favourite songs, 'Home Sweet Home', at the same time trying to balance the empty bottle on his thumb.

Some servants, as 'Harriet' well knew, were seeking freedom from the restrictions of domestic service. Many found that freedom by working in hotels, and the Savoy was one of the most popular. By the time it celebrated its twenty-first year in 1910 it employed a thousand people who in the course of each year prepared half a million meals and made a cumulative total of 125,000 beds in the rooms adjoining 244 bathrooms. Wally Allen was the chief pageboy, and while he received only half a crown a week for putting out footstools for ladies to rest their tired feet on, he was often tipped as much as a sovereign.

Hwfa Williams had helped form the Savoy Group, which included Simpsons in the Strand, Claridge's and The Berkeley as well as The Savoy. To promote the hotel restaurants Mrs Williams used to take parties of her good friends – and those whom she planned would become her good friends – to dine. The Savoy's reputation soared after Edward VII implored the famous French chef Escoffier to leave his Paris restaurant and come to London to introduce the English to his exquisite cooking. Escoffier was determined not to alarm what he believed to be an unsophisticated clientele with such novel delicacies as frogs' legs, so in the summer of 1911 he capitalised on the glamour of the Russian ballet with a dish he called 'nymph à la rose' (after Nijinsky's famous 'Spectre'), in which the amphibians' legs were cleverly disguised in a pink paprika sauce. The dish was the hit of the menu until the day someone realised what those protruding 'jambes' really were. Mrs Hwfa was as disgusted as Escoffier by the fickle tastes of the diners. 'So foolish is popular prejudice', chastised Mrs Hwfa, 'that a dish people enjoyed one day is revolted at the next.'

Most of the hotel's innovations won more lasting acclaim, including the paved courtyard at the front, lined with rubber to muffle the sound of vehicles. Traffic circulated to the right – the only such road in London – to keep the adjoining theatre entrance free and ease the tight turn into the Strand. The restaurant did not demand evening dress of its patrons, and the racy novelist Elinor Glyn, wearing one of her sister's 'Madame Lucille' gowns, would drop in at the end of the day on the Savoy's Café de Paris after calling at the offices of her publishers Duckworth, near the hotel in Henrietta Street. Guests enjoyed the American-style mail chutes on each floor and were delighted by the new, mirrored lifts. Mrs Hwfa was thrilled to see that those who thronged the hotel on Sunday evenings often included such fashionable people as the actress Ellen Terry, the millionaire Aga Khan, and more than a few dukes and princes. An American lady challenged the hotel by asking for any fruit '*not* in season'. Nellie Melba gave a dinner party with a scintillating literary guest list including the Australian-born writer and anti-suffrage campaigner Mrs Humphry Ward, Jerome K. Jerome, author of the Victorian comic masterpiece *Three Men in a Boat*, and the writer of humorous short stories W. W. Jacobs.

Many of the staff were so intrigued by the hotel's labour-saving devices that they decided to cross the Atlantic to find work in America where such marvels as vacuum cleaners, lifts or 'elevators' and telephones were commonplace, and instead of coal fires, houses were 'steam heated'. Here was a country where the 'no talking' rule at staff meals was unknown and where, unlike the hierarchical custom of an English servants' hall, all servants were considered equal. The Home Secretary Winston Churchill's butler was among those to have joined the exodus, but this was not enough to convince Eric to think life abroad was a choice he would make.

J. M. Barrie lived round the corner at Adelphi Terrace, and was often to be found in the Savoy's excellent Grill Room. He was recently divorced and just beginning to emerge from mourning the death of Sylvia Llewellyn Davies, mother of the boys who had provided him with the models for those in his 1904 play *Peter Pan* (the novel based on the play was due out later that year, but he planned to take the boys up to a remote part of Scotland in August to escape all the unhappiness associated with London). Barrie revelled in the incongruity of someone who had started life in a weaver's cottage spending time in a place as opulent as the Savoy, and at the same time was grateful to the hotel for having provided him with the inspiration for *The Admirable Crichton*.

Sir George Reeves Smith was the managing director of the Savoy Group and, though far too grand to be told so to his face, certainly the grandest 'butler' in the country. He already spoke French, and had been taking Italian lessons to enable him to communicate with his many foreign staff. He was a kindly man, always ready to give an employee the benefit of the doubt, but for his one obsession, an intolerance for an unevenly-tied bow tie. Wearing a morning coat and high collar, Reeves Smith walked to work through Green Park, and a policeman would hold up the traffic for him as he crossed to the grass-lined Embankment. At ease in an erudite conversation with a customer about philosophy or literature, he also kept an eye on the daily market prices of meat and vegetables and, like all the best butlers, was a connoisseur of the finest wines. There was something of the air of an old-world diplomat about Sir George, but he never forgot that he was there to serve. In the summer of 1911 two diners in the Savoy restaurant stood up at once, suddenly taken by the celebratory frenzy of the season, and began to dance in the open space between the tables. It was not long before Sir George had had the chairs and tables moved back towards the walls, creating the novelty of a restaurant with a dance-floor. Twenty-three-year-old Irving Berlin happened to be staying in the hotel, and to the surprise and delight of the assembled guests he took to the piano. Duchesses in tiaras danced to the composer's own hit of that summer, *Alexander's Ragtime Band*, and to counteract the July heat, the dancers were sprayed with ozone from iced cylinders. The Savoy was definitely the 'in' place to be that summer.

By the end of July the combined effects of lack of rain and scorching sun had resulted in a dangerous scarcity of grass for herds and flocks. Pastures had turned brown. Farmers were being forced to raise the price of milk. On 28 July the nature correspondent of *The Times* reported that even in the deepest, most sheltered lanes it was impossible to find green leaves and with a note of despair that 'the crannies and rifts in walled Sussex hedgerows where one looks for rare ferns and other treasures hold only handfuls of dry dust'. Nor was that all: 'The most sorrowful sign of all is the silence of the singing birds. July is never a very musical month. This year however all the sylvan music has been mute. The silence of a parched countryside.'

The Royal family's tour had come to an end and Queen Alexandra was established for the late summer months in the big house at Sandringham. The London social season had long been over, apart from the odd July wedding (Viscount Anson, son of the Earl of Lichfield, had married in splendour at St Margaret's, Westminster) and a grand memorial service (for the Dowager Duchess of Devonshire at All Saints, Margaret Street, after she died of a seizure at Sandown races). The social press had been full of announcements: the Begum of Bhopal had left England to travel but would return to India for the Delhi Durbar later in the year; the Duke of Hamilton had left London for Hamilton; the Earl of Minto was on his way to Minto in Roxburghshire; and Sir

E. P. Morris, Premier of Newfoundland, had left Liverpool for home by steamer. On 17 July, as the rich were leaving London to enjoy themselves, Canon H. S. Holland sent a letter to *The Times* reminding readers of the 'Factory Girls Country Holiday Fund' and appealing to their charitable instincts: 'How can we better relieve our hearts of the excess of our thanksgivings', he asked, 'than by letting loose into those delicious fields and woods the poor girls who are cooped up in London workshops slaving for our needs.'

But the increasingly troubling situation both in the docks and on the North African coast demanded that Members of Parliament and George V (who had been looking forward to some racing at Goodwood) defer their holidays. On 21 July Lloyd George as Chancellor made an unexpected speech at The Mansion House in which he stepped out of his domestic role in the Cabinet to comment on the continuing German aggression towards the French in Morocco and – what was perhaps more significant – on the German expectation that England would leave France to handle her aggressor alone. 'I say emphatically that peace at that price would be a humiliation intolerable for a great country like ours to endure,' he thundered. The speech was received with surprise and dismay in Berlin, and the next day Sir Edward Grey told the Cabinet he had just received 'a communication from the German ambassador so stiff that the British fleet may be attacked at any moment.' The Army and Navy were alerted immediately, and the tunnels and bridges of the South Eastern and Chatham Railway lines were guarded day and night.

Meanwhile the Parliament Bill intended to curtail the powers of the House of Lords, and ease the passage of Asquith's and Lloyd George's Liberal reforms, had been causing havoc in both chambers, and the question of Home Rule in Ireland had further divided Conservatives and Liberals. The majority of the Conservative party, the Conservative peers in particular, had long been determined to prevent the granting of Irish Home Rule, seeing it as a threatened erosion of British power. If Ireland were to break away from the control of central Government, from what quarter might the next bid for freedom come? A group of cross-party MPs opposed to Home Rule (the majority of them Conservative) led by the future Prime Minister Andrew Bonar Law joined together, calling themselves the Unionist Party. Asquith was in a difficult position. Not a keen advocate of Irish Home Rule himself, during the last election he had nevertheless promised John Redmond, leader of the Irish Nationalist Party, that he would advance his case for Home Rule in exchange for Redmond's support for the Liberal Government. The passing of the Parliament Act, Asquith told Redmond, and with it the limiting of the Lords' voting powers, would ensure the passage of the legislation with little objection. On 21 July the Duke of Devonshire noted in his diary that his father-in-law, Lord Lansdowne, had shown him a letter that the Conservative leader Balfour had received from Asquith, warning him that 'the King had agreed to the tactical move of creating the extra peers. St Albans, Curzon, Harris, Galway and myself for moderation, Selborne, Salisbury, Halsbury, Somerset for extreme steps. Norfolk and Bedford moderate.'

On Monday 24 July Asquith went to the House to announce that to force the Bill through he had been promised the King's co-operation in creating four hundred extra Liberal peers. New members of the House of Lords would include the writer J. M. Barrie, the playwright Bernard Shaw and the novelist Thomas Hardy. Cries of 'traitor' and 'divide' drowned the Prime Minister's speech and he flung down his notes, declaring as loudly as he could, 'I am not going to degrade myself by addressing an Opposition which is obviously determined not to listen to me.' As he tried to return to his seat, there was 'a fearful uproar'. The Duke of Devonshire thought the behaviour of the 'Ditchers' of the Bill a 'great mistake morally and strategically'. Writing to his wife Evie at Chatsworth he concluded: 'People are nearly off their heads. Really Hugh Cecil and Co. ought to be ashamed of themselves and what a scorn for the government. This sort of conduct must do untold harm in the country.' On 26 July *The Times* published a letter from Mr Lockwood, Conservative MP for West Essex, in which he disassociated himself from those of his party members who had in his view behaved in an 'unseemly and indecent way to the PM'.

The proposed National Insurance Act was also being debated in both Houses almost daily during those July weeks, the most important of a series of reforms for the disadvantaged put forward by Lloyd George. Under the terms of the proposed Act, which would provide medical treatment and sickness benefit to millions, the Government would contribute 2*d.* a week, employees 4*d.* a week, and employers 3*d.* The Act was a favourite topic of discussion in the servants' hall that summer. Eric considered the whole thing 'a farce as far as servants are concerned', and detected 'a false sense of security being offered. If a servant does not feel well, can he or she join up in the queue to see the doctor at 9 a.m. or at 6 p.m., the surgery hours?' he asked sceptically, and provided the answer: 'they may do it once, but will soon get the order of the "Boot" as the gentry will not have unhealthy servants in their houses.' At no level of society could sympathy in another person's ailments be guaranteed, and Eric knew of one cook who had ordered a girl with a sprained ankle to come downstairs. 'You'll come down to your meals, my girl,' she cried, 'if not on your feet, on your bottom.'

Objections to the compulsory contribution by anyone earning under £160 sometimes had the unintended effect of narrowing the gulf between employee and his mistress. For all his cynicism Eric was prepared to admit, albeit reluctantly, that the necessary familiarity of the servant/master relationship sometimes created a beneficial dependency of servant on master. Servants expected to be taken care of when they fell ill, as part of their employment perks, and the resentment felt by employers at the prospect of the enforced contributions was often subtly disguised by encouraging staff to believe they might be worse off if responsibility for their welfare was taken out of employers' hands and transferred to the state. The leading society hostess Lady Desart was planning a demonstration in November in the Albert Hall, at which she hoped to gather up to 20,000 servants and employers to protest against the impending destruction of 'that beautiful intimacy which had hitherto so often existed between mistress and servants.'

The *Daily Mail,* a newspaper with no sympathies for the German way of thinking, frequently reproduced in its pages the German version of the national insurance card, to demonstrate how low England would sink. Futhermore, the paper argued, the exchange of cards containing stamps licked by employees or employers suffering from consumption, diphtheria, smallpox or scarlet fever might result in a series of terrible epidemics. Eric well knew that 'gentry didn't like servants being ill or dying in their houses', but there was some truth in the argument that loyal staff were treated well. Lord Willoughby de Broke at Compton Verney guaranteed his staff 'a certainty of employment for as long as they chose to work', and they were to be 'looked after when sick and pensioned when they could work no longer.' He explained his belief that 'There was a mutual bond of affection that has existed between their families and the families of their employer, a bond that cannot be valued in terms of money.' Since the middle of the nineteenth century each outgoing headmaster at the village school of Edensor, attended by the children of Chatsworth estate workers, had been guaranteed an annual pension of a third of his salary. The cook of a house was frequently a dispenser to ailing fellow-servants of home-made medicines, including rosemary paste for eczema, an infusion of honeysuckle for asthma, elder-flower tea for throat infections, a poultice made from the flowers of golden rod for arthritis, and sage for menstrual pains and nervous anxiety. At Longleat, medicinal drinks and beef tea were provided especially if the wage earner was indisposed. And Eric's hard-hearted cook was probably the exception: mutual compassion in the servant community was not uncommon. The butler at Cliveden was appalled by the demands imposed on the scullery maids, whom he thought 'poor little devils washing up and scrubbing away, their hands red raw with the soda.'

On 22 July Mr Henry Rundle from Southsea pointed out in a letter to *The Times* that servants working in a doctor's family would be attended by their employer, so he and his staff should be exempted from paying the tax. Diana Manners knew that her father the Duke of Rutland believed making employers responsible for servants paying their contributions would 'disrupt the harmony between servant and employer'. He and many others felt the collection of the tax should be administered directly by the State. Mrs Havelock Ellis suggested the setting-up of a central Domestic Service, by means of which the supply of servants could be regulated by the State. Not that employers were universally benevolent. Eric's own father had also been in service, and had been killed when a heavy load from a crane fell on top of him, driving his ribs into his lungs and killing him instantly. There was no insurance policy to cover accidental death, and Eric considered the family lucky that The Foresters Club paid the £12 to cover the funeral expenses.

By the end of the month *The Times* was thinking of discontinuing their 'Deaths from Heat' column – not because such deaths were no longer occurring, but rather because their frequency meant they were no longer particularly newsworthy. On Thursday 27 July hailstones fell in London. Balls of ice weighing up to a pound hurtled from a blue sky towards the earth at ninety miles an hour. The stones fell so thickly and the subsequent rain storm was so dense that all traffic was halted at The Mansion House, London's (and the country's) largest and busiest traffic interchange. On the last day of July a great wind accompanied by a huge dust cloud swept along the Welsh coast, and clothes left on the seashore by bathers were blown away.

The dockers' dispute which had begun in June in Southampton and spread to other docks in the North of England had been temporarily settled at the end of that month, but now the threat of strike action erupted again. On Friday 28 July the London dockers had a meeting with the dock owners in Mile End Road and a rally in Trafalgar Square, and were persuaded to call a temporary halt to their action. The dockers in Cardiff and Tilbury were also back at work, and it seemed to the dock owners that the angry mood of the men was being gradually defused. With cautious relief the King finally left London for Cowes, and Balfour went off to the Continent, but Lloyd George and Winston Churchill did not yet feel the political situation was stable enough to allow them to leave the city. Churchill was disappointed not to be joining his children and Clemmie in building sandcastles on the beach in Kent, but took comfort in the knowledge that the new swimming pool and beautiful Turkish steam room at the RAC Club would provide the three perspiring MPs of Eccleston Square with some relief from the heat.

8

Early August

There is an imminent danger of famine and the whole thing
is as insanely foolish as it is wicked.

The Times, 9 August 1911

A T THE BEGINNING of August the constitutional health of
England was beginning to falter badly in the continuing heat.
Only at the London Zoo in Regent's Park were there any signs
of enjoyment of the oppressive temperatures. Although the
keepers' thick uniforms had been replaced with special light-
weight jackets their charges were thriving in the heat wave. The
lion cubs, cheetahs, leopards and jackals in the King's Collection
had become unusually active and the lordly ungulates, the rhinoc-
eros and giraffe, strode round their enclosures happier than they
had been since leaving the large sunny plains of their homelands.

The Royal party had arrived at Cowes for the Regatta, 'an
enchanting picture of gleaming sails and gently swaying masts',
and the King and the Prince of Wales had taken to cooling themselves with a pre-breakfast swim in Osborne Bay. But the press
had quickly discovered this secluded place, and as cameramen
jostled to get their shots of the sovereign and his heir in bathing
dress, a statement was issued by Buckingham Palace: 'If less objec-
tionable behaviour is not observed by the photographers they are
warned that steps will be taken to stop the nuisance.'

Many miles from the seashore, an infinitely more newsworthy
if less obviously photogenic sequence of events was taking place.

In London on the first day of the month the temperature maintained a steady 81 degrees, and just as the dock owners were hoping that the strike action of earlier in the summer was a thing of the past, between four and five thousand men employed in the Victoria and Albert Docks stopped work, and the place was at a standstill. For a day or two the Government seemed not to notice, all its attention concentrated on the Parliament Bill scheduled to pass through the House of Lords on 10 August. The King, away at the seaside, was also oblivious of the true seriousness of the developments at the docks.

Among the seven hundred families that owned a quarter of the country there was a colossal ignorance of the problems facing the poor, who were ubiquitous but required to be invisible. In the words of E.M. Forster's novel *Howards End*, they had become 'unthinkable and only to be approached by the statistician or the poet.' The anger felt by the under-classes was not directed solely at those men whose names were synonymous with whole counties and were attempting to hold on to the lands and privileges enjoyed by their families for several centuries – it was aimed equally at the new breed of millionaire, the industrialists of the great English towns who ran the pits, the docks and the railways and amassed great wealth and power, but were indifferent to the fortunes of those individuals whose hard work had built their empires. Increasingly the vocal and physical activities of the trade unions seemed to be the only way of improving wages and conditions. Ben Tillett, co-founder in 1910 of the weighty and powerful National Transport Workers' Federation (which included the dock workers) and one of the most powerful union men alive, was an advocate of the effectiveness of strike action.

Poor pay and lack of job security, the two main grievances in the docks, meant that groups of able-bodied men standing listless on street corners for several hours a day, waiting for the chance of employment, had long been a familiar sight in London, Liverpool, Hull and all the other main British ports. If a man was lucky enough to find a week's work, at sixpence an hour, his take-home pay might amount to as little as £1 5s. – often only enough to rent one room for an entire family. It no longer seemed tolerable to live in this way. The acute anguish felt in being poor, of a working life spent either under-employed or without any prospect of work at all, had been gathering momentum, and in the overwhelming heat of an unnaturally warm English summer it swelled into a tidal wave of anger and resolve. A guaranteed job with a minimum wage of eightpence an hour, plus overtime rates of up to a shilling, became the common goal.

The banks of the Thames, usually a scurrying, seething ant-hill of activity with men coming and going about the business of the dockyard, suddenly fell still, and the immense black doors at the entrance to the docks were swung shut. Cranes and jibs and loads stood motionless; as Ben Tillett observed, 'the coughings and hoarse mumblings of machinery ceased.'

The largest mechanical sign in Europe, the electrically-wired metal figure of a Brobdingnagian Scotsman in kilt and criss-crossed patterned socks that towered above the London Wharf, a huge glass of Dewar's whisky in his hand, seemed a cruel taunt, reminding the thousands of men below that even had they been able to afford a drink, there was nothing in their lives worth celebrating. Persistently over that summer of 1911 the *Daily Mail*, priced at only half a penny and with a circulation of three-quarters of a million readers, many of them among the poorer workers, had emphasised the chasm between the champagne-drinkers and the thirsty have-nots of London. Ben Tillett later recognised this as a summer in which 'the dispossessed and the disinherited class in various parts of the country were all simultaneously moved to assert their claims upon society.'

The working man's weekly budget, precariously balanced even in a full working week, was dangerously threatened by the slightest unforeseen event; injury, the birth of another child and redundancy were its severest enemies. A voluntary strike backed by an uncertain and paltry strike fund meant no money at all. A striker in 1911 might with some justification be accused of foolhardiness, but never of lacking courage. For the first few days of August the men of the docks relied on their wives and daughters to earn enough money for rent and food. But as Emmeline Pankhurst, who with her daughter Christabel was leading the struggle to win voting rights for women, was so emphatically demonstrating, female tolerance of unfairness would not endure indefinitely.

A small, insomniac asthma sufferer with an unnaturally pale face, but a man of great charisma, Ben Tillett, was born in 1860, the son of an alcoholic cart polisher. He grew up in the murky shadow of the Easton coal pit in Bristol, and his Irish mother died 'of hunger and the drudgery of life' when he was only a year old. When he was eight, a 'tired penniless little tramp and homeless little waif', he ran away to join a circus. He joined the Royal Navy at 13, then ill-health moved him to the merchant navy and later, in his early twenties, to a job as a tea-porter in the London docks. Though his body ached after a day's work and he had to starve to save the money to buy books, he taught himself to read and write, and went on to master Greek and Latin too. As a young member of the Tea Coopers' Union he was well aware of the effect of scarcity of employment on his fellow members' lives, and felt impelled to address the dismal state of affairs on their behalf.

'There is nothing refining in the thought that to obtain employment we are driven into a shed iron-barred from end to end, outside of which a contractor or a foreman walks up and down with an air of a dealer in a cattle market.' Inhibited at first by a terrible stammer, which he found 'tripping me the more rapidly I spoke', he described the pain and shame of needing to beg for work, and moved all those who heard him. He never forgot the humiliating scenes in that shed, which was referred to as 'The Cage', an inhuman place where men 'like rats – human rats who saw food in the ticket' – were jammed in together as 'this struggling mass fought desperately and tigerishly, elbowing each other, punching each other, using their last remnants of strength to get work for an hour or half hour for a few pence.' By the summer of 1911 Tillett had long since conquered his stammer and become a much-respected orator. He believed the ports, harbours and docks of his native land to be amongst the wonders of the world and valued and applauded the importance of transport workers. They, for him, represented 'the circulation of the blood in the life of the body' of England, and he felt about them as he believed 'Napoleon must have felt when he ordered a lady out of a porter's way with the words, "Respect the burden, Madam."'

Ben was an inspiration and hero to his union's quarter of a million members, having successfully overseen a dockers' strike the year before. He guaranteed them that 'if the necessity demands I will protect my home, my interests, my wages by means of violent or pacific measures.' To his enemies he was the personification of aggressive class-consciousness. A great favourite with the ladies, at 22 Tillett had married Jane Tompkins, and they had had nine children. His early years in the circus meant that music and showmanship were in his veins, so it was perhaps not surprising that on a fact-finding trip to Australia in 1898 he should have fallen in love with a voluptuous Australian opera singer, Eva Newton. Tillett brought her secretly to London and as yet, to his surprise and relief, neither their affair nor the four children he had with Eva had been discovered by Mrs Tillett.

At talks held in June and July the dock owners had tried to persuade the dockers against taking further industrial action, but by early August the men were still unsatisfied with what they saw as meaningless offers. The basic 8d. an hour they were seeking had not yet been agreed on, and the workers and the Union leaders, among them Ben Tillett, felt they had been waiting too long for final proposals from Sir Albert Rollitt, the Government-appointed arbitrator.

On 3 August, far from London, near the quiet calm of the swimming pond known as Byron's Pool at the Old Vicarage in Grantchester, Rupert Brooke had just written to his girlfriend Ka Cox: 'I was fairly on my last legs. I'd been working for ten days alone at this beastly poetry . . . I had reached the lowest depths possible to man.' He was finishing the final verses for his first volume of poems, and had celebrated his twenty-fourth birthday that day by signing a contract with the publisher Frank Sidgwick for a 500-copy edition at a personal financial risk of £9 17s. 6d. – equivalent to 36 full days of work for a docker.

Though Ben Tillett had led the dockers to victory in the strike of 1889, membership had remained patchy and many of the casual dockyard workers – the lightermen who unloaded cargo from large ships into their smaller boats and took it directly to the quay, the coal porters and tugmen, the ship repairers and bargemen, and the carters who pulled the loaded carts carrying goods that had been delivered to land – had no form of representation or protection at all. But under Tillett's unflagging leadership, the numbers were increasing.

In 1911, as Tillett once again led his men in procession through the City to demonstrate at Tower Hill and Trafalgar Square, he recognised they were 'ragged and weary'. Although they managed to march 'with head erect, with vigorous swinging steps', their jauntiness was in part due to the reassuring continuity of Ben's presence and his determination to push through their claims once and for all. 'The Class war is the most brutal of wars,' he wrote, 'and the most pitiless. Capitalism is capitalism as a tiger is a tiger and both are savage and pitiless towards the weak.'

That August the striking men were at least relieved to be out in the open wider streets of central London. With its narrow alleys, cramped and airless at the best of times, the East End had become intolerable in the August weather. In filthy six-storey tenement buildings with narrow stone staircases, four or five people might share not just one room but one bed, crammed into a twelve-foot by ten-foot space, a baby squashed in one corner, a banana crate for its cot. Even if a family could afford more than one room, a bedroom was indistinguishable from a sitting room because beds filled all available floor space – the Blenheim ballroom would have accommodated several dormitories of families. The air was thick with the rankness of unwashed bedding and stale food. Even during the stifling summer nights there was little chance of rest, according to one exhausted mother, for 'throughout the hours of darkness – which were not hours of silence – the sleepless folk talked incessantly.'

Alexander Paterson, an assistant teacher in a council elementary school, had been living for several years in a tenement building among the very poorest residents of south London, an area where, as he wryly observed, 'It is not possible to find a good tailor or a big hotel.' Few of the long riverside streets of Southwark, Lambeth, Vauxhall or Bermondsey, where many more dockworkers and their families lived, 'seemed suitable for a royal procession.' Smells filled the air – the smell of frying fish and chips, the smell of manure, the smell of factory effluent – and in the narrow streets with their crowded terraces, the smell of disinfectant failed to mask the ever-present stink of dirt and poverty. For Paterson, it was the smell that symbolised everything these people had to endure. In the heat of July and August the smells were intensified, so that, as Paterson observed, 'the vapour of the slum is so indefinable as to be more of an atmosphere than a smell,' continuing 'It is the constant reminder of poverty and grinding life, of shut windows and small inadequate washing basins, of last week's rain, of crowded homes and long working hours.' In addition to the combined stench there was the depressing effect of relentless grime, 'the soft gentle shower of dirt which falls and creeps and covers and chokes. No man can cope with it.'

With one feebly flowing standpipe and a barely usable lavatory between 25 houses, one-third of the 900,000 people of East London were described in a report published in 1909 by the Poor Law Commission as living in conditions of 'extreme poverty'. The report went on to decry the words A.C. Benson had supplied to Elgar's popular and patriotic *Coronation Ode* of 1902, 'Land of Hope and Glory', as 'a mockery and a falsehood' to 'certain classes of the community.'

There was no system in place to catch those as they fell into extreme poverty except sporadic charity, and the workhouse. Some women from the privileged classes, in particular Queen Mary herself, took their charitable work very seriously, but others salved their consciences and filled in time by going 'slumming', travelling by carriage to poor areas to spend an hour ladling soup. In the country, Lady Salisbury did her part by mixing port with the residents of Hatfield's left-over medicines and distributing the concoction to her infirm tenants.

Exhaustive and invaluable studies into the lives of the poor by Seebohm Rowntree and Charles Booth showed that the living standards of 30 per cent of the population fell below those at which the barest needs were met. Churchill as Home Secretary had been told of lodgings where beds were let on a relay system, for eight hours at a time. Violet Asquith had seen 'children in rags fluttering like feathers when the wind blew through them'. Alexander Paterson had noticed that 'here and there a gifted woman keeps pace with the tide, cleaning and cleaning with the same uncomplaining consistency that some men show in drinking beer.'

In scenes of such bleakness the lights of the public house were always burning, an oasis of deceptive cheeriness, for rarely was there enough slack in the uncertain and variable wage packet to justify entry, and 95,000 drunks and debtors were currently taking up spaces in English prisons. Churchill was aware that it was in part a victimisation of the poor that resulted in such high numbers, since poor men were often sent to gaol for the slightest misdemeanour. Churchill roundly told the rich young Irish peer-MP Lord Winterton, who was unsympathetic to the problem, that if he had committed some trivial but imprisonable offence while at college, 'he would not have been subjected to the slightest degree of inconvenience.'

Over the Bank Holiday weekend of Saturday 5 to Monday 7 August, the section of the English population who worked for 51 weeks of the year was on the move. The Shop Act of that year had legitimised paid days off and the new luxury of what became known as 'early closing day', in addition to the national holidays, and after so many weeks of heat people were more determined than ever to enjoy fresh sea air. Thousands of holiday-makers unable to afford a car or taxi but anxious to travel some distance to the coast depended on the excellent network of punctual, reliable and affordable railways that criss-crossed the country. Many of the railway companies had doubled and even trebled their services over the Bank Holiday weekend, with The South Coast Railway Company taking exceptionally high bookings for Folkestone, Ramsgate and Margate. Reservations for journeys to Scotland and the Yorkshire coast were substantially up on the year before.

All through that weekend the dockers remained on strike, and the temperature remained steadily in the 80s. On Sunday the 6th, in response to an appeal from the city's hospitals, Ben authorised the workers to break the picket lines and unload ice from the refrigerated ships sitting full to the gunwales in the ports. That afternoon, at an enormous rally in Trafalgar Square, the Government arbitrator Sir Albert Rollitt spoke quietly on a corner of the platform to Harry Gosling, co-founder with Ben of the National Transport Workers' Federation, before Harry turned to address the crowd of men assembled below. They had spent three days without work and three days without pay and now, dressed in their Sunday suits and bowler hats, they were waiting to hear of any improvement of the hourly rate of 6d., and whether there was to be any provision above that for overtime.

'I don't want to keep you a moment in suspense,' Harry said to the still and silent gathering. 'I am going to make the announcement first and talk to you as soon as you will let me afterwards.' He paused for a moment, looking out over acres of black hats. 'You have won the 8d. and the one shilling [for overtime].' In one simultaneous movement, thousands of those bowler hats were sent spinning up towards Nelson's Column, and a euphoric chorus of 'For he's a jolly good fellow' was heard for miles around London.

But as soon as the noise died down, Harry and Ben indicated to the men that they should temper their jubilation: the union leaders were not prepared to sign off on the negotiations yet. They reminded the men of the outstanding, unsettled claims of the casual labourers in the dockyards, whose pay remained frozen. The stalemate continued, and such was the solidarity among these men that according to Ben Tillett, 'pickets were unnecessary because there were no workers to be found willing to blackleg upon their fellows.'

One hundred and fifty ships full of imports remained unloaded at their moorings. Refrigerated container ships that had managed to get hold of enough fuel to keep their freezing mechanism functioning for a short time began to run out, and their contents to grow warm. There was such a scarcity of meat at Smithfield and of fruit and vegetables at Covent Garden that whispers of famine were gradually becoming more audible in the cramped backstreets. Any hope that emergency needs might be met by British cattle were disappointed: supplies of beef had dwindled, not just because of the recent drought but in the face of competition from abroad over the last several decades. A frantic meat supplier with Argentine beef worth £100,000 turning 'musty and nearly green' on the quayside tried to sell his stock to the Government for the troops, but was met with a blunt refusal – Churchill could not risk having battalions of soldiers falling ill at this critical moment. All over the dockside lay piles of putrefying tomatoes, bananas, peaches and pears. Argentine butter turned to stinking liquid in its unrefrigerated barrels. Motor-bus services were suspended for lack of oil supplies, and motorised taxis hiked up their prices in accordance with demand. Essentials such as coal, water, gas and electricity all began to fail. Hospitals were becoming anxious about their depleting stores of medical supplies.

Moving through a motionless London, Ben Tillett described how 'the great markets of the city were idle; the rush and turmoil of the City's traffic congesting the principal ways dwindling to a little trickle as motor buses, motor cars and private vehicles of all kinds felt the pressure of a shortage of petrol and all the immense volume of trading traffic through the City streets from the docks to the warehouses and the great railway terminals ceased to move.' The country was in danger of collapse.

Across the country the sun continued to burn down, and the hum of activity in meadow and field ceased. The water pump and the well in the village of High Easter in Dunmow in Essex both ran dry. Taking advantage of cloudless skies, many keen but inexperienced car drivers had saved up their petrol and took their chance on the roads. Mr and Mrs George Cain from Yarmouth skidded on the hot slippery tarmacadam surface of the Yarmouth streets and struck an electric cable. The car was hurled across the pavement and Mrs Cain's sister, Miss Smith, was impaled on the adjoining railings. A driver in Farnham in Surrey failed to spot the bridge over the river at Tilford and drove straight into the water. At Ditchling in Sussex a newspaper delivery boy drove into an oncoming horse, his van crumpling on impact as the horse was crushed to death on the bonnet.

Queen Mary and George V returned from Cowes to London by train. As the severity of the dock crisis escalated, the King knew his place was in the capital. The Lords' vote on the Parliament Bill was imminent, and Asquith, Churchill and Lloyd George, already facing a momentous day at Westminster, were unable to ignore the painful symmetry: at one end of the hierarchical ladder the hereditary Lords were objecting to the threatened curtailment of their powers and wealth, while at the other the trade unionists in the transport industry were asking for theirs to be increased. The two polar ends of society were simultaneously asking for and objecting to change.

In the middle of this turmoil Churchill heard that an electrical fault had resulted in a serious fire at the Carlton Hotel, on the corner of Haymarket and Pall Mall. Flames were leaping from the roof, and the billowing smoke could be seen as far away as Islington in North London. He could not resist rushing to the scene, but when he was spotted for the second time that year in the thick of fire-fighting activities he was jeered loudly by the sceptical crowd demanding that he return quickly to the House to deal with issues which more rightly concerned him as Home Secretary. On 7 August – the high summer Bank Holiday, and the day after the Trafalgar Square meeting – the political leaders hardly dared to acknowledge to each other that in Liverpool Central Railway station four thousand men, mainly railway porters, had started strike action, resulting in an announcement by the Mayor that there would be a 'considerable interruption in the distribution of goods'. The Lancashire railway workers had warned that they would soon follow. There were early reports that the Liverpudlians were beginning to behave like madmen, cracking open the enormous kegs of beer that lay on the platforms awaiting delivery to pubs, and helping themselves. These were the sympathy strikes that Churchill had feared so much, touch-paper action that had no predictable end.

On Wednesday 9 August Queen Mary conceded in her diary 'heat perfectly awful': the thermometer reached 95°F in the shade by 2 p.m. George Askwith, Churchill's successor at the Board of Trade, was brought in to take over negotiations from Sir Arthur Rollitt. Ben was sceptical of Askwith's ability, thinking him 'a patient plodding man with pigeon holes in his brain who listened without signs of being bored or absorbed, who concealed his mind like a Chinaman, emotionless except that he would peer through his glasses.' He nevertheless felt Askwith to be 'the most dangerous man in the country' during those precarious days, and was appalled to be told 'in icy tones that unless we gave in troops would be let loose on the struggling men and women.'

Such was the determined mood of the strikers that Ben Tillett and Harry Gosling feared violence of a desperate kind if troops were sent in to the docks. Tillett had some respect for Churchill, considering him 'the sanest minister of the crown' and applauding him for refusing 'to listen to the clamour of class hatred', unlike those other 'fire-eating blood-thirsty gentlemen, sitting in their clubs and offices apoplectic with indignation against the dockers.' But he was well aware of Churchill's propensity for aggressive action, and in the hope of avoiding any implementation of Askwith's threat he went to visit Churchill at the House of Commons. In his office there he found the younger man, 'slightly bent, hesitant of breath, almost an apologetic manner, youth left in his mobile features, ready for boyish fun, the cares of office sitting lightly on a good sized brow, eyes that sparkle with a wishfulness almost sweet. This was the modern Nero whose terrible power had been threatened against us.'

Tillett set up a camp at Tower Hill with Harry Gosling and Will Godfrey from which to direct the next moves of the now ten million men of the Thames Valley who were caught up in the strike. He attended nightly meetings at Tower Hill, and travelled up and down the country to speak at the volatile, potentially violent meetings resulting from the threatened intervention of troops, riding the crisis. *The Times* saw the gravity of the situation and was both angry and unsympathetic. 'There is an imminent danger of famine,' it warned. In its view, 'the whole thing is as insanely foolish as it is wicked. The trade union leaders talk of putting an end to poverty. Are they really so hopelessly ignorant as to imagine that destroying property, stopping trade and dislocating the whole machinery of civilisation is the way to benefit the poor?'

By an unpredictable and almost unbelievable clash of events, the Lords' vote on the Parliament Bill was scheduled for 10 August, a day that found the entire structure of the country teetering towards breakdown. If that were not enough, on this most politically critical day of the summer the temperature, reflecting cruelly the drama of events, broke all known records. An announcement from the Royal Observatory at Greenwich claimed 'the *doubtful* honour of reporting for the first time in its history, a shade temperature officially returned as 100 degrees Fahrenheit'. Farmers in Cheshire reported that their cattle were now being fed on expensive corn, as there were no pastures fit for grazing, and the milk yield was 25 per cent below average for the time of year. Men repairing the roof of Lincoln Minster had to drop their tools and return to the ground when the lead started melting at 130 °F and became impossible to handle. That same day Stepney Crown Court dealt with seven inquests on children, all found to have died from violent diarrhoea attacks caused by rotting food and bad milk. There were 548 reported deaths from childhood diarrhoea that month, nearly three times the usual annual average. *The Times* reported the case of six-year-old Charles Maslan, sent to the Western Fever Hospital at Fulham in London, near the Brompton Cemetery, where he died of 'spotted fever', due to 'congestion of the brain' brought on by the high temperatures.

On 10 August Queen Mary recorded in her diary the outcome of the preceding day's vote: 'At 11 a.m. we heard that the Parliament Bill had passed, thus avoiding the creation of peers, a great relief to our minds.' The tension in the House of Lords before the vote had been extreme. Peers who rarely left their country seats came to town to take part in this historic occasion; some even had to ask for directions to the Houses of Parliament. Sir Thomas Eamonde, MP, startled his sober-suited fellows by appearing for a day of exceptional parliamentary business dressed in a suit of 'snow white drill': the *Daily Mail* noted approvingly that such 'holiday-wear' was at least 'impeccably cut'.

The vote was taken and the result was announced: 131 peers had voted in favour of the Bill, 114 against. From now on the House of Lords would be unable in law to block for more than two years any bill that had already passed through the Commons. Some Lords dared not think where this erosion of their powers might eventually lead.

Queen Mary was relieved that her husband had not been compelled to exercise the Royal Prerogative to force the Bill through the second chamber, and now felt free to make her own plans, to leave a stifling London and spend a few days at Windsor sitting in the garden, picking roses, rowing on the lake, and arranging her photograph albums. Feeling he had been 'spared a humiliation which I should never have survived', the King embraced the chance to celebrate the first day of grouse-shooting, the Glorious Twelfth, and left for the open moors of Studley Royal in

Yorkshire to enjoy himself on the estate of his friend Lord Ripon.
There, according to the Prince of Wales, he was 'stimulated by
the bracing air and hard exercise and on the alert for a flushed
bird, and he would put aside the cares of State.' His host's wife
Gladys tolerated the visit though it kept her on the hated moors.
Nothing about shooting endeared itself to her, even when it
involved the honour of a visit from the Sovereign.

Lloyd George was relieved by the result of the Lords' vote and
the resulting restrictions on the power of the second chamber.
The aristocracy, he felt, bore a strong resemblance to cheese in
as much as 'the older it was the higher it smelt.' In the same
Parliamentary sitting MPs were for the first time awarded a salary,
making it feasible for men from less wealthy families to stand for
election. The apparent ease with which this financial award was
authorised, and the fact that it was paid regardless of an MP's other
income, did not go unnoticed by the men and women of
Bermondsey in East London, nor by those in Liverpool, Hull,
Bristol and Southampton who were unable to pay their rent or
call a doctor to their sick children. Pawnbrokers in the vicinity of
the Victoria and Albert docks announced that they would enter
into no more transactions: they had simply run out of room to
store the possessions of thousands of desperate people. The Dean
of a local church spoke about the daily effect of the strike on the
most vulnerable, the strikers' families: 'It is impossible for the
outside world to realise all the ghastly horror of this strike. The
people are literally starving to death by thousands . . . they have
nothing left to buy food with, no clothes to go out in, and no furniture and no fuel. They just sit on the floor in speechless despair,
day and night, waiting for something to come and end it all.'

By 11 August George Askwith had unravelled the skein of
claims put forward by the various workers and had come up with
offers that seemed to be acceptable to most. Wages were raised
and cautious guarantees of employment were given by the dock
owners, and this was enough, in conjunction with the benefits to
be incorporated in Lloyd George's National Insurance Act, to

ensure that much of the machinery at the docks began to move once again. But the mood of distrust prevailed, and disruption continued. A crowd of roughs in London's Gray's Inn Road, still fired up and aggressive, attacked a heavy closed wagon – but when they found it to contain a cage occupied by a full-grown lion they willingly allowed it to proceed, unmolested.

Detachments of troops had been mobilised for strike duty in case the tension should develop into violence. In Hyde Park, soldiers were camping once again on the same grass where only a couple of months earlier they had gathered for their ceremonial role in the Coronation. Battersea Park, Hackney Marshes and Regent's Park were all filled with men sweltering in helmets and bearskins. To the amusement of railway passengers, an unprecedented 'Changing of the Guard' ceremony took place on the platform at Clapham Junction. A chain of Army signallers on tall buildings communicated by flag-waving during the day and torch-light at night. A look-out had been established on the golden gallery of St Paul's, the highest point in the City.

On 11 August the House was told that the Prime Minister was suffering from laryngitis brought on by strain and had been advised by his doctor to rest his voice. But the events that had caused this strain continued to develop. The passionate intention of the Liverpool railway workers to demonstrate their unhappiness found expression at Central Station, where a cart containing herrings was attacked and hundreds of fish were sent skimming through the air to land in shimmering slithery, silvery piles all over the street. There was a sense of barely contained violence in the city, and on the 13th, a Sunday, Churchill decided that military intervention was the only possible way to relieve the situation. At a request for help from the Lord Mayors of Liverpool and Birkenhead who were thought by some MPs to be 'hysterical' – the warship HMS *Antrim* sailed up the coast to anchor off Birkenhead: 2,300 troops and cavalry officers, representing the entire Aldershot garrison, had arrived on the Mersey. The streets were teeming with angry men. The 1715 Riot Act was read aloud, that famous injunction to a rioting crowd to disperse or risk not less than three years in prison. But that day the ominous words carried no deterrent. One hundred thousand workers assembled in the heart of the city outside the magnificent pillared Victorian St George's Hall, on St George's Plateau. Forty speakers, including Jimmy Thomas, the MP for Derby, took their turn on four special platforms, and at first the meeting was peaceful, until a soldier spotted a man leaning from a window in a threatening manner. The man refused to come down when ordered to do so, and this challenge sparked a sudden sense of panic in the crowd. The police were ordered to charge the crowd, and to move them from the Plateau. The Riot Act was read twice more, and hundreds were injured as glass and stones and logs were hurled at the police.

By 15 August the determination of the Liverpool workers had become still more entrenched. A prison van containing several demonstrators under arrest was attacked, and in the mayhem two men were killed. Churchill was told that there was 'a revolution in progress', and during the week that followed, workers in every part of the city stopped work in sympathetic protest. On the same day notice was given by union leaders that the first-ever national rail strike would begin the following evening. The gunmakers of St James's Street and Pall Mall sold out of their stock of revolvers within 48 hours as nervousness spread to the residents of central London. The King, who had moved his shooting party across the moors to the Duke of Devonshire's estate at Bolton Abbey, sent Churchill an anxious telegram: 'Accounts from Liverpool show that the situation there is more like revolution than a strike.' Churchill telegraphed back: 'The difficulty is not to maintain order but to maintain order without loss of life.'

At Bolton, despite temperatures reminiscent of the tropics, the Royal party dressed in their thick tweed knickerbockers and tightly fitting shooting-jackets, and went out onto the Yorkshire moors. That evening a satisfying bag of 390 brace of grouse was recorded by the head gamekeeper. The General Steam Navigation Company announced that their services were operating as normal, and holidaymakers continued to make journeys to resorts up and down the British coast, apparently oblivious of the prospect that with a stoppage of all transport by train, they ran the risk of being stranded far from home once the strike began. By Thursday 17 August the railway network had ceased to operate. Tom Mann was Ben Tillett's counterpart, representing the railwaymen. Meetings were held in Hull, Cardiff, Salford, Bristol, Glasgow, Cardiff and Swansea. George Askwith was alarmed by reports that in Hull women 'with their hair streaming and half nude' were reeling through the streets, smashing and destroying shop windows.

The Prime Minister, still suffering from a sore throat and exhausted by the events of the past few months, not least the strain of the days leading to the passing of the Parliament Bill, was mis-handling the Union leaders. He promised to hold an investigation into the railwaymen's grievances, but undermined their trust by his evident determination to keep the railways running at all costs; he did not seem prepared to give the Union time to agree to back down, and to wait for the results of the investigation. The mili-tary presence remained, serving only to inflame the heady atmos-phere. The Home Secretary, already considered by many to be a loose cannon, merely compounded Asquith's high-handed behaviour. Lucy Masterman, industrious and observant recorder of her MP husband's colleagues, noted with some alarm that Churchill was evidently 'enjoying mapping the country and directing the movement of troops.'

To the relief of many, the Chancellor Lloyd George now inter-vened for the second time that summer. Having spoken out in July about the German threats to Agadir, emphasising Britain's posi-tion of solidarity with France, he now threw his weight into the domestic crisis. At his instigation Asquith called a Cabinet meeting, at which the Chancellor explained that he did not think the strike could possibly be settled by force; he advised a return to mediation. He also believed it possible that an appeal to patriotism and a reminder of the danger posed to every Englishman's liberty by the German activity in Morocco might prove persuasive. Patriotism was, he believed, the key to unification.

On Friday 18 August the War Minister, Lord Haldane, described to Lucy Masterman the level of anxiety that was building at desks throughout the War Office, with 'a General in each room with his ear glued to the telephone receiving reports as to military arrangements.' Suddenly Lloyd George burst excitedly into the room: 'A glass of champagne! I've done it. Don't ask me how, but I've done it. The strike is settled.' The patriotic card had been well played, and it had worked.

A message had already reached Churchill, who was packing to leave London for the weekend. He telephoned almost at once, asking to speak to the triumphant mediator. 'I'm very sorry to hear it,' Churchill spluttered. 'It would have been better to have gone on and given these men a good thrashing.' And having made his own feelings clear, he left to play golf.

The King was deeply grateful, and telegraphed at some length from Bolton to acknowledge his Chancellor's invaluable intervention: 'Very glad to hear that it was largely due to your energy and skill that a settlement with regard to this very serious strike has been brought about,' he said. 'I heartily congratulate you and feel that the whole country will be most grateful to you for averting a most disastrous calamity. It has caused me the greatest possible anxiety.'

The 1911 strikes had a markedly beneficial effect on union power. Many of the transport unions doubled in size, and the overall number of people in trade unions increased from 2,565,000 in 1910 to 3,139,000 in 1911. More than a million trade union members were involved in the 1911 strikes. There had never before been solidarity between workers on such a scale, and several union leaders were committed to continue working together. But the settlement came too late to prevent a dreadful event that took place the very same afternoon in Lloyd George's own part of the United Kingdom. In the small town of Llanelli a mild confrontation between the armed forces and the pickets that had brought a train to a standstill ended with two innocent bystanders being shot and killed by soldiers from the Worcestershire Regiment. Looting then broke out, a cargo of combustible carbide packed on one of the trucks exploded. Four more people including a woman bystander were killed, and another man was burned beyond recognition.

And the repercussions were not at an end. Thousands who had considered themselves lucky to be able to afford a short holiday now found themselves stranded in waiting rooms and on railway platforms across the land. In Lancashire some people walked for over twenty miles to the nearest town of Preston looking for some form of transport. The elderly found it impossible to continue in the heat, limping with raw blisters from their heavy shoes. One woman carried her five-year-old, who had a broken leg, ten miles across the Yorkshire moors. Farmers were powerless to object as hundreds of holiday makers cut suddenly adrift lay down in the dry fields, too exhausted to continue the long journey home.

By the middle of August the militant atmosphere of that perfect summer of 1911 had seeped into the confectionery factories of East London. The women workers of Bermondsey, 'the black patch of London' according to the pre-eminent surveyor of the poor and their life in the City, Charles Booth, were about to join their husbands on strike. For those women the holiday month of August presented no prospect of fruit-filled silver dishes on the white linen cloths laid for luncheon aboard a yacht or sunny afternoons in rose gardens, or even of days out to the music halls of the coastal resorts of Brighton and Blackpool. The working life of the very poor was monotonous, and did not allow for days off. Some men looked for escape in the Army, recently flooded with enquiries, many from unsuitable, unhealthy and elderly applicants, all of whom sought steady employment. The comradeship of the new Boy Scout movement had also encouraged younger men to consider an eventual military career. Women had almost no such opportunity, with the Girl Guide movement merely a fledgling year old in 1911.

With so many men in uncertain employment, it was often the women who took control of the weekly household budget. Rent and burial insurance, the cost of living and dying, took priority, while the sum spent on food varied depending on what was left after such other expenses as wood, gas, coal and cleaning materials had been taken care of. Clothes were never allocated a fixed sum. A canny mother had been known to tape a penny to her baby's small body, concealed beneath the nappy and retrieved only in desperate need. Maud Pember Reeves, a sympathetic Fabian compiling a report on the poor of Lambeth, would on occasion unstitch the lining of her coat and hand over the coin she had placed there to weight the hem, leaving the house with her coat-tails flapping.

Insurance for funerals and burial, the second largest fixed household cost after rent, was considered essential. The death of a child, especially during hot summer days when disease spread so rapidly, was an agonising if familiar part of daily life. The cost of a decent funeral for a little girl dead of cholera that August was at least five times the weekly wage of a woman factory worker, but a pauper's funeral was an indignity few would tolerate. A bereaved mother would rather borrow, then starve for the months it took her to repay the loan. Kindly neighbours would often show their respect by contributing to the cost of a wreath and the men, black diamonds of cloth sewn to their sleeves, would line the street, their hats tucked under their arms, as the hearse passed by.

A funeral sometimes served as an emotional unifier. *Across the Bridges*, Alexander Paterson's study of life in Kennington, was published that year. In it he wrote that 'The cord is tightened and ideals are found to be true in these dark days which in brighter ones are almost lost to sight.' The costs of death were broken down as follows:

The funeral service	£1 12s.
Death Certificate	1s. 3d.
Gravediggers	2s.
Hearse attendants	2s.
Woman to lay the body out	2s.
Insurance agent	1s.
Flowers	6d.
Black tie for father	1s.
Total	£2 1s. 9d.

There was rarely any money left over for a private grave, and the child would be buried in a common plot with two others. If a child had died very young, the undertaker might take pity on a poor family and save them the cost of a hearse by driving the coffin to the church wedged beneath the seat of his van.

One day Maud Pember Reeves glimpsed something unexpectedly beautiful, cutting into the unrelenting struggle of the streets just as a rainbow illuminates a sky dominated by dark cloud. She saw a seven-year-old lad hopping, crutch in one hand, the other encircling 'a pot in which was a lovely, blooming fuchsia whose flowers swung to his movement.' Something at that moment about his look 'of glorified beatitude' in the middle of a world of extraordinary hardship gave Miss Pember Reeves 'a pang of the sharpest envy'. Even a child seemed to recognise that there was hope for another dimension to life, if only he could reach it. As she watched the crowd milled around him and he hopped away, vanishing as quickly as he had appeared.

If the women were to take any action to alter the poverty of their lives, many knew that a second missing wage packet would place an extraordinary strain on the family budget. Those most fearful of the repercussions of voluntary idleness strung several large ragged bed sheets across Tower Bridge Road with the cautionary words 'No work, No rent' written across them. But a great many women had suffered enough hardship, and were ready to risk their income for what they believed in. The factory workers of Bermondsey, in particular, were no longer prepared to spend long days sitting on hard wooden benches, filling earthenware jars with sticky jam, without objecting.

Industrial action on the part of women was not new. In 1888, the year Jack the Ripper was stalking prostitutes in Whitechapel, 700 female workers in the Bryant & May match factory had lit 'the small spark that ignited the blaze of revolt'. The theosophist and women's rights campaigner Annie Besant had been to the factory to interview women for her article 'White Slavery in London', and found conditions beyond her belief. Pay was derisory and unreliable (less than five shillings for a 70-hour week), but the most disgraceful aspect was that the phosphorous used in making the matches was ruining the women's health. Skin turned yellow, hair fell out, and the jaw turned first green and then black with 'phossy jaw', a type of bone cancer. Death always followed. Annie Besant helped the women to organise a union, and persuaded George Bernard Shaw to be the treasurer of the strike fund. They were successful, and phosphorus was dropped from the production process of matches.

At around the same time, women cigar makers in Nottingham and cotton workers in Dundee were joined in strike action by women in a tin-box factory in London who pelted the men with red ochre and flour when they refused to join in but remained behind on the shop floor. Conditions in women's work places were intolerable. At Murrays, where white sugar mice were assembled into after-dinner *bonnes bouches* for the salons of Belgravia, women emerging from their factory shift looking as if they had been drenched in volcanic ash were a commonplace sight. The sugar seeped into every crevice and the workers never felt properly clean.

The Idris soft drinks factory provided the lemonade that was drunk on velvet lawns at summer country-house lunch parties. The women who bottled it stood ankle deep in poorly drained water, and the weak tea served at their short midday break was boiled from the same water that had already been used to slop down the floor. In 1910 the proud resilience to such conditions finally failed these women and they walked out of the factory gates singing their own strike anthem to the tune 'Every Nice Girl Loves a Sailor'.

> Oh you great King in the palace,
> And you statesman at the top;
> When you're drinking soda water,
> Or imbibing ginger pop;
> Think of some who work at Idris,
> For very little pay;

And who only get nine bob for a most unpleasant job,
A lack a day! A lack a day!
Now then girls all join the Union,
Whatever you may be;
In pickles, jam, or chocolate,
Or packing pounds of tea;
For we want better wages,
And this is what we say –
We're out to right the wrong, and now we shan't be long,
Hip hurrah! Hip hurrah!

The employees at the chain-making factory in Cradley Heath near Birmingham moulded iron rods into plough chains, work described by one observer as 'the process of grinding the faces of the poor.' Babies wrapped in filthy makeshift hammocks were hung from hooks in the ceiling while slightly older children lurked among the dangerous embers spilling onto the floor at their mothers' feet. Sweat poured down the womens' arms and legs, and flying sparks continually burned through their clothes and on to their flesh. In 1910 500 women chain-makers – half of all those employed in the industry – decided they had endured enough, and went on strike. The courage of the women of Cradley Heath, led by a young Scottish trade unionist called Mary Macarthur, played a significant part in raising the morale of other undervalued, victimised workers in the Midlands, both male and female, thousands of whom, with Mary's help, began to organise themselves into unions. But conditions and rates of pay in the 'sweated industries', whether home-based or in the factories and workshops, were still intolerable in 1911. In the manufacture of match-boxes, umbrellas, bicycles, paper bags, coffin tassels, safety pins and baby clothes, women were rewarded with a wage even lower than the derisory amount received by a man doing the same work. A lucky woman might earn between seven and nine shillings a week, but thousands of girls earned as little as three shillings. With rent at an average of five shillings a week, and a hundredweight of coal at a shilling and threepence, the sums required for a half-way decent standard of living did not add up.

Jam-bottling, traditionally a female occupation, was inevitably seasonal. Work in the cold winter months was scarce, but during the cloudless days of the late spring and summer of 1911 the soft fruit had ripened speedily in England's sun-drenched fields, and gooseberries and strawberries, raspberries, redcurrants and black-currents in succession had piled in from the countryside. The unpacking rooms at Pink's factory in the Old Kent Road, a hated place nicknamed 'The Bastille' by the locals, were filled with women with red-stained fingers preparing the raw fruit for steam-ing. Alexander Paterson was familiar with these workers. 'The jam maker betrays his whereabouts to everyone within half a mile,' he wrote. 'The flavour of strawberry lives in every mouth . . . It comes in through the window in the sultry night, fills the streets and lurks in the very police station.'

Here was a sisterhood, a circle of good-humoured women not averse to a joke. According to a study in the *Christian Commonwealth Magazine*, these women knew they would be teased if they didn't talk in the dialect of their district, but it noted that 'there may be occasions on which factory workers wish to talk fine and the result is often amusing.' With affectionate though patronising tolerance, the magazine admitted that 'to the refined the everyday language of women factory workers will sound shocking and their general behaviour will appear coarse and vulgar,' but cautioned sternly that 'they are not so in reality' and, further, that 'it is very unfair to judge the lives of factory workers from the standpoint of a cultured lady. They are hardworking honest sober faithful wives and good mothers.'

Pride was their dominant emotion. And pride manifested itself in appearance. Their Sunday-best clothes were an outer symbol of self-respect, summed up in the motto, 'better be out of the world than out of fashion.' One factory worker, Priscilla E. Moulder, described her colleagues' fascination with modishness and their 'delight in sudden change' in appearance. 'One year the hats are severely plain in shape, very little trimming, scarcely any brim, and small in size; the very next season the shapes are the most fantastic imaginable. In size they may be akin to car wheels and as for trimming – why, they look like walking flower gardens, while the brims flop up and down with every movement of the head.' Miss Moulder celebrated her co-workers' love of colour: 'at one period greens are all the rage', whereas 'in recent years heliotrope has been a favourite.' On the women's return to work after a Sunday or a rare day off, the *Christian Commonwealth Magazine* observed, 'strong iron shod clogs have taken the place of glacé kid boots, harden mill skirts [to protect the dress] and shawls over the head and shoulders are worn instead of tailor made costumes.' They were determined not to be outshone by the beautifully turned out suffragettes for whom nothing less than their immaculate uniforms would do when they marched to express their own demands for equality and fairness. The fashion-conscious factory worker saved every spare penny she could to dress as becomingly as possible. As Miss Moulder explained, they 'love pretty things just as do the women who occupy higher social planes, and they experience the same craving to gratify the instinct.'

Word spread of the collective intention of the women of London's East End to go on strike, and in the middle of August a very large woman pushed beyond the limits of her own endurance dressed herself up in all her Sunday finery. Her striking docker husband had not been bringing money home, she was exhausted by working so hard for so little, and these evils were exacerbated by the effect of the intense heat on a woman of her size. She called in at more than twenty factories in the Bermondsey neighbourhood, and wherever she went, she beckoned to the girls inside to come out and join her. Into the stiflingly hot streets came the pickle-makers, the biscuit-makers, the tea-packers, the cocoa-makers, the glue-mixers and the girls from Pink's, walking out into the brilliant sunshine to join their men.

Fifteen thousand women left their work places that hot August day, ready for the signal to abandon work, defiant and already wearing the best clothes in their possession, irrespective of the heat. In fur coats, with fur stoles or 'tippets' draped around their

shoulders, in feather decked hats, starched skirts and heavy polished boots, smelling collectively like some great unrefined sugar
mountain over which a tidal wave of molasses had been poured,
they began to march. Their jaunty song and sweet stench filled the
streets of the East End as they walked, an exhilarated, liberated
crowd of women. Behind them in the silent factories ripe fruit
rotted, biscuits lay unbaked, tea remained unpacked and cocoa
powder unmixed. The factory owners, not anticipating the
strength of feeling to last, locked the factory gates after them,
expecting that the women would soon realise they could not afford
to miss their wages and return, begging for the gates to be opened.

Their walk-out coincided with the near-paralysis of the country
through the transport strike, and there was an atmosphere of gaiety
as the women joined the men gathered in Southwark Park, chanting as at a football match the question 'Are we downhearted?' to
be met with the resounding refrain 'NO'!

There, even before Ben Tillett had climbed on the platform to
address the crowd, Mary Macarthur, a vivacious blonde woman
with an infectious laugh, stood before them to pledge her unwavering encouragement. Mary, the heroine of the successful
Cradley Heath chain workers' strike, was the daughter of a committed Conservative Glaswegian shopkeeper. At the age of 15 and
to the horror of her father Mary had revealed socialist sensibil-
ities, and her political convictions were further enhanced when
she fell in love with Will Anderson, a member of the Independent
Labour Party. Refusing Will's proposal of marriage, she threw
herself with confidence not only into her job as Secretary to the
Women's Trade Union League but also into founding a monthly
newspaper called *The Women Workers*. In 1906 she had organised
an exhibition at the Queen's Hall in London for the 'Sweated
Industries' which Queen Mary, as Princess of Wales, had visited.
The women and children whose story was told in the exhibition
inhabited a world of which she knew very little, and the Royal
visitor had been deeply affected by Mary Macarthur's conviction,
and by the evidence she had produced both of appalling working

conditions and of derisory wages that paid one woman sixpence for a shirt that would be sold in Bond Street for 25 shillings.

By 1911 Mary Macarthur had become Secretary of the National Federation of Women Workers (their badge declared they were there 'to fight, to struggle, to right the wrong'), and Will was chairman of the ILP. Mary was seriously (if privately) considering his proposal of marriage.

If the London dockers had a defender in Ben Tillett, their wives now had their own champion in this young Scottish woman. At first she could scarcely be heard above the sound of cheering, but on Monday 14 August she went straight into action and set up a small office in Clerkenwell Row as the administrative nerve centre for the women's strike. Barely sleeping or eating for the next few days, she worked non-stop in the office, outside the factory gates, cheering on the dispirited, advising on the health and well-being of the women and of their children too. She enrolled four thousand new union members that week. Much of her time was spent either in direct negotiation with the employers, or in raising funds for the strike subsidy accounts (the Peel Male Choir gave an impromptu concert on Clerkenwell Green and took a collection for the cause). Like Ben, 'our Mary', as she was always referred to, was able to hold an audience.

Most people responded to Mary Macarthur. Despite the severe shortages brought about by the dockers and railwaymen's actions, she appealed for food for the strikers and their families. Well aware of the power of the press, she wrote to the editors of the national newspapers: 'We want at least a 1,000 loaves of bread at the Labour Institute, Fort Road, Bermondsey, SE. If possible by noon on Monday. Who will send them?' The papers published her appeal and the Federation headquarters were swamped with supplies. Not only did the bread arrive on time, but crates packed with cans of condensed milk were delivered to her office, as were six full barrels of herrings from a Fleetwood fish merchant, who addressed his offering to 'Mary, Wholesale Fish Merchant' so it would not be stopped en route. The queues of women and children waiting to receive the thousands of loaves and other supplies that appeared, as if by biblical intervention, stretched far into the distance. Any sign of unpleasant behaviour, of anyone trying to jump the queue, or of parents using babies who were seen to be doing double duty by being handed from 'mother' to 'mother', received a swift jab from a Sunday-best hat-pin.

One man was impervious to Mary's charm, however: Lloyd George was unaffected and 'rated her like a schoolgirl'. He was irritated by Mary's unconstrained appeals through the newspapers, and by the fact that she gave the union's financial figures to the press and they were published before he had had a chance to see them himself. Mary felt forced to hand over negotiations to her colleagues Constance Smith and Marion Phillips, while she concentrated on the immediate welfare of the women.

Most of the women returned to work in the last week of August, following many hours spent by Mary and her colleagues in negotiation with the employers. They emerged pleased with the result. Wage increases ranging from one to four shillings a week amounted to a collective minimum of £7,000 a year. Mary felt the greatest achievement was 'the new sense of self reliance, solidarity, and comradeship which has been so gained, making it certain that whatever the difficulties they will never again be, like those of the past, without hope.'

The momentous events of the month of August had, however, not prevented all those who were rich enough, had saved enough, or were young and carefree enough from spending some time mucking about at the seaside, a part of the summer that few were prepared to forego.

9

Late August

The exquisite print of the sand and shingle underwater, luxuriously hurting you.

A.L. Rowse, *A Cornish Childhood*

B Y LATE AUGUST lassitude had begun to further weaken the nation's energy, as the hot weather hung over England like a brocade curtain. The relentless sunshine seemed to have bleached the colour from life, replacing it with an oppressive haze. City dwellers were worst affected, and that year holidays as a means of escape were in fashion as never before. Summer holidays had been increasing in popularity over the years since the 1871 Bank Holiday Act had entitled everyone to a day off on Whit Monday in May and another in early August, just as everyone was due days off at Christmas and Easter. But these new work-free days were intended for unrestricted freedom in the sun, rather than for religious contemplation.

On 9 August two days after the 1911 Bank Holiday, *The Times* remarked somewhat tetchily on the new habits of the new generation. 'In our grandfather's and great-grandfather's day, man was content with the annual expedition from the country to London or the town to the seaside, and those who could not afford this stayed quietly at home,' the correspondent grunted, continuing: 'Now, not only is the annual holiday a recognised necessity for every middle class household but the weekend habit is more and more invading our periods of work and people seem to be always

on the move.' The frequency and reliability of trains and the avail-
abilty of cheap tickets meant that for the last fifty years travel had
been available to almost all classes. If the very rich did not go
abroad to the stylish resorts of Biarritz and Monte Carlo, they
visited the spa towns of Bath, Cheltenham, Harrogate, Leaming-
ton Spa and Tunbridge Wells. The middle classes often went on
bicycling tours, and picnics became increasingly popular, more
practical now thanks to the new travelling gas stoves and the inven-
tion of the paper bag. Many others stayed at home in the semi-
rural comfort of Garden City suburbs like Letchworth, which
offered the recreational facilities of tennis and golf. The poor, if
they could manage to make savings, went to the seaside. If the
budget could not stretch to a day or two on the beach, the East
Enders of London went hop-picking.

Augustus John and his family seemed that summer to live life as
if the whole thing were one long holiday. Augustus was one of the
most famous painters of the decade, acknowledged by his contem-
poraries to be the most talented draughtsman of his generation.
An authoritarian upbringing in Wales had been alleviated by a less
conventional grandfather, William John, who encouraged his
grandchildren to 'Talk! If you can't think of anything to say, lie!'
The itinerant Irish tinkers who came to camp in the fields near
Augustus's Tenby home held an immediate attraction for him, and
from his earliest years he planned to embrace the travellers' way of
life. He taught himself the Romany language, and his fluency
brought him a rare acceptance in the gypsy community, a *bouilla-
baisse* of Eastern European races that criss-crossed Europe in their
brilliantly painted caravans, united in their shared love of the open
road. Untrammelled by the bureaucratic restrictions that seemed
to be encroaching on so many aspects of twentieth-century life,
gypsies, the essential anti-capitalists, demonstrated their belief in
an asset-free life by their insistence on the burning of all personal
belongings at death. Physically Augustus sometimes seemed indistinguishable from the true gypsy, an intensely male presence, and
although not quite reaching six foot, he appeared taller with his

slim build, long red beard and exotic violet eyes. For many years his own existence had been itinerant, travelling through Europe and England in vivid blue and canary-yellow caravans, returning irregularly to London and to his studio just off the King's Road in Chelsea. During the spring of 1911 his caravans and their six horses had been parked in a corner of Battersea Park, convenient for his frequent escapes. Putting on his large black felt hat and giving his family no notice, Augustus would clatter out of the Park in the direction of the Home Counties, or across the Channel to France. His fame and his reputation as the English counterpart of Gauguin and Matisse notwithstanding, most of the Bloomsbury circle were suspicious of him. Lytton Strachey was entirely unnerved in his presence: 'When I think of him,' he admitted, 'I often feel that the only thing to do is to chuck up everything and make a dash for some safe secluded office stool.'

Augustus's wife Ida, the mother of five of his children, had died after giving birth to their last child in 1907, and he was now living with his long-term mistress Dorelia McNeill, by whom he had another two sons. The extended John family had always shared their father's exhilaration with the gypsy existence, but travelling the roads in the burnt-out lands of the Mediterranean, as they had the previous year, had begun to lose its charm for Augustus. 'There are no green fields here,' he wrote in August 1910 to his friend Ottoline Morrell. 'Scratch the ground and you come to rock; a green meadow smells sweet to me.'

In August 1911 Dorelia was determined to take the whole family out of London where, as Augustus acknowledged, 'she tends to get poor'. His impromptu absences had begun to cause her some distress. Nor did she feel that the dusty streets of Chelsea, the airlessness and lack of open spaces were suitable for the six children under ten who lived with them, David, Caspar, Robin, Edwin, Pyramis and Romilly (Henry, the seventh, had been abducted by his maternal grandmother, to give him what she believed to be a more appropriate way of life). The Church Street house was claustrophobic, often filled with the unpredictable hangers-on who always surrounded Augustus. When one of his gypsy friends who lived with them in Church Street, a Spanish musician named Fabian de Castro, started spitting in the bath, it was the last straw. Fabian was an exotic adventurer, admiringly described by Augustus as having done 'everything except kill a man'. Dorelia, while acknowledging Fabian's genius as a guitarist, found the spitting habit intolerable. Fabian persistently ignored the large sign she placed above the bath warning him not to continue with his disgusting habit, and Dorelia began to feel she had put up with him and with life in Church Street for long enough.

On 16 August, three months pregnant with her third child, she moved the whole family out of London to Poole in Dorset, to Alderney Manor, a long, low, pink one-storey house with a tall crenellated sandcastle-like construction at one end. The rent was £50 a year. Shortly after their arrival, their landlady called by, unannounced, to meet her new tenants. Lady Cornelia Wimborne, sister of Lord Randolph Churchill and aunt to the Home Secretary, was confronted in the driveway by six small, male, scarlet-and-black-paint-bedaubed naked bodies. The boys had been decorating the gardener's cottage, and were scrubbing their bodies with turpentine soap to try to remove the dye they were using to paint the walls and furniture. The matriarch Dorelia presented a no less startling appearance in her 'tight fitting, hand-sewn, canary coloured bodice above a dark gathered flowing skirt, and her hair very black and gleaming, emphasiz[ing] the long silver earrings which were her only adornment.' Children's author Kathleen Hale, who knew Dorelia, thought her the most beautiful woman she had ever seen: 'her warm brown skin glowed in the whiteness of her softly gathered white bodice.' But Lady Cornelia was unfazed by such lack of convention. An open-minded woman, she had supported her nephew's exchange of the Tory benches for the Liberal, and was delighted by the arrival at Alderney of one of England's most celebrated if controversial artists.

And so it was that the wild and beautiful Englishness of the gardens and surrounding fields of Alderney provided Augustus,

Dorelia and the boys with air and freedom, and also with a reassuring stability for which they had perhaps unconsciously been yearning. It soon became clear to Lady Cornelia that the tenancy would last well beyond the holiday season of 1911.

Despite her pregnancy, Dorelia had a lover that summer, Henry Lamb (also a one-time object of Ottoline Morrell's passion, and friend of Lytton Strachey). The fair, slim painter with pale golden hair was one of Alderney's first visitors and described the John refuge in a letter to Lytton Strachey as 'an amazing place'. He wrote enthusiastically of 'a vast secluded park of prairies, pine woods, birch woods, dells and moors with a house, cottages and a circular walled garden.' There were only eight rooms, so the life of the house spilled easily into the surrounding country, and Dorelia turned her creative gifts upon the overgrown garden. Her second son Romilly recognised its natural, anarchic beauty. 'Great masses of lavender, and other smelling plants sprawled outwards from the concentric beds,' he later wrote, 'until in some places the pathways were almost concealed. Tangled masses of rose and clematis heaved up into the air or hung droopingly from the wall.' Delicious smells of Mediterranean, garlic-infused dishes drifted through the open kitchen windows, to the sound of a Mozart duet played by Dorelia and her constant visitor, Henry Lamb.

Further away, in the untamed woodland, the boys would run naked into the frog-filled pond, climb trees, and make a cart-horse of one of the pedigree saddleback pigs, harnessing its broad bristly haunches to the tin bath. As the pig pulled the tub with its human cargo through the bushes, the boys' shrieks could be heard as far away as the house. There were other animals, cows that provided them with caramel-tasting cream, donkeys, ponies, cats, and hives of vicious bees. The boys had long, blond hair with, Romilly also remembered, 'a fringe in front that came down to our eyebrows', and wore matching outfits designed by Dorelia, described by Romilly as 'pink pinafores reaching to just below the waist and leaving our necks bare; brown corduroy knickers, red socks and black boots.' They would play for hours in the nearby brickyard, pushing miniature trolleys along the miniature railway lines – it was almost the only railway in the country operating that week. After supper they would join in with their father as he sang gypsy songs around a camp-fire, then collapse in exhausted contentment in wigwams in the orchard. Neither cloud nor rain marred those carefree days, and Augustus John's sons found themselves living the sort of Peter Pan-like existence that J. M. Barrie's play had made so bewitching. If you were under ten years old, Alderney was Neverland made real, and Augustus recorded those weeks in his paintings 'Washing Day' and 'The Blue Pool'.

Augustus attracted women that summer as he had all his life, and during his less frequent but still solo caravan absences from the family unknown girls would arrive on the Alderney doorstep, only to be charmingly turned away by Dorelia. While at Alderney, however, Augustus determined to impose some academic discipline on his sons even during that holiday time, and hired a tutor. John Hope-Johnstone, an impoverished dilettante in his late twenties, arrived at Alderney on 16 August pushing a pram filled with grammar books and much-read editions of the works of the metaphysical poets, possessed of an eager willingness to adapt to the John way of life. Even his name gave a double emphasis to his suitability: John Hope-Johnstone seemed perfect for Alderney. He was eager to learn, and his enthusiasm for knowledge made him 'an excellent and charming youth' in Augustus's eyes, as well as an ideal tutor. Adopting his own Alderney style of dress – corduroy frock-coat, black felt hat and a coloured neckerchief, with a pair of distinctive horn-rimmed glasses – he began his day alone at dawn with a private seminar for himself on four-dimensional geometry. By the time he had finished, the children would have vanished into the open country, and (with the complicit encouragement of Dorelia) lessons were abandoned before they had begun. Instead Hope-Johnstone would conduct mysterious evil-smelling experiments with coloured liquids in a home-made laboratory in the kitchen of a nearby empty cottage, or help Dorelia in the garden. Occasionally he would corral the boys for long enough to teach them the names of the Hebrew kings, or encourage them to memorise chunks of the Book of Job.

But Augustus eventually tired of Hope-Johnstone's exhaustive repertoire, and became bored by his relish for an argument. 'He's a garrulous creature and extremely irritating sometimes,' he grumbled to Dorelia. The boys were fed up with the way he hogged the cream at lunch, the 'accidental' spilling into his own pudding plate of most of the contents of the jug. Books began to disappear from Augustus's library, and Hope-Johnstone proved quite inept at operating the expensive camera he had persuaded Augustus to buy, promising to photograph his paintings with it. As the young man's popularity began to wane, so Augustus himself became less inclined to insist on lessons, leaving the boys more time to revel in summer-holiday freedom. Quite soon Hope-Johnstone found no discouraging voices raised against his often-expressed ambition to visit Outer Mongolia.

In the adjoining county of Somerset, the Bloomsbury hostess Lady Ottoline Morrell was spending her holidays with her MP husband Philip near Frome, in the village of Mells. The Elizabethan Mells, home of the Horner family for more than 350 years, had a 'lovely medieval garden with its grass paths and flower beds within its frame of grey walls'.

Ottoline was feeling inadequate. Nothing about the visit was going well. She had packed her best dresses, only to decide that 'when shaken out and worn they seemed absurdly fantastic and unfitting for the company and the surroundings.' Wearing one of the ridiculous outfits while sitting on the terrace in a creaky wicker basket-chair beside Raymond Asquith – son of the Prime Minister, Horner son-in-law and acknowledged leader of the formidable Corrupt Coterie – she was conscious of her companion's superior intellectual stature. Raymond was reading the just-published novel *The White Peacock* by D.H. Lawrence, son of a Nottinghamshire miner. From time to time he commented aloud on the book: though admirable in parts, it was quite inauthentic, since it was unlikely that 'peasants could talk as Lawrence made them talk' and could not possibly be expected to have opinions on either art or music. He was quite forgetting Lawrence's own origins. Ottoline remained silent, hating herself for having 'entirely failed in courage to express what I really thought' – for one found Raymond too daunting to contradict. Her sense of inadequacy drove her to escape up to her own room, where she would cry out loud 'Oh to be free, free!' before returning 'sedately' to her creaky chair. An uneasy feeling overtook her as she watched the Asquiths and Horners basking 'in the sunshine and peace and beauty of this lovely English garden and smoking cigarettes and scheming, planning, doubting, criticising.' She felt that there was a nearby voice whispering 'Your dreams and efforts are but as the smoke of your cigarettes'. None of them could hope to capture and hold the precious, elusive evanescence of an English summer's day for ever.

Ottoline's Bloomsbury neighbour Virginia Stephen was trying to concentrate on her first book *Night and Day* while spending a few more days in Grantchester with Rupert Brooke. She wrote to her sister Vanessa on 16 August that 'It is the greatest difficulty to get pen and paper here because Rupert apparently writes all his poems in pencil on the back of envelopes.'

In 1911 the seaside provided an experience that most could share, irrespective of income. A little further down the English coast from Poole, Alfred Leslie Rowse was looking forward to spending some time at the beach. He was always known by his second name after his adored elder sister had a crush on a teacher named Leslie; he was eight years old, and lived with his parents at the family village shop at Tregonissey, in Cornwall. His father was a clay worker and his mother, before her marriage, had been in service at St Michael's Mount, a house in Leslie's view the 'most romantic in its associations and memories of all places in Cornish history'. One year, on Midsummer's Day, Leslie's mother and the other maids left the white of an egg in a glass of water overnight on a window sill, in accordance with an age-old local myth; by the next morning it had formed a shape resembling rigging, which they took to mean that they would all marry sailors.

Leslie craved solitude, and his favourite activities were very different from the boisterous games of the John boys at Alderney. Leslie found joy in 'an occasional seagull passing over, or a cruising rook' or a day spent as uninterrupted as possible at the beach. In 1911 the attitude to the sea and to sea-water was ambivalent: a stretch of sand or shingle promised pleasure or fear, depending on association. In her thick black silk coat with a large stiff black ribbon tied at the neck in a bow, Leslie's grandmother made no concessions either to the weather or to the ten years that had elapsed since the death of Queen Victoria. She lived near her grandson at Crinnis Beach, on the curve of St Austell Bay, 'the magnificent stretch of white, glistening sand almost a mile long, with the red-brown, tin-and-copper-stained cliffs enclosing it.' Granny Vanson did not trust this beautiful deserted place, and would not allow her grandchildren go to there unaccompanied. Her husband's brother Christopher had been drowned there and a cousin, Uncle Rowse's brother Joe, disillusioned with life and sotted with drink, had chosen Crinnis Beach as the place from which to give up altogether on his miserable existence. The occasional chaperoned trip to this 'melancholy place' was never much fun for Leslie. The Rowses would team up with another family that included girls – in itself, Leslie felt, a deterrent to enjoyment. Even without girls, Leslie found the 'vast spaces' of Crinnis Beach 'shapeless' and 'positively forbidding . . . the small groups of picnickers were lost in its immense perspectives'.

But if he was discouraged and disinclined to bathe in this 'crooel sea', this 'ungry sea', the excitement of a busy day at Porthpean, two miles from the town of St Austell, was not to be surpassed. Shy, slightly overweight and self-conscious, Leslie was never happier than when, bootless and stocking-free, he and the other men and boys rolled up their trouser-legs and paddled. They climbed on the rocks. They sat in the sand with the rest of his family and made sandcastles. They ate homemade pasties from the shop at lunchtime and later, at tea time, ravenous from the sea air, devoured 'an enormous round saffron bun corrugated with currants and flavoured with lemon peel.' The return journey home by donkey and trap was all part of the excitement of the day. Inhaling the scent of warm summer rain 'upon the pines and fuchsias, soaking into the thirsty summer earth', they travelled back 'through the mysterious and lovely shadow of Gewings Wood'. Later in the evening, in bed, Leslie had the delicious illusory sensation that his feet were still planted firmly on the beach and he could still feel the 'exquisite print of the sand and shingle underwater, luxuriously hurting'. These seaside days represented for A. L. Rowse 'the high-water mark of childhood'.

The simplicity of a day at the beach that Leslie Rowse and his family enjoyed was not enough to satisfy all holidaymakers. The countryside motor-bus service which had been running for the past eight years gave Cornish adventurers in 1911 the opportunity to go a little further than the Rowse donkey and trap would allow. With petrol at 3 d. a gallon and the expensive replacement of tyres there were costs to be met and the tickets were not cheap, but the bus was always packed. The front seat was reserved strictly for smokers, to discourage the ladies who were otherwise apt to engage Mr Charles Bolton, the worn-out driver, in ceaseless conversation.

Until the national network of railway lines opened up in the Victorian age mankind had never been able to move faster on land than on horseback. Trains represented speed, adventure and freedom. Arriving at King's Cross Station, Margaret Schlegel in E. M. Forster's novel *Howards End* felt exhilarated by 'those two great arches, colourless, indifferent, shouldering beneath them an unlovely clock' because she knew they were 'fit portals for some eternal adventure'. Improvements were being made to the railway service all the time. As recently as May 1911 picture windows had been installed for the first time, allowing passengers a magnificent view of the countryside. The current handbook for the South-Eastern and Chatham Railway announced that Vestibule Car Trains ran a first-class service, with carriages exquisitely furnished in the style of Louis XV, featuring richly upholstered chairs, lounges or settees on Axminster carpets and hung with genuine oil paintings and plate-glass mirrors. All cars were fitted with lavatories, and bells to summon attendants.

With the end of the rail strike the southern seaside resorts were left with twelve days of August in which to pull out all the stops for visitors, although there was still some disruptive after-shock to the services in the north. On 21 August the *Daily Telegraph* reported hundreds of people travelling to and from Blackpool by motor drays and furniture vans. Taxicabs, revelling in the opportunity to raise their fares, charged £5 for a journey from Blackpool to Manchester. Happily for schoolboy Brian Calkin, however, the Eastern branch line to Felixstowe Beach from Broad Street via Ipswich reported no delays.

Brian, the young chorister who had sung for the King and the Kaiser in Westminster Abbey on the day of the Coronation, was excited. His family owned a holiday house in Felixstowe, and every August they prepared to leave London for the coast, cramming the five-foot portable tin bath with boots, tennis rackets, stumps, kites, model yachts and roller skates. Brian's brother John had designed an ingenious smooth-fitting lid which slotted over the top of the bath and was tied in place with rope. Perched on top of the dome-topped trunks the bath was wheeled by the Calkins' valet Carrey on a trolley through the streets to the Finchley Road station. There Carrey would meet the Calkin family, who had travelled to the station in one of the few remaining horse-drawn buses, before they boarded the train for the Suffolk coast.

The Calkin boys' excitement at the prospect of their holiday was tempered by the loathsome grey powders their nanny forced them to swallow before the journey, the disgusting taste scarcely concealed by the added teaspoon of jam. This vile medicine was intended to loosen the bowels, for it was feared that the excitement of the journey combined with sudden exposure to the sea air might wreak havoc with their 'systems'. The boys dreaded the inevitability of spending several unhappy hours on arrival in Felixstowe in the pink carbolic-reeking water-closet. Brian had another reservation about this annual expedition: he was secretly terrified that one day the donkeys on the beach would break into a sudden canter and carry him towards the waves. But donkeys and donkey-rides were part of the essence of a summer holiday, and he knew better than to protest.

Services on the London, Victoria to Brighton line had also returned to normal – which was just as well, for Brighton, with its specially-built three mile protected sea front and its tantalising Victorian aquarium, had recently become the most frequented resort in the British Isles. The town's popularity had waned briefly at the beginning of the century, its associations with Queen Victoria seeming to give it an outdated air. Most of the tourist attractions had been built during her reign, and she had sold the Pavilion itself to the town in 1850 for £53,000. By the time of her death the imposing houses on the sea front suddenly seemed too huge to manage, the expense of bringing the necessary number of servants down for a few days prohibitive. But Edward VII became a regular visitor in 1908, and the town's status was restored. In gratitude Marine Parade was renamed 'Kingscliffe', and Brunswick Terrace, in the adjacent town of Hove, was thenceforward known as 'Kingsway'. Baedeker revised his guidebook entry, refuting the town's old reputation as a place made up of 'wind, glare and fashion' by describing the newly planted windbreak of thousands of shrubs, and recommending the grounds of the Pavilion for shelter from the sun. 'On a fine day', the guide pronounced, 'the scene here is of a most animated character.' The Palace Pier built in 1899, 1,760 feet long, with filigree arches and minaret corner towers, had that summer extended the repertoire offered in its 1500-seat auditorium to include concerts as well as the usual music hall turns, plays both modern and Shakespearean, opera, ballet, and boxing matches. With a resident population of 173,000 and an average annual influx of 50,000 tourists, Brighton's chief attractions as recommended by Baedeker were 'clear and bracing air, a fine expanse of sea bordered by white chalk cliffs, its bathing facilities and its gay crowd of visitors.'

In 1911, 55 per cent of the British population were taking the minimum of a one-day trip to the sea in the summer. Some work places, including paradoxically the railway companies themselves, had begun to introduce paid holidays longer than the customary half-day, and the double advantages of good weather and financial security for sometimes as much as a week combined with the ever-improving transport services to make England's coastline a crowded place that August. There, in the simple, cost-free pleasures of sunshine, sand and water, a fleetingly realisable equality was to be found by the poor, the suffragettes, the trade unionists, and even the parliamentarians.

As with everything in a class-structured England, inevitably the standard of resorts was graded. The 1911 Baedeker stresses for example that Margate is 'one of the most popular though not one of the most fashionable watering places in England', while Ramsgate, just along the coast, is 'a somewhat less cockneyfied edition of Margate.' Blackpool and Skegness were considered by gentry to be unquestionably vulgar, and the charms of towns like Bootle and Swansea were ruined by their proximity to industrial development.

For many years the rich had spent their August holidays taking a fashionable 'Spa-Cure'. Most spa towns were based inland, but the treatments they offered began to spring up in the coastal resorts. At the best hotels the staff included medical attendants to supervise those embarking on 'the Cure'. Ladies and gentlemen ingested quantities of sulphurous water four times a day, and also immersed themselves in the water itself, and sat with their hands packed in sulphurous mud. 'Electropathic repertoria' and treatments involving the use of ozone were also offered. The food served was usually somewhat at odds with the health-giving properties of the waters. Mouth-watering menus included salmon, sweetbread, duck, salad, and ices; those taking 'the Cure' were advised to avoid these delights, and some found the monotony of plain chicken and a lightly grilled sole a very poor alternative.

When they were not swallowing the sulphurous waters people relaxed in the pretty hotel gardens and read, or listened to music, and sometimes made expeditions to places of local interest. In the evening they might go to the theatre. At Harrogate, *The Prisoner of Zenda* was proving popular that August. The inland spa cure tended to be preferred by the older generation, who saw more disadvantages than advantages in a seaside holiday. Sun-darkened skin was still considered most undesirable, the give-away sign of an outside labourer, and special creams to counteract accidental tanning were advertised in the women's magazines. *The Lady* helpfully advised the use of 'Sulpholine' lotion, 'a simple remedy for clearing the skin of eruptions, roughness and skin discoloration.' A greater hazard even than sunburn was the risk of exposing naked flesh in public. On many bathing beaches the sexes were still segregated, although at Bexhill the experiment of mixed bathing had attracted much excited comment.

A cautious entry from a bathing-machine was the recognised means of making bodily contact with the sea, though at a shilling a time it was not cheap. In the Town Hall at Broadstairs, a conservative-minded town (in 1911 it was still being promoted in the *South Eastern and Chatham Railway Handbook* as Charles Dickens's favourite resort), a large unmissable notice in the hall cautioned that 'No female over eight years shall bathe from any machine except within the bounds marked for females.' It hung next to a second poster warning that 'Bathing dresses must extend from the neck to the knees.' These rules were accepted unquestioningly and were clearly not seen as restrictions, for the editor of the *Handbook* felt able to boast that Broadstairs was 'one of the freshest and freest little places in the world.'

The fully enclosed bathing machine was a sort of garden shed with wheels at one end, its walls and roof made either of wood or canvas. Sunlight Soap advertised their product on the side of some machines, cleverly targeting consumers whose awareness of personal hygiene might be enhanced when in a state of undress. Men and women would enter the machine from the back, while it was parked high up from the water line on the gender-segregated beach. In the pitch black hut, windowless in order to discourage any peering in, bathers would remove their clothes and put them up high on a shelf inside the machine to keep them dry, before struggling in the dark with the elaborate costume required for swimming.

The corseted bathing-dress, mirroring the corseted daywear, was beginning to loosen its laces, although until 1906 some had considered the wearing of stockings and shoes necessary for adequate decorum. But stockings as well as the full-length sleeves and knickerbockers beneath the bathing skirt had gradually been abandoned. In 1911 floaty pairs of shorts, which peeped out no more than three or four inches below the skirt, were enough to preserve modesty while the sleeve had shrunk from wrist to elbow. The weight of the clothes when wet ensured that swimming, at least for ladies, was impractical as a competitive sport. Men on the other hand wore far less cumbersome outfits, in a material that when wet clung to the body in a way that made some wonder why men bothered to dress for swimming at all. A sharp tap from inside was the agreed signal for a horse, a muscley man or even occasionally a mechanical pulley-contraption to drag the whole machine and its human contents to a line just beyond the surf. There the bather could slip discreetly into water up to the neck, with no chance of any part of the body being exposed to the view of those who remained on the beach. At the point of entry there was usually an attendant, irrationally sometimes of the opposite sex and some ladies looked forward to the moment of being lifted into the sea by strong local arms more than any other part of their holiday. After the swim, a little flag raised at the side of the machine indicated that it was time for welcoming arms to lift the bather back into the dark sanctuary of the dry, beach-bound dressing room.

As ever, rules were made to be broken and Clemmie Churchill was not one to allow any gold-chained Town Hall official to restrict her enjoyment of the water. Neville Lytton, brother-in-law of Winston's first girlfriend Pamela, was much struck by

Clemmie's emancipated ways during a short break at his brother Victor's house in stuffy Broadstairs itself: 'It was a broiling day,' he recorded, 'and the water was heavenly. Clemmie came forth like the re-incarnation of Venus re-entering the sea. Her form is most beautiful. I had no idea she had such a splendid body. She joined in a game of water polo with Victor and me and then she and I swam half-way across the channel and had an animated conversation bobbing up and down in the waves.'

The Home Secretary's wife was unusual in the social ease she demonstrated in the water; other more modest holidaymakers were more comfortable on dry land. Royalty could be deliciously accessible there, and *The Lady* was delighted to report that during the week of 20 August Princess Victoria, the King's sister, was frequently to be observed walking her black Aberdeen terrier up and down the promenade at Harrogate. Kings and queens, princes and princesses went frequently to the sea-side and to spa towns, and their presence was a recommendation to and attraction for visitors. The social press had correspondents in every fashionable resort, and local newspapers would publish the names of the aristocracy and the places where they were staying, to alert those who enjoyed gawping at the rich and famous. The promenade was the place to be seen, and the place to watch those wishing to be seen. Ladies floated past in white summer gowns, beneath matching silk parasols. The relaxed holiday mood of their immaculately turned-out male companions was reflected in an unaccustomed jauntiness in dress, their striped blazers, white flannels and boater hats all originally made fashionable by the late King. The rich promenaded on foot, in carriages or by motor-car as humbler onlookers played the game of identifying them as they passed by. *The Lady* published a splendid photograph of Queen Alexandra and her party gathered outside her commodious bungalow at Snettisham Beach, a few hundred yards from Sandringham, but by that time the dowager Queen was on her way up to Yorkshire to join her friend Lady Ripon at Studley Royal. Victoria Eugenia,

Queen of Spain, a granddaughter of Queen Victoria, was staying on at Osborne Cottage in the Isle of Wight, where an enjoyable garden party was given by Mr and Mrs Douglas Hall at Ryde. Tea was served on the Douglases' lower lawns in the cool shade of the trees, and a programme of tennis, croquet and bowls was overseen by the hostess, who according to *The Lady* was 'effectively gowned in bright blue, and a black hat trimmed with ostrich feathers.'

Inconveniences such as the drought and the railway strikes were stoically handled. The King left Bolton Abbey by car since the train he had planned to take was still not running, but he managed to catch a connection at Carlisle that set him well on his way to Inverness and his next host, The Mackintosh of Mackintosh. The Duke of Sutherland's polo match in Shropshire went ahead as planned despite the unfortunate absence of the Royal Scots Greys' team: the regiment had been on strike duty in Liverpool, and found they could not get there in time.

The Lady reported from Brighton that Mrs Norman of Holcombe had drifted across the lawn at her own party wearing 'crushed strawberry charmeuse' while her guests admired the late summer flowers and trees laden with fruit 'in spite of the drought which is affecting the country rather badly', and in Liverpool the pretty wedding of Miss Winifred Mabel Horsefall on 24 August 'afforded an agreeable break in the social stagnation of the past weeks.' The lawn tennis tournament in Folkestone opened on the 28th with a record 126 entries.

It was on the beach that the more humble holidaymaker found true liberation, mingling on an equal footing with those in a class or two above. Here on the crowded sands a children's paradise was on offer to all, though chimney-sweep lads were cautioned by *Punch* to keep their smudged faces from the cleansing water or risk accusations of being 'inauthentic' at their trade. The infinite pleasure of clambering over rock pools, shrimping nets and wooden spades clutched in the hand, collecting sea anemones and shells and building castles in the sand was to be had in resorts all along the English coastline. As well as the rides on often unkempt and ill-tempered donkeys that Brian Calkin so dreaded – and in some cases an uncomfortable canter on a reluctant harnessed and saddled goat – there were numerous entertainments and refreshments available for children. Here was the Punch and Judy stall, where screams of laughter accompanied the marital battering of poor resilient Judy, here were the conjurors, the whelk vendors, the ice-cream seller with his cart, the ginger-beer men, the hawkers with sweet sticks of rock, lollipops and bullseyes, and here were women selling straw baskets covered in small ridged cream-coloured scallop shells. Here, hustling for business, were the newspaper boys, the weighing-machine men, and the evangelists. The travelling photographer was particularly popular for his ability to turn a snapshot quickly into a much-valued picture-postcard. During that last week of August, test runs were being carried out for the first aerial post, between Hendon and Windsor, due to be launched officially on 9 September. The onlookers watching excitedly saw a postman in full Royal Mail uniform and cap clinging on precariously behind the pilot as they wobbled through the sky.

At the edge of the beach next to the helter-skelter, which was clamped in mock Tudor beams, were the candy-striped stalls advertising palmistry, crystal-ball gazing, phrenology, and the chance to see a two-headed mermaid. The century-old practice of phrenology, the interpretation of the lumps and bumps to be found by rubbing the hand over the skull, was an extremely busy attraction. Deep, clearly-defined lines on the forehead might indicate a high degree of mental concentration, while an elevation of the crown of the head signified decision-making powers and evidence of self esteem. At the age of 20 the butler Eric Horne had consulted a phrenologist about his future career. The expert's view, after he had 'felt my bumps', was that Eric was fit to be 'an actor, a lawyer or a parson'. Although 'fate destined that I should be neither', Eric appreciated in hindsight that the predicted acting skills had come in useful for concealing his views about certain employers.

The tent containing mermaids induced awe in the young and scepticism in the old. A careful examination would reveal these fish-women to be real live girls with rubber tails stretched over their legs. One particularly famous and convincing example, discovered years before and embalmed by Japanese fishermen, was brought from the Pacific to London for authentication. When Sir Everard Home, President of the Royal College of Surgeons, examined the creature he discovered it to have been made up from the head and arms of an orang-utan, with human finger nails attached to the ape's fingers, human teeth inside the jawbone of a baboon, a torso of stuffed hose, and the tail and fins of a large Pacific fish. The head had been ingeniously covered with synthetic skin, with the eyes and nose added in paint. But Sir Everard's exposure of the fake mermaid did nothing to obliterate the fascination such mythic beauties held for those who strolled the Margate sands.

Adults did different things on the beach. Men rarely removed their hats, and the poorer female holidaymaker, possessing neither a special holiday outfit nor light-weight summer clothes, was con-strained by the weight of her 'Sunday best' – since women dressed for a holiday as they did for a strike – from scrambling over the rocks. These women made an arresting sight against the backdrop of a sparkling blue sea in their elaborate artificial-flower-laden hats, their long black skirts brushing the sand as they stood, stifling, in their sturdy black shoes.

There was a good deal of standing about, for not all could afford to rent a deck chair. Those lucky enough to have 3 d. to spare would sit comfortably with a book or a newspaper. Here was a place for chatting, dozing, flirting, reading, gazing, sleeping. Older gentle-men of some means might bring out their telescopes and train them on the horizon, contentedly looking at nothing. If at last they saw a cloud of smoke they were able, fancying a steamer behind it, to feel the day's activity had been worthwhile. Younger blades might train their telescopic eyes on the activity surrounding the female bathing-machines, or put a penny in the saucy strip-tease slot machines.

> Oh just let me be beside the seaside!
> I'll be beside myself with glee.
> There are lots of girls, besides,
> That I'd like to be beside,
> Beside the seaside, beside the sea.

The noise of music and song emanating from a holiday resort could sometimes be overwhelming; even in the 1880s, Charles Dickens had considered staying away from his own Bleak House at Broadstairs because of 'the most excruciating organs, fiddles, and bells, violins, music boxes and voices.' But for most people, music emphasised the merriment of the seaside. There was music to listen to, and music to dance to. Dancing was a famous highlight of the Blackpool Pier, known for its all-encompassing gaiety as 'The People's Pier'. Revellers whirled away the holiday evening hours in polkas, barn dances, lancers and quadrilles. A military brass band was a familiar sight in all resorts, playing at regular intervals on piers, in the bandstands, and in the steamy fern and palm tree conservatories known as 'Winter Gardens'. As a schoolboy on holiday Osbert Lancaster was fond of these soldierly musicians, 'plump elderly gentlemen with long hair and thick glasses clad rather improbably in tight braided hussar uniforms.' In competition with them were the equally noisy white-ruffed, pierrot-costumed players who blacked up their faces and appeared as 'Nigger Minstrels'. Strumming their banjos and squeezing their concertinas, they were immensely popular, and merited a line of their own in one jolly sing-along song:

> Oh I love to sit a-gyzing on the boundless blue horizing
> When the scorching sun is blyzing down on sand and ships and sea!
> And to watch the busy figgers of the happy little diggers
> Or to listen to the niggers when they choose to come to me!

The Times did not recommend the musical aspects of seaside life. An article published at the end of August recognised that 'the modern holidaymaker wants rather more gaiety than was sufficient for his ancestors, the solemn shadowy personages who followed

George III to Weymouth for a course of sea bathing.' But the correspondent was disconcerted to notice that although some south coast resorts had gone so far as 'to make use of a "Publicity Manager" to use the American term, there is no "Entertainment Manager", so seaside music is the worst music in the country. The nigger on the sands who blacks his face is a tradition as English as Morris Dancing.' And, he might have spelled out, no more musically distinguished. Local papers in Eastbourne, Brighton and Hastings had reported for several seasons that the persistent playing of the Salvation Army Brass Band on Sundays – the day they felt rightfully theirs to proclaim the Saviour as the Lord – had been driving the local residents mad. An Act of Parliament had been passed restricting 'religious acclamation in the streets on the Sabbath', but fierce cymbal-clashing protests had resulted when residents tried to enforce the rule, and the restriction was now completely ignored.

If the Promenade and the beach were heaving with activity, the piers were no less crowded. A stroll along these fixed platforms was an enjoyable way of going a considerable way out over the water, without getting in a boat. There was usually a welcome breeze in the heat – though an unpleasant smell of shellfish and vinegar carried on the wind was apt to drift over the Palace Pier at Brighton.

Visitors to Ramsgate might take a picnic to Pegwell Bay, about a mile and a half to the west of the town and well known for its lovely picnic spots and plentiful shrimp. The adventurous would hire a sailing boat to take them seven miles out into the Channel, where at low tide the usually dangerous Goodwin Sands offered a benign open space suitable for an impromptu game of cricket. The evening saw day trippers returning home, but those who could afford to spend a few nights away would have booked a room in one of the many new coastal hotels. The Skelmersdale in Folkestone boasted of its fine cuisine and French wines (available in all the best hotels, except of course those reserved for the Temperance observer) but this year also made much of the charms of its recently completed smoking room. The new facility attracted the attention of the *Folkestone Herald*, in which it was praised as ' a

veritable paradise for lovers of the fragrant weed.' Many establishments advertised 'matchless views of the Channel with its never-
ending panorama of shipping'. The Fort Lodge Hotel,
conveniently situated opposite the Fort Promenade and the new
bandstand, had 'long been commended by the leading medical
men as the most healthy position in Margate.' Bathrooms were not
yet plentiful, however, and unless, like the Calkin family (and hop-
pickers), you packed a bath in your luggage, it might be necessary
to make an appointment with the chambermaid authorised to
prepare baths. She was often a source of irritation, filling baths too
full or making them too hot. Baths were not permitted after ten at
night lest the noise disturb the other guests.

Some working-class families could only manage to leave the city if
they were guaranteed paid work. Hop-picking was a popular alternative to a break at the seaside, particularly for Londoners, as the
heart of hop-picking country was in the south-east corner of
England. On 26 August *Country Life* announced that the season
had begun a fortnight earlier than usual because of the advanced
growth of the crop in the hop gardens. Messrs·L. May, hop suppli-
ers from the Weald of Kent Gardens Company, reported that 'the
hops are fully matured and are full of lupulin' – the sticky yellow
powder found in the hop cone that gives beer its bitter taste –
leading them to anticipate that the 1911 crop would be 'the best
we have had for many years.'

The start of the hop-picking season was the signal for hundreds
of families to leave the cramped tenements of the East End and
head for the fields. Women and children made up more than half
the numbers. Some, gathering first for a farewell drink in the local
pub, laughing, chatting, and excited, would board a special bus to
take them out into the country. Others would borrow a barrow
from the greengrocer, piling it high with bedding and pots and pans
packed into old tin baths and tea chests and then wheeling the
precarious load through the streets all the way to the train at
London Bridge. Throughout the hop gardens of Sussex and Kent

several generations, including children barely old enough to walk, spent two weeks together in the country air. Farmers would provide the displaced communities with little huts and bedding straw, but everyone disliked the walk through stinging nettles and thistles to the inadequate makeshift sanitary facility known as the 'Thunder Box'. Inside the flimsy wooden shack, three feet wide by two feet long, a plank of wood was supported over a huge and smelly hole into which children were terrified of falling. During a long working day punctuated by cups of tea brewed on a portable, methylated-spirit primus stove the pickers moved along the dark green hop-alleys, pulling down the crop-laden bines from the twelve-foot poles, their arms scratched by the rough twine of the hop garlands and their clothes covered in the thick yellow pollen. But the familiar, musty, unmistakable smell of the bright green hops and the welcome change from the grey lives that so many led in the city were so enjoyable that families returned every year, often to the same farm for many generations.

Politicians who felt unable to leave London during August were often to be found cooling off in the basement pool at the RAC Club in Pall Mall, and they were not the only ones to enjoy indoor swimming. On the occasional day that Lady Diana Manners was in London she would visit the Bath Club, just off Bond Street. Swimming was for her 'the only athletic pleasure I have ever known', and she was usually in such a hurry to 'plunge into that delectable green pool' that she would start undoing her belt and unfastening buttons while still in the street. She was taking lessons to improve her technique, and became good enough to dive in displays in front of Royalty. And what went on afterwards was as much fun as the lesson. 'After an hour's tuition my friends and I, wrapped in bath towels, would stagger into the hottest room of the Turkish, send for large strawberry ices from Gunter's next door and shock the older fatter ladies with our giggling gossip.'

For others, a few hours on Hampstead Heath were enough to provide a change of scene. Despite initial opposition from the Hampstead Heath Protection Society, worried that the underground trains would shake the living daylights out of the trees, in 1908 Lloyd George had opened the new extension from Charing Cross to Heath Street, sophisticated engineering enabling it to be sunk 150 feet below the earth. 'Take your Son and Heir where there is Sun and Air' an Underground poster urged irresistibly, and on the August Bank Holiday of 1911 more than 300,000 people took up the invitation. On this magnificent non-urban hilly expanse where shaggy sheep grazed and organ grinders turned their wheels, the cockney holidaymaker sang 'Happy Hampstead' at the top of his voice.

In the city the music halls provided entertainment for a summer evening out. Lady Ottoline Morrell loved to go and watch the tartan-clad, walking-stick twirling, singing star Harry Lauder at the Tivoli. Victoria Monks, whose energetic cheeky presence embodied cockney London, would join the Edinburgh born Harry on the stage: Ottoline, a bohemian queen of flamboyance herself, thought Victoria Monks a wonderful sight with her 'vulgarity, vitality, human kindness, tragedy, and humour and recklessness.' Inviting the audience 'in her hoarse thrilling voice' to join her in song, she strutted 'her vulgar body in a tight red satin dress, short skirt with flounces and spangles, brown hair done up on high with a huge fringe.'

The weather had remained consistently fine, though the intolerable heat of earlier in the month had eased, and on 23 August, for the first time in 53 days, the recording instrument in South Kensington failed to register a single trace of bright sunshine. But the balmy late August weather continued, and on 26 August a correspondent wrote to the editor of *Country Life* to ask about the possible harmful effects of sleeping out-of-doors: 'During the recent period of full moon my head one night was exposed to its full rays and I was conscious in sleep of discomfort sufficient to cause wakefulness,' a Mr Leveson-Scarth noted anxiously, going on to ask 'whether the moon's rays are known scientifically to have an effect upon sleepers and if so do animals feel it also? My dog awoke too and moved for a time into the shade.'

During the August of 1911 there were those who did not need a holiday from anything except the relentless pressure of their own busy minds. On the 16th *Punch* invited several personalities to describe their favourite holiday occupations. Clement K. Shorter, editor of *The Sphere*, wanted to live on a diet of light paperback novels, without ever mentioning Charlotte Brontë or George Meredith, while the delight of the dandy actor-manager Sir George Alexander, knighted just that summer, was to 'don garments snatched at the last moment from their appropriate rag bag and do all I can to emulate the sartorial nonchalance of a tramp.' The composer Sir Edward Elgar also relished the refreshment of a complete contrast, confessing that he loved 'Like Apollo to unbend my bow and indulge in frivolous compositions.' He was proud to tell *Punch* that he had had some recent successes, and in the last fortnight alone had produced 'A ragtime rhapsody, a burlesque of Brahms, and a symphonic cake-walk polka.'

But if these carefree days held enduringly happy memories for some, the elemental summer of 1911 had not yet loosened its grip. The seaside air might be intoxicating, but the sea itself could be dangerous. *The Times* had followed its column 'Deaths by Heat' with another headed 'Deaths by Water', and found no shortage of material with which to fill it. On 29 August a 12-year-old boy out boating on his own in Ramsgate was drowned, despite the best efforts of an old deck-chair attendant to save his life. On the same day in Southampton Water, a leaking boat sank too rapidly for the coastguard to reach it. The three passengers, unable to swim, lost their lives. The river provided an end to the misery of a young courting couple from Southwark. With her handkerchief Lizzie Morgan bound her wrist to that of her sweetheart James Chipps, a boot repair boy, and together they jumped off Vauxhall Bridge into the Thames. Lizzie's mother found a note beneath her daughter's pillow: 'As you would not let Jem and I be together we thought we would end it all. Please do not blame Jem.'

News from across the Channel was hitting the headlines in England, and readers were gripped by the drama of the unfolding story. It had been announced in Paris that on Tuesday 22 August a bric-à-brac seller with a stall a couple of hundred yards from the Louvre had been approached by a middle-aged man of appearance 'indéterminé' and asked whether he was interested in buying 'an old picture of a woman' which the seller had rolled up in a piece of cloth and tucked under his arm. The bric-à-brac man did not even bother to look at the painting. Shortly afterwards the Louvre authorities announced that the *Mona Lisa* was missing. They had narrowed the time of the theft down to the hours between 7 and 8.30 a.m. on the previous day, and had not alerted the police until they were sure it not been removed to elsewhere in the museum by the official photographer. The hope was that the theft would prove to be the work either of a lunatic, who would return da Vinci's masterpiece as soon as he had had his last laugh, or of someone anxious to demonstrate the museum's poor security. The staff had begun an intensive search of the Louvre itself, but the building covered 49 acres and the search was expected to last at least a week. The frame that had encased the world's most famous picture was discovered empty near a cloakroom. A reward of £400 (the equivalent of six years' salary for a British policeman) had been offered for information. No one had yet come forward, but they were questioning a young artist (well known and admired by Augustus John) who a few months earlier had inadvertently bought some sculptures that turned out to be works of art stolen from the museum. His name was Pablo Picasso.

The Mona Lisa might be absent from her customary surroundings, but the still-rumbling German threat to French interests in Morocco, the aftermath of the strikes and the as yet unresolved question of Irish Home Rule kept many politicians in or near London. The Prime Minister managed an occasional few days at Easton Grey, his sister-in-law's house, near Newbury in Berkshire. But on 21 August Asquith was in the back seat of the car reading while being driven back to London at moderate speed by Hayward, his chauffeur, when there was a collision. The car hit a young nurse on her bicycle, an orphan named Nellie Green, so the papers reported, only 20 years old. Highly distressed, Asquith explained in a letter to his daughter Violet, who was holidaying in Munich, that Nellie was 'very badly wounded in the face and head and has not yet recovered consciousness, but there is now a faint hope that she may live.' Over the next few days her condition remained critical, and although there were glimpses of consciousness, her prospects were not encouraging.

That same day, in the House of Commons, Winston Churchill made a speech justifying the use of troops in Llanelli on the afternoon the railway strike was settled, without a request for military help from the local authorities. He said the strike had threatened 'a swift and certain degeneration of all the means, of all the structure, social and economic, on which the life of the people depends. ' Trying to justify the loss of six lives at Llanelli, he continued by comparing the railway strike to the breaching of the Nimrod Dam on the Euphrates, 'when the enormous population who had lived by that artificial means were absolutely wiped from the book of human life.' Seen as typical Winston hyperbole and oratory misplaced, this was not well received by the handful of MPs who remained in the House.

The *Daily Telegraph* and *The Lady*, meanwhile, reported on 24 August in concerned vein a worrying tendency to 'overuse the top most note' that had crept into the pattern of daily speech. Pointing in particular to the language heard over the past few tumultuous weeks in both the Upper and the Lower House, notably during the animated debates over the Parliament Bill, these publications worried that it was 'threatening the significance of the finest words with extinction.' A theoretical exchange cited as an example of the absurd lengths to which people might go had one woman saying 'I simply adore loganberries, they are so exquisitely subtle!', to be answered by her friend: 'Dear basketfuls of the beloved things! How perfectly wonderful!' The *Telegraph* and *The Lady* joined their considerable forces to call for the founding of 'The Society for the Abolition of the Top Note'. That perfect summer had overreached itself in excessive heat and drama, and as if in response the language of the nation's people had become affected. 'Utterly,

utterly' was how the Souls might have described that summer; they remained serenely unmoved by the newspapers' reproving words, and their extravagant exchanges continued in dismissive and self-satisfied fluency.

After Churchill's speech on 21 August the last MPs finally abandoned the House, but the Home and Foreign Secretaries remained in London. On the 23rd there was a meeting of the Defence Committee, Sir Edward Grey, the Foreign Secretary, reluctantly denying himself the bird-watching expeditions he so loved to continue working long hours at his desk. Churchill kept an eye on his diligent colleague and lodger, who noted gratefully how 'late in the afternoon he would call for me and take me to the Automobile Club which was thinly populated like other clubs at that season. There after what had been to me a weary and perhaps anxious day he would cool his ardour and I revive my spirits in the swimming bath.'

Winston's attention was increasingly drawn to the problems of North Africa, yet he remained unable to resist becoming involved in the smallest detail of the problems of his own ministry. On 31 August he issued a special dispensation in favour of a Mr James Garfield Crake, aged 33, a tradesman who had developed an inordinate crush on a Mrs Florence Egan Newcombe, of Rutland Gate in Knightsbridge and had been imprisoned for causing the poor lady a nuisance, Winston took pity on the man for a penalty that seemed to him harsh for a simple declaration of passion, ignoring a report from the Chief Medical Officer, who had concluded that Mr Crake was 'an imbecile and dangerous'. Liberated, Mr Crake immediately hot-footed it back to Knightsbridge, gained entry to Mrs Newcombe's house, and terrified her by flinging his arms around her neck and kissing her. *The Times* took a dim view, calling it 'a most disgraceful case'. Winston in his turn hot-footed it to Broadstairs for a day, to build sandcastles with Clemmie and the children.

On 28 August the press reported that Nellie Green had partially recovered consciousness after her accident involving the Prime

Minister's car, but her condition was still critical. Mrs Asquith had paid her several visits, and Mr Asquith had telephoned daily. Three days later, at the Prime Minister's request, an eminent specialist named Mr Rock Carling travelled from London to visit the young woman in Newbury Hospital. He confirmed that she had intervals of consciousness and that there was a chance she might recover.

Apart from the odd day in Broadstairs with his family, Churchill had spent most of August in London. According to Grey, it was because of his 'love of the crisis', in North Africa. On the second to last day of the month Churchill went to immerse himself in the peace of the Horners' house at Mells, but could not clear his mind of the danger of the situation in Morocco. Writing to Grey, he confessed that 'I could not think of anything else but the peril of war . . . there was only one field of interest fiercely illuminated in my mind. Sitting on a hilltop in the smiling country which stretches round Mells, the lines I have copied kept running through my mind.' They were from A. E. Housman's *Shropshire Lad*:

> On the idle hill of summer
> Sleepy with the flow of streams,
> Far I hear the steady drummer
> Drumming like a noise in dreams
> Far and near and low and louder
> On the roads of earth go by,
> Dear to friends and food for powder,
> Soldiers marching, all to die.

On the last day of the month Lady Diana Manners went up to a Yorkshire houseparty staying with a family friend, Mr Frank Green, who owned The Treasure House, the beautiful early Tudor building next to York Minster. The Queen spent a day shopping in London before heading north to join her husband at Balmoral. Augustus John wondered whether he might send some of the boys away to school. For sportsmen, notable among them the King, the official opening of the partridge season on 1 September was a sign that the summer was coming to an end.

10

Early September

There was no sign of anything amiss. No sudden chilling of
the blood.

Osbert Sitwell, *Great Morning*

ELINOR GLYN HAD not been enjoying her summer. At the age
of 46, the leading romantic novelist of her decade was still
thrillingly beautiful, a startling example of youth preserved in
middle age. Aware that the muscles of the face would slacken with
the years, she had taught herself to strengthen them by moving
the scalp up and down and wriggling her ears, and these exercises
seemed to have had a remarkable braking effect on the sag that
afflicts all women. Her unblemished white skin and 'Venetian red'
hair had captivated any number of men, among them Lord
Curzon, widowed former Viceroy of India. But although com-
pliments flowed – many directed at the glorious 'snowy ampli-
tudes' of her décolletée – Curzon made no formal declaration. By
early September, Elinor was beginning to conclude that her love
life was once again proving to be a disappointment.

Elinor's elder sister Lucy Duff Gordon, the haute couturier
Madame Lucille to her customers, had been abroad for most of
the summer, preparing to open a new salon in Paris. The French
were affronted that an Englishwoman should have the impudence
to think she might set up shop among them, and she watched
with some amusement as 'their wax moustaches quivered with
wrath and ample satin bosoms heaved with indignation.' She had

found it difficult to get away to spend some of the summer with her sister in England. Elinor had been lonely. She had been hoping that her three-year affair with George Curzon might at last be moving into a new phase of steadiness. He had always been reluctant to reassure her where she stood in his vacillating affections, and over the years this hesitancy had unsettled her deeply. 'Rather in the spirit in which other men like a good horse or fine wine or beautiful things to embellish a man's leisure', she observed, were women allocated their place in Curzon's scheme of things. 'There was more for a man to do in the world than to fall in love with a beautiful woman and live happily ever after.' Elinor was well aware that he did not regard women as 'equal souls worthy of being seriously considered or treated with that scrupulous sense of honour with which he would deal with a man.' Paradoxically, Elinor's perceptiveness and intelligence were the very qualities about her that so attracted this contradictory man who loved women as much as he despised them.

Curzon had spent a challenging summer too, deeply opposed to the plan for Home Rule in Ireland, and preoccupied with the difficult passage of the Parliament Bill through the House of Lords, but at the end of August he had asked Elinor to stay at Hackwood, his Palladian country house near Basingstoke in Hampshire, accompanied by her elder daughter Margot, aged 16. During that weekend, while she helped him remove the hated plantains from the Hackwood drive, Elinor redoubled her energetic attempts to woo Curzon into thinking of her as a future wife and step-mother. She had made a tremendous effort with his daughters, especially the younger two, Cimmie and Baba, who accepted her role in their father's life and had become very fond of her. She had taught Baba to paint, and took the girls on exciting picnics, building open fires on which, to the girls' delight, she would cook bacon and potatoes. For their father's entertainment she arranged for a distinguished clairvoyant to visit Hackwood, knowing that Curzon shared her fascination with the spiritual world. Side-tables began to float above the ground in the dark-

ened library, and the eerie knocking noises heard in the dim light
of the sitting-room were identified as specific individuals returning to Hackwood from the spirit world with messages. Ping-pong
balls bobbed up and down of their own accord above the
Hackwood dining room table. Elinor was so obviously enthralled
with the spiritual world that there were those who thought she
herself possessed occult powers. She was a passionate believer in
reincarnation, convinced that 'there is something fundamentally
irreligious in the idea that so amazing a miracle as the creation of
a human soul should depend for its occurrence upon the whim
of a pair of earthly lovers, or worse, upon the accident of a faulty
contraceptive appliance.' Sometimes she would conduct a séance,
and enjoyed giving a full analysis of her opinion of particularly
disagreeable returnees.

Elinor was not sure that her campaign to make Curzon love her
was having much success. Officially, marriage was out of the
question. Elinor was already married. Her husband Clayton Glyn
was nearly 60, a spendthrift and an alcoholic, and for many years
Elinor had supported him and their two children, Margot and
Juliet. But she was an optimist and a romantic, in life as well as in
the pages of her novels: Curzon's wife had been dead for five
years, and Clayton's health was not good. Nevertheless, as she was
horribly aware, invitations to stay at Hackwood were a precious
rarity. Curzon's habit was to select his end-of-the-week guests
according to his and their various interests. Old friends from India
did not overlap with family parties, people invited for shooting
were segregated from neighbourly get-togethers. Her exclusion
from most of these gatherings did not greatly disturb Elinor, but
there was one group she longed to be accepted by – Curzon's
inner set, 'The Souls'.

She was well aware that they considered her vulgar and an
embarrassment, and that she would never be welcome in their
exclusive circle. Curzon's American wife Mary Leiter had also
found herself disapproved of by the group of women she called
'the thorns', but Mary had at least been an heiress: Elinor was

usually short of money and earned her living by writing, in the Souls' view, novels of questionable quality and taste. She longed for her daughter Margot to become a friend of Lady Diana Manners, daughter of the leading Soul, the Duchess of Rutland, and entirely at ease at Hackwood; but as the two young women were never invited to stay at the same time, a friendship was out of the question.

By the summer of 1911 Elinor was the author of ten published novels, but had made her name just four years earlier with *Three Weeks*, the story of a highly erotic affair between an Englishman and a mysterious older woman referred to throughout the book as 'The Lady'. From across a restaurant in Switzerland Paul Verdayn was transfixed by the mesmeric appearance of a fellow diner whose mouth was 'straight and chiselled and red, red, red'. He watched The Lady toy with her caviar, *truite bleu* and quail, her figure 'so supple in its lines it made him think of a snake'. Later, after four glasses of port and an after-dinner cigar alone on the terrace, Paul, 'a splendid young English animal of the best class', found that his 'heart seemed to swell with some emotion, [and] a faint scent of tuberoses filled the air.' The following day the notorious seduction scene took place on a huge tiger skin, a present Paul had sent to The Lady's room earlier. Reclining on the part of the animal 'where the hair turned white and black at the side and was deep and soft', The Lady emitted a sound similar to the purr of that formidable wild beast in the satisfaction of conquest. Elinor's own response to a tiger skin played a significant part in the plot, as she confided in a letter to the portrait painter Philip de László. 'If you knew the strange effect tiger skins have on me! The touch of the tiger awakens some far off savagery – some former life when I was unhampered and could kill or love when I desired, without having to consider civilisation.' Reviewers of *Three Weeks* were amazed that such a story had been written by an author already established as a highly readable and entertaining observer of contemporary manners. She usually wrote 'lightly and trippingly', and her departure from her customary style caused literary consternation. 'Squalid!' the reviewers cried when *Three Weeks* appeared. 'There is little in the book but a mawkish display of sickly sentimentalism misnamed love', said the *Globe*, dismissively. 'To get an artistic result out of such a subject', the *Westminster Gazette* pronounced, 'it is necessary for a writer to show delicacy and self restraint. Neither of these qualities are displayed in this book.' It became an immediate best-seller.

Elinor was prepared neither for such success, nor for such a hostile reaction. She began to realise that she had miscalculated the Edwardian talent for hypocrisy. 'It was secretly considered quite normal in society circles for a married woman to have a succession of illicit love affairs during the intervals of which, if not simultaneously, intimate relations with her husband were resumed,' she wrote in puzzlement, a while after the initial commotion had died down. She was genuinely mystified that 'a novel in which an exotic foreign character is depicted in the throes of a single passionate romance, for which she pays willingly with her life, should be condemned as highly immoral.' The adverse publicity continued to provide a terrific boost for sales. Edward VII would not allow the book to be mentioned in his presence. The Head Master of Eton, Dr Edward Lyttelton, banned it from his school after staff reported that boys, inattentive with so little sleep, had been discovered reading it by torchlight beneath the bedclothes. He later admitted sheepishly that he had not actually read the book himself, and Elinor persuaded him to do so by sending him an inscribed copy. To his credit, he felt even more sheepish when he then admitted he had rather enjoyed it. An anonymous poem was widely circulated:

> Would you like to sin
> With Elinor Glyn
> On a tiger skin?
> Or would you prefer
> To err
> With her
> On some other fur?

Rosa Lewis of the Cavendish Hotel in Jermyn Street designed a seductive sitting room containing a sumptuous purple sofa and named it The Elinor Glyn Room. A parody of the novel – *Too Weak*, by Elluva Gryn – was followed in 1908 by a stage adaptation at the Adelphi Theatre in London's West End, and the cream of society was invited to the gala night. At the last minute, with a self-confessed 'amazing temerity', Elinor took the lead role of The Lady, dressed in a silky gown especially designed by her sister Lucy.

Curzon was in the audience for the gala performance that evening, and was mesmerised by Elinor's flamboyantly beautiful and youthful face, her red hair clashing magnificently with her purple robe. The following day, he sent her 'the kindest note of real appreciation' and, with the letter, a complete tiger skin taken from a magnificent beast he had shot in India when he was Viceroy. They met for the first time at a party shortly afterwards, and Curzon was impressed not only by her beauty but by her intelligence. Elinor in her turn was 'dazzled by his marvellous brain'. She saw at once how his 'delightful outbursts of humour and fun' would be tempered by his irritating 'contemptuous manner and assumption of natural superiority in every known respect and on every occasion' but was prepared to forgive him everything, in part because of the pain she knew he suffered from a troublesome back, in part because of his adherence to 'the duty of the individual to the state, of man to humanity.' In his strange accent, 'an eccentric amalgam of Derbyshire and Eton', he would read Aristotle aloud to her in the evenings. She began to feel he 'stood above other men as St Paul's above village churches'; she called him 'Milor'; and then she fell in love with him, and was unfaithful to her husband for the first time.

Clayton had not always been the depressing, shaming and worrying drain on her finances and spirits that he had become by 1911. At their first meeting, twenty years earlier, she had been reminded of Cinderella's Prince. Clayton had lost his original brown hair in a gas explosion at his prep school and it grew back bleached of its colour. Elinor's romantic spirit quivered: now thick but silver, the hair was 'like the powdered wigs of the eighteenth century'. He claimed to be a gentleman farmer, insisted (to Elinor's delight) on first-class travel, and produced a splendid diamond engagement ring. What he appeared to offer was sufficiently tempting for Elinor, a poor girl from Jersey encouraged by a determined mother with material ambitions, to agree to marry him; what they did not know was that he was already heavily in debt and living way beyond his means, and that the Glyn estate at Harlow in Essex was impoverished.

When Clayton arranged for the tenant farmers with their 'Newgate frill beards and shaved upper lips like Abraham Lincoln' to line the drive to greet the newly-weds she was most touched. And she felt life to be perfect when, on their honeymoon, he hired the Brighton swimming baths simply for the pleasure of watching her swim up and down naked, her knee-length hair streaming mermaid-like behind her. But Clayton's devoted attention did not last long, and his strange disengaged attitude began to worry her. Shortly after their marriage the Glyns went to stay at Easton, home of the Warwicks. Walking with her in the rose garden, Lord Warwick suddenly tried to kiss Elinor. She was deeply shaken, more so after she had confided the facts to Clayton. Instead of being outraged, he turned to her while tying his white tie for dinner, 'his whimsical face lit by a delightful smile. "No, did he? Dear old Brookie" was all he said, and went back to his tie-fixing.' Almost worse was the time he abandoned her alone upstairs in bed, to spend the entire night in the dining room simply in anticipation of eating a pear at the precise moment it ripened.

The money Elinor made from *Three Weeks* was consumed by her husband's mounting debts, but she still had to run the household and pay the school fees for her two daughters. Those years were 'one long nightmare of recurring financial crises as fresh debts of Clayton's came to light.' In June 1911 Elinor's money worries had reached a climax. The summer months of the Coronation and the festival of dance and colour brought by the Ballets Russes, had been blighted by the necessity of dealing with her spendthrift husband's latest financial indiscretion. In the red leather journal she kept locked in a purple velvet bag, secured with a gold chain, she admitted that Clayton's cheeks had begun to acquire 'the violet tinge which one associates with serious heart trouble.' The excessive consumption of brandy that had contributed to his financial troubles was also affecting his health. In the spring Elinor had visited her American publisher in New York, then enjoyed a cultural holiday in Italy, returning to discover not only that Clayton's health had deteriorated as a result of his reluctance to give up 'shooting grouse under an August sun, travel in hot climates, Turkish baths, rich food, perfect wine and strong cigars', but that he had extended his borrowing by a further £1,000. Finding the bank unwilling to bail him out again, this time he had arranged a loan with a friend. Elinor was aware of the identity of this friend, but determined that his name be kept secret, describing him to her sister as someone 'who had often paid attentions to me, and who had never ceased to show his devotion'. Lucy guessed correctly that the friend was Curzon. Frantic with worry that the loan would further derail her already precarious relationship with him, Elinor swallowed her pride and contacted R. D. Blumenfeld, editor of the *Daily Express*. He willingly co-operated, telling her that if she wrote him a book in three weeks, he would serialise it in June. In exchange for ninety thousand words he would pay her exactly the sum she needed to pay back Clayton's debt. She agreed. Tucking herself away into her Louis XVI bed, its bed-head garlanded with Lucy Duff Gordon's signature silk rosebuds, and wearing a lace mob cap, Elinor assembled a pile of new writing blocks beside her. For the next eighteen days she lived on sandwiches and reviving tumblers of brandy brought up on a tray while under 'superhuman strain' producing a novel she called *The Reason Why*. This indeed was exploiting what Curzon called her 'cursed facility' with plot and words. The novel contained all the Glyn elements her readers loved: a proud handsome hero, a beautiful savage heroine, an enigmatic financier with a heart of gold, a foolish stepfather, and a sickly child of genius dying in a garret. Elinor felt sick with herself for having debased her art, and conscious of the most wounding criticism she had ever received. The *Times Literary Supplement* pronounced *The Reason Why* 'A variant of no great originality, on the familiar theme of a marriage bargain becoming a marriage of love.' The book was, predictably, a hit.

In September the idea of new beginnings coinciding with a new season seemed appealing: it was the time for a whole new approach to the Curzon campaign, and Elinor embarked on something serious. On holiday in 1910 she had met the distinguished metaphysician Professor F. H. Bradley who had recently promised her that he would supply her with authentic Greek quotations to give a new book intellectual weight, as well as agreeing to help her choose a picture of Aphrodite for the frontispiece.

She was determined that this autumn she would write a novel that would elevate her in the eyes of her lover and force him to admire her intellect. She already knew what he thought of her body, for he was an extremely passionate lover with a highly developed libido; what she was interested in vanquishing was his mind. Inexplicably, however, in *Halcyone* she chose to write about a character who was not only selfish and egotistical but who put his ambitions before everything else, an anti-hero who believed that only men had souls. Elinor was intent only on impressing Curzon, and all her instinctive caution and judgement seemed to leave her. The manuscript copy of the misguided novel that arrived at Hackwood received a curt response. Curzon pointed out two spelling mistakes in Elinor's accompanying letter; there were no other remarks attached.

On 1 September 1911 the early-morning autumnal mist began gradually to clear, like the dry ice used for dramatic effect on a stage, leaving the sky as blue as a gentian. All along the hedgerows spider webs elaborate as spinnakers glistened with dew in the low sunlight. The day marked the beginning of two popular seasons: partridges and oysters would soon be appearing on all the most gastronomically-inclined tables. Essex oyster farmers agreed that there had rarely been a better spatting season in the famous Pyefleet beds. The 370-year-old ceremony of toasting the Sovereign in gin and gingerbread was successfully conducted by the Mayor of Colchester, who felt a flicker of personal greatness when he sent a telegram to the King at Balmoral to announce that 'According to ancient Custom and Charter dating back to Norman times, the Mayor and Councillors of the Colchester Borough Council will formally proclaim the Opening of the Colne Oyster Fishery for the coming season and will drink to your Majesty's long life and health and request respectfully to offer to your Majesty their expressions of dutiful loyalty and devotion.'

Ingredients for breakfast were suddenly deliciously available to the early-morning country riser, who found the lanes full of ripe blackberries and the undergrowth at the outer edges of the woods packed with fleshy mushrooms. The bright green aftermath was pushing up between the stubble in the harvested fields, and for a few weeks before ploughing began there was a strange sense that a couple of seasons had been skipped over, and spring was already on the way.

In the cities, however, summer was not quite ready to release its long hold on the year. In London's Hyde Park the bandstands were still humming with the Wednesday and Saturday concerts, elderly and deaf members of the audience sitting in deck chairs as close as possible to the musicians while the younger men and women flirted on the perimeter. In Kensington Gardens children played around Sir George Frampton's new statue of Peter Pan. Only a few of the smarter carriages had returned to the Park after the summer holiday, their habitual occupants still away on the grouse moors, as in London the temperatures continued to defy normal expectations for mid September. Some enthusiasts were still looking for opportunities to swim, and the *Spectator* was a little concerned by the news that 'the once decorous shores of the Serpentine have been invaded by bathers at unwonted hours', imagining the consequences of a second hot summer – it 'would probably see the practice of mixed bathing imported from the coast to our metropolitan waters!' The magazine was also anxious that the monotonous blue skies would result in an erosion of the natural flow of an Englishman's 'customary conversational resource'. With the unnatural climate that had descended on this island, 'when weeks and months pass by with no variation in the tropical heat, and the Sahara-like dryness, when drought follows drought and every atmospheric record is distanced again and again', the magazine feared circumstances when 'the humblest talker begins to doubt whether even for him the weather has not lost its novelty.'

For Lady Cynthia Asquith, a young woman of the slightly insecure temperament that comes from social inexperience, the shooting season brought with it a whole set of social challenges. Some robust members of her sex seemed to enjoy accompanying the men out to the field. The sort of girl who might be branded a 'good sort', she explained, 'took immense vicarious pride in the number of birds brought down by the particular gun she stood behind.' But Lady Cynthia was sickened by the 'holocaust of birds' and reluctant to deal with 'a disappointed hence surly sportsman', being quite uncertain of the etiquette, not knowing whether she should engage the 'Gun' in conversation, or if it was wiser not to make any comment at all. Something seemed required but, unable to tell whether skill or chance had been in play when a bird was hit, she hesitated to cry out her congratulations. 'Bad luck:' did not sound the right sort of response to a missed bird, 'yet silence seemed so unsympathetic'.

New challenges were confronting those even younger than Lady Cynthia. Children expected for the start of the new term were reluctant to let the summer slip away, and for it to be replaced by schoolbooks. One exasperated Kentish headmaster reported that 'owing to hop tying, attendance is very bad indeed. I have visited the school managers and parents and also sent lists of irregularities to the board meeting but with the exception of the kind help from the Rector I am not backed up in any way.' He was not the only frustrated headmaster to be dealing with rebellion at the start of the new academic year: another, puzzled to know why his geography class was so lethargic, was told on investigation that 'Percy Topliss brought in a bottle of laudanum, sir, and passed it round the class.' An opportunity not only to express their views about school discipline but to be listened to was what the schoolboys of Llanelli were after. When the new timetables were handed out, the boys discovered that their lunchtime break had been eroded by a full quarter of an hour, and a group of incipient Ben Tilletts decided to act (coincidentally, their inspiration was himself in Wales at the time, soothing and encouraging the union men still sore from the antagonisms and tragedies of the last month).

The strikes of August had given the schoolboys irresistible role models, and they had serious grievances. Conditions in some schools were as unacceptable as the conditions in which they worked were unacceptable to their parents. Brian Calkin, survivor of a summer free of malevolent donkeys, was happy in the authority of his new role as editor of the St Paul's Choir School Magazine, but at his school near Bristol his younger brother was not so content. Kenneth Calkin had suffered from severe claustrophobia since being punished for some minor offence by being locked in a basement cupboard. He felt picked on and lonely. He did not know who to talk to about the persistent stares directed at him by the Latin master during prayers. Once, during a walk on Durdham Downs not far from the school, the housemaster knocked Kenneth's straw hat off his head and twirled it in the air on the end of his walking stick. Alarmed by this behaviour, Kenneth bolted. On his return to school he was given six strokes for running away, the reason for his punishment 'unseemly behaviour in public'.

There was no means of voicing the general grievances harboured by schoolboys, among which unfair and extreme penalties and excessive homework headed the list. On 5 September, the second day of term, the schoolboys of Llanelli went into action. Thirty-two boys failed to turn up for their history lesson, appearing instead on Murray Street, dancing and singing and causing something of a local stir. They were objecting to corporal punishment as well as the cut in their lunch break, and demanding payment of a halfpenny a week for the monitors. The ring-leader climbed onto the top of the park railing to make himself heard, and *The South Wales Press* reported a speech delivered in commendable, though flowery, language. Marching through the streets the boys, Pied-Piper-like, reminiscent of the robust lady leader of the striking jam-workers of Bermondsey only a few weeks earlier, persuaded two other schools to join in. Only when the headmaster appeared, flexing in threat the very weapon against which they had been protesting, did the oratory dry up.

But the power of adolescent dissatisfaction was not exhausted; it spread. The *Educational Times* ticked off local papers for encouraging such action by reporting every development. Boys in Hartlepool were the next to make their complaints heard. At Newcastle's Sandyford Road Council School the total abolition of homework was called for; at Middlesbrough, where demands for the abolition of both canes and homework were chalked neatly onto the pavement, the meetings were dispersed by the police. At Stoke-on-Trent there was talk of military intervention. Convinced that maturity and adulthood were theirs for the taking, schoolboys from Hull burst into a local hotel and helped themselves to cigars, whisky and stout. Some wags marvelled jokingly over the Home Secretary's absence from the scene of all this excitement. But according to the *The Times*'s Court Circular, Churchill had left the country on 6 September 'for the Continent'.

Burton-on-Trent was the next school to rebel, followed by Portsmouth. Adolescent unrest was racing through the country. Six county council schools in the London districts of Shoreditch and Islington sent a hundred boys into the streets, drumming up local support by chanting 'Fall in and follow me'. At the Latchmere school in Battersea the arrival of the most muscular policemen on the force sent the children rushing for the safety of the school playground. Eventually a group possessing even more authority than the powerful arm of the law appeared to resolve the unrest: mothers arrived at the school gates. Clutching them by the ear, they dragged their reluctant children home. Further humiliation awaited many who returned to school on 15 September, carrying notes assuring the staff that suitable punishments had already been delivered. The strikes came to an end without any negotiation. Trade Union recruiting officers noted that senior schools might make a good enrolling ground.

There was a feeling that September of a youthful boldness, a feeling which stretched beyond the school walls. On 6 September Thomas W. Burgess, aged 37, covered in lard and stark naked except for a pair of thick motorist's goggles and a black rubber bathing cap, stepped into the sea at Folkestone to make his sixteenth attempt to reach France by swimming across the Channel. Despite numerous attempts over the last 36 years, no one had succeeded in this since Matthew Webb reached Calais in August 1875. Webb was not on the beach to wave Burgess into the water; he had been killed in 1883 trying to swim the Niagara Falls in Canada.

Averaging a mile and three-quarters an hour and accompanied by a boat whose crew fed him a grape from time to time and eleven drops of Champagne every thirty minutes, Burgess followed the irregular course dictated by the tide, a route he described as 'a figure of a badly written capital M with a loop on first down stroke'. After 37 miles and with only two and a half left to swim he sensed himself entering foreign waters, and was promptly stung badly by a cluster of poisonous pink French jellyfish. To show he was in no way offended, he asked the boat crew to start singing 'La Marseillaise', and to their accompaniment he landed on the beautiful deserted beach at Le Chatelet near Sangatte.

On the day of the swim the temperature recorder at South Kensington registered 92 °F, and people found themselves crossing over to the shady side of the street. There was still a severe water shortage in pockets of the country, wool workers in Bradford Mills being laid off because there was no water for the night-time cleaning of the wool.

The debonair pilot Gustav Hamel, 'gold haired intrepid Swede', darling of the Corrupt Coterie and so handsome that

Diana Manners still shuddered with desire at the very thought of him, had been given the job of carrying the first-ever aerial post. On 9 September he arrived at the small bi-plane parked beside a Royal Mail collection point in the middle of the tarmac runway at Hendon, just 30 minutes by car from central London. His destination was the East Lawn at Windsor Castle. Inside the mail box on the tarmac were letters gathered from the aerial mail collection points that had been installed in the leading London stores. Harrods in Knightsbridge, Arding and Hobbs in Clapham, Whiteleys in Westbourne Grove, Gamages in Holborn and Barkers in Kensington had all collected letters from the public to send to Hendon; they included one from the Suffragette headquarters marked for the attention of the Prime Minister, prompting him to keep his promise and 'Remember Votes for women 1912'. As Hamel climbed on board, the gusting wind suddenly dropped, the spectators raised their hats, and the band struck up the National Anthem. When the closing bars sounded, at two minutes to four in the afternoon, Hamel lifted the plane from the ground, the postbag strapped firmly round his waist.

Twelve minutes later the plane was seen hovering over the East Terrace, but the wind suddenly strengthened, and Hamel was forced to bring his plane down in a meadow next to the Mausoleum at Frogmore House where Queen Victoria lay buried, beside a rather surprised cow chewing a few blades of late-summer grass. The dashing airman sauntered through the meadow and arrived unruffled on the East Terrace to present the mailbag to a beaming Lord Mayor of Windsor. The brass band burst into a lively rendition of 'See the Conquering Hero Comes'. Anxious to get back to base, Hamel refused a cup of tea. He returned safely to Hendon, and a telegram of congratulation was sent down from Balmoral. The deputy pilot attempted to repeat the triumph the following day, but the wind was stronger and the plane crashed, crushing the pilot beneath it, lucky to escape with two broken legs. On 13 September the fledgling service was still having trouble keeping to the timetable. Neither weather nor engine could be relied upon, and the pilot took three attempts to land in deep fog at Hendon, having guessed at his whereabouts by the lights of the White City sports stadium below him.

Lady Diana Manners was not at Windsor to see her hero's great achievement. She had returned to London from Yorkshire anxious to begin her own new term, having enrolled in The Slade School of Art, an institution 40 years old that summer. Diana was to take lessons from Ambrose McEvoy, a 'dear myopic man' and alumnus of the art college, a graduate of the same year as Augustus John and his first wife Ida. One-time lover of Augustus's sister Gwen, Ambrose was used to being teased by Augustus for his declared ambition to paint every holder of the Victoria Cross, and every debutante beautiful enough to be commemorated on canvas. In the spring of 1911 he had grown a moustache, which according to Augustus resembled 'an old blacking brush', and with his 'cracked voice, limp body, dancing pumps, monocle and high collar' his appearance was eccentric enough for him to command a special place in Diana's affections. He had a tiny makeshift studio, and was so short-sighted that he had hung a naked light bulb dangerously low and alarmingly near his canvases. His favourite and most beautiful students were invited to visit him: these included Diana, and they 'prattled and laughed' about 'the infinitely inexhaustible subjects of scandal and art and love' as he smoothed an almost finished portrait into his characteristically lovely 'strange etherealness' with the help of a battered toothbrush.

Another Slade teacher, Professor Henry Tonks, inspired terror in some of the students. Diana dreaded his approach down the corridor, for it 'set me trembling as though he were Justice itself.' As she sat in the Life Class in front of dispiriting models (which she described as 'cold and livid and sagging and goose fleshed'), Tonks's corpse-like yet commanding appearance reminded her of a nineteenth-century cardinal. He would stand, apparently baffled, in front of a nervous student's easel, enquiring 'WHAT is it? . . . Is it an insect?', reducing the poor deflated artist to tears.

Henry Tonks had been a Fellow of the Royal College of Surgeons and through his work had become fascinated with drawing the bodies both alive and dead that came his way, and eventually a highly accomplished teacher of figurative portraiture. While he tolerated the petrified Diana, not all Slade students were allowed to flourish in his teaching studio. One look at Augustus John's landlady Mrs Everett, who arrived to enrol carrying a bag that contained a bible, a loaf of bread, a Spanish dagger, a spirit lamp and a saucepan was enough for him to banish her at once to the cellar, where she remained for years, becoming the doyenne of the Slade Skeleton Room. But Tonks was a marvellous teacher and Augustus John, also subjected on occasion to his withering scorn, had been among those to benefit from his tutelage. Indeed, he was such a favoured pupil that Tonks once told him, to his embarrassment, that he would become the greatest draughtsman since Michelangelo.

On the 11th the average temperature suddenly dropped by 20 degrees and *The Times* forecast good news: 'The condition over the kingdom as a whole is no longer of the fine settled type of last week and the prospects of rain before long appear to be more hopeful for all districts.' *The Lady* magazine was already devoting several pages to the new autumn fashions. The hobble skirt seemed to have vanished entirely, and a distinctive fitted and streamlined shape with a slight kick at the hem was making the headlines. Sumptuous furs had arrived on the rails of Peter Robinson's. The break in the weather coincided with the end of the cricket season, and the press offered the English team their best wishes for a safe and successful journey: they were departing imminently for Australia, where they would try to win back the Ashes, after two series in which the Australians had beaten them. There were high hopes this year of the British batsman Jack Hobbs, who was determined to bring back the tiny symbolic sporting trophy for his country.

The flat dry pitches of that summer had made it a vintage year for batsmen. The season had been as enjoyable for Siegfried

Sassoon's village team as for the national players, in large part because of the endless unbroken sunny days, but a disturbing new habit had been observed which *The Times* felt should be addressed. 'The modern practice of the batsman covering the wicket with their legs', the newspaper advised, 'ought to make the authorities re-open the old question of leg before wicket.' Dismissal for LBW had first been introduced in the late eighteenth century, but the labyrinthine debate over the rule had never been concluded. Lately the increased bulk of the leg pads worn by batsmen had made the precise interpretation of when ball made contact with body even more ambivalent, and during the Gentlemen v. Players matches at Lords the unpopular LBW dismissal rate had risen from six in the 1870s to five times as many in the preceding few years. As the English team prepared to travel to the other side of the world, no satisfactory resolution had yet been found to the debate over the LBW rule.

The English sporting calendar moved into its autumnal phase. At Renishaw, the Sitwell family house twenty miles from Doncaster Racecourse, the annual race meeting in the second week of September provided a focal point for a late-summer house party. This was an event Osbert Sitwell's father deplored, finding no amusement at all in racing, but Sir George tolerated the week for the sake of Lady Ida, who loved a flutter as it injected amusement into the monotony of a life of indolence and boredom. A house party was assembled, and The Blue Hungarian Hussars would arrive by train to spend the week in digs at the nearby Sitwell Arms. Each morning they walked through the village and up the drive towards the big house, carrying suitcases containing their 'frogged sling-jackets and cherry-coloured britches.' Locals took the sallow-skinned, dark-haired musicians for Armenian carpet-pedlars. They played for the entertainment of the guests at every meal except breakfast, and Sir George was very pleased with the temporary addition to the staff. 'The music makes things go,' he beamed, 'and prevents people from feeling they *have* to make conversation.' In the late afternoon, as the race-goers returned from the track for a sustaining tea before going upstairs to change for dinner, the summer seemed to Osbert 'to return in epitome so that it was impossible to believe we stood on the very brink of Autumn in this high country.' Outside in the garden, where the rose bushes were still 'swooning under a special weight of flowers', elderly guests would collapse onto garden benches as the scent of summer flowers still filled the air 'while the fruit ripening on the dark red-brick walls appeared to shine in its own radiance and heat.' Refusing like the season to acknowledge their age, they ascribed their creaking joints to the day's activity. 'Racing makes one very rheumatic,' they would mutter to one another as they sat in the warmth of the setting sun.

Eric Horne, after a lifetime of English summers spent attending to the owners of knees in various stages of decrepitude, was beginning to conclude that he had been a butler for long enough. Not at all anxious to continue his experimental employment as a taxi driver, he had been working for an Indian Prince who was spending seven months in England with his 'suite, aide de camp, secretary, type-writer and two valets.' The Prince 'must have been a big bug in his own country'; he was well-connected, a personal friend of George V, and Eric had enjoyed himself in this job though it was only temporary. A man 'of a splendid disposition, sharp as a needle', the Prince was possessed of an intelligence that 'far surpassed [that of] any Englishman' Eric had ever met. He was decent to his temporary butler, showing him the respect Eric knew he deserved.

A full complement of staff was employed in the Prince's large rented West End house, and Eric had been made responsible for the hiring and firing of all the servants, a state of affairs that suited his belief in himself as a good judge of character. There was a pleasing bustle about the establishment, a sense of importance as visitors came and went throughout the day. It satisfied Eric to note in his diary that 'a dozen Indian officers would call at one time

from Hampton Court', in addition to 'well connected old generals who the Prince had known in India.' The British military top
brass certainly had a thirst, and the generals' chauffeurs lacked the
manners that Eric expected of servants, being typical, however,
of the boorish type their profession attracted, throwing 'ends of
cigarettes and burnt matches all over the place.' The occupation
of some of the Prince's evening visitors was less immediately
identifiable, though Eric allowed himself make a guess. 'I am not
sure that some of the ladies who came to supper after the theatre',
he surmised a little coyly, 'were not pretty actresses.'

For the shooting month of August the Prince had rented a substantial castle in Scotland and had asked Eric to accompany him.
There had been a tricky patch when the whisky supply ran very
low during the railway strike, but Eric had made good friends
with a local merchant in the nearest town and they had just about
scraped through. No lady guests had been invited for the shooting, and this Eric counted a blessing, as it meant there were no
demanding lady's maids to deal with.

The Prince had been very particular that the castle should be
run strictly according to Scottish custom, and Eric's violin
accompaniment during the nightly exclusively male reeling
parties proved very popular. Haggis had been served almost
every night, and there had been a plentiful supply of early local
oysters. One night the Prince held a competition to find who
could eat the most oysters. Washing the slippery molluscs down
with plenty of Champagne, 'the old generals kept steadily on'
until a veteran Paymaster, a captain from the Indian Army,
became horribly ill. In the absence of female staff, Eric volunteered to be nursemaid. He persuaded the distinguished but
retching old gent to drink a thick brownish cocktail of mustard
and hot water and made sure he was properly sick, before
tucking the now relieved old gentleman into bed. Oysters were
off the menu for everyone else that night. No one could face the
thought of them.

★

Towards the end of the month a surprise telephone call to the Prince from the very grandest Scottish residence of them all informed the staff that the King and Queen would be motoring over from Balmoral the day before the Prince was due to return south. The Royals had heard of the beauty of the grounds and wished to come to enjoy the gardens. All preparations were made for a sumptuous luncheon, but by 5 p.m. on the appointed day there had been no sign of the Royal party. No word came from Balmoral and the Prince, mystified but too polite to make any sort of complaint, returned as planned to London. Eric stayed behind for one more day to do the final packing-up before taking the train south himself. To his horror, at precisely lunch-time the following day he looked out of the window to see the royal car approaching up the drive. There had been a mistake about the dates: the King and Queen were coming to lunch, and there was nothing to eat.

Quickly Eric banked up the fires and made the place as welcoming as possible before the door of the royal car opened and its unexpected passengers emerged. By great good fortune the boot of the royal car contained an emergency picnic, and this was eaten on the remarkably accommodating Royal knees in front of the welcoming fire, accompanied by some grapes that the gardener had rushed over from the hothouse. Eric's skills as a host, learned from years of observation, proved exemplary, as he conducted the Royal couple around the principal rooms of the castle and discussed the season's grouse coverts. As they left, the King gave Eric his photograph as a memento, and the Queen shook his hand.

The Prince's summer was ending, and with it his stay in England. He was returning to India to help with the preparations for the Delhi Durbar to be held in November, when millions of George V's subjects on the sub-continent would celebrate the Coronation. The Prince tried to persuade Eric to go with him to the new capital, and take up full-time employment there. The proposition was tempting: professional respect and financial security, not to mention heat, and transport by elephant, all added up to an enticing offer. Above all else, the Prince treated him 'like a human being'. Eric knew it would be difficult to find an employer who outclassed the Prince, or was such a pleasure to serve. 'He could teach English gentry a wrinkle or two as to the way servants should be treated.' But Eric was tired. He had been in service for several decades. He would have had to abandon his wife and child. And after playing solo host to the King and Queen of England he felt a special connection and duty to his country, and a reluctance to leave it so long as it needed him.

In the middle of September, the last weekend she could persuade herself to justify calling summer, Virginia Stephen took the opportunity presented by the fine weather to invite a guest to stay at her small rented red-brick house in the village street of Firle in Sussex. A few days earlier she had been camping with Rupert Brooke on the river Teign in Dartmoor, and it had not been a success. All the 'sleeping on the ground, waking at dawn and swimming in a river' held no appeal for Virginia. During her stay the preceding month in Grantchester she had found Rupert 'all that could be kind and interesting and substantial and good hearted', and had enjoyed the atmosphere of innocent sexy exhibitionism she had found there. It was a refreshing contrast to the intellectual scepticism of many of her other friends. But she was revising her opinion of Rupert. During the rail strike he had failed to convince her that he felt any 'socialist enthusiasm', and she was looking forward to the contrast of a few days spent in the company of Leonard Woolf, her brother Toby's Cambridge friend. She had been feeling anxious and her writing was not going well. She confided to her elder sister Vanessa that in those moods 'all the devils came out – hairy black ones.' She was also worried that there would be war with Germany, although she could not find many people to take this worry seriously. The weekend with Leonard was a success. He calmed her, and the early autumn countryside was beautiful. The corn sheaves had already been cleared from the stubble, and the hazy sun had lost the power to burn off the dew, so that even by noon it was still lying on the grass as they walked across the Downs and back along the banks of the river Ouse. On the way they passed a remote, elegant Regency house called Asheham, surprisingly empty, tucked into a fold of the Downs, with a wonderful view over the Sussex countryside, and near a place where mushrooms were growing in profusion. Leonard thought it 'an extraordinarily romantic looking house', and with his encouragement Virginia determined to rent it. At the end of the weekend they promised each other that they would get tickets for the new season of Russian ballet due to begin the following month, and Leonard realised that he was falling in love with Virginia.

Mary Macarthur, joint Secretary of the Women's Trade Union League, was not impervious to the late summer mood. Her friends had noticed how this determined and driven young woman had softened over the course of the summer. Despite the demands of the August strike, when she had often worked up to twenty hours a day, the presence of Will Anderson had given her the glow of a woman in love. In early September she was mourning the death of the much loved joint secretary of the league, Margaret Macdonald. A great friend of both Mary and Will, and the wife of the leader of the Independent Labour Party, Ramsay Macdonald, Margaret had died after a short illness on 6 September. The fragility of life suddenly confronting her, Mary Macarthur determined at last to seize the moment and live a little for her own happiness. She agreed to marry Will, and a date was set at the City Temple for the third week of September. Mary planned to buy a new coat and hat in pale brown for the occasion.

George V had gone straight to Balmoral from Yorkshire, having managed to avoid spending any time in London during the difficult weeks of the strike. He had been shooting almost continuously since the end of the Coronation tour but was happiest when indulging in his favourite hobby in the Highlands, where he liked to affect a Scottish accent. The telegraph, the advent of the telephone and the prospect of an aerial post (even if it was sometimes unreliable) kept him in communication with London while leaving him free to spend his days on the moors eliminating wildlife. Public Life, he realised with some relief, could function without his presence in the capital. His wife and children joined him at Balmoral on 2 September, and the next day a telegram arrived with the news that the liberal-minded Russian Prime Minister Peter Stolypin had been gunned down in the presence of his cousin the Tsar at a festival in Kiev. This eruption of unwelcome events into his untroubled holiday alarmed George, reminding him how grateful he was that he lived in a country essentially at peace with itself and with the outside world. Stolypin remained in a critical state, and George was kept informed of his condition. But enamel fragments from the badge of the Order of St Vladimir pinned to Stolypin's chest had splintered into his chest cavity on the bullet's impact, and they entered and poisoned his blood stream; he died on 4 September.

Press photographs of the King's new car were a happier reminder of life outside Balmoral. A six-cylinder landaulette of twenty horse-power, its interior finished in mole-coloured Bedford cord with ivory and silver fittings, its exterior in the Coronation colours of dark blue with a crimson line, had gone on display in the front hall at Harrods. It would shortly be shipped to Delhi to await his arrival in November.

According to end-of-summer custom, leading Cabinet ministers arrived to spend a day or two with the King at Balmoral. The Chancellor Lloyd George, the War Minister Lord Haldane and of course the Home Secretary Winston Churchill and the Foreign Secretary Sir Edward Grey were all among the Royal Family's guests. The state of affairs in Morocco continued to preoccupy the Government, and the King was aware that disagreements over policy between his Army and Navy chiefs and the War Office would soon have to be resolved. The Prime Minister was already in Scotland, staying at Archerfield in East Lothian, his brother-in-law's house, which boasted its own nine-hole golf course and was popular with guests. Asquith was planning to discuss a Cabinet re-shuffle there with his key ministers. Churchill had his eye on the post of First Lord of the Admiralty, currently held by Reginald McKenna, because (as Grey noticed yet again) 'his high-mettled spirit was exhilarated by the air of crisis and high events.' Haldane had no confidence in McKenna or his management of the naval chiefs – 'Admirals live in a world of their own', he wrote to Asquith in September – and wanted him urgently replaced. Churchill seemed a strong candidate, but Haldane did not get on well with him and suspected that a working relationship would be difficult to achieve.

Haldane, who at 55 was 18 years older than Churchill, was, like his younger Cabinet colleague, physically a gift to the caricaturists. Osbert Sitwell said he 'entered the room with the air of a whole procession', Violet Asquith was reminded by his 'pneumatic bulk' of a character from Edward Lear's book of nonsense, and the young diarist newly arrived at the Foreign Office, Harold Nicolson, compared his walk to 'the epicene waddle of a Balinese dancer'. Haldane had little in common with Churchill except a love of food, hard work and cigars. A lawyer, mathematician and scientist, he considered the Home Secretary uneducated. Haldane spoke German fluently (Churchill thought the language 'beastly') and was on very friendly terms with the Kaiser, for whom he had given a dinner party during the Coronation at his lovely house in Queen Anne's Gate. Haldane was sceptical about Churchill's suitability, thinking he lacked the experience and knowledge to take over the Admiralty job, but deferred to Asquith's decision. The two men met at Archerfield, and Haldane was pleased to note that they parted 'in a very friendly spirit.'

Queen Mary found that the extended summer days at Balmoral hung a little heavy after her arrival on 2 September. She was not happy to be 'sitting on a mountain' in a very cold house, surrounded by décor that had been designed to suit the taste of two earlier queens. She was longing to redecorate the rooms but did not dare upset her husband's currently benign frame of mind. In the 'tartan drenched' décor, she braced herself for the stream of guests, and worried about her wardrobe for the Indian visit two months hence. The Durbar required a display of all the glamour and glitter the Emperor and Empress of India could muster, and May discovered to her horror that a seventeenth-century law prohibited the Crown Jewels leaving the country. As an alternative, Garrards, the Royal jewellers, were to make her a complete parure that included necklaces, a choker, a stomacher, earrings, bracelets, and a magnificent tiara, using the thousands of diamonds given her in South Africa on a world tour in 1901. The diamonds were to be set to May's own design of forget-me-nots and lyres.

Elinor Glyn was disturbed by Curzon's increasingly frequent observations that the servants were beginning to gossip about their love affair. As a man in a prominent public position in politics and society, he told her, he could not risk being associated with a scandal; but Elinor suspected that he was trying to end their liaison. Her new book had not achieved what she had intended: it had not made him love and respect her enough to ask her to marry him. In fact, her plan had completely backfired. To add to these worries, she realised that her sister Lucy was becoming increasingly interested in the possibilities of a life in America. She was thinking of opening a branch of Madame Lucille in New York, and had planned a trip for the following spring. Cunard had just announced the sailing dates for the maiden voyage of their new super-liner, and Lucy thought she would book tickets for herself and her husband, Sir Cosmo Duff Gordon. The ship had been given a suitably impressive name: *Titanic*. Lucy hoped the next few years would open up the world for herself and her unhappy sister. Elinor was not the only one for whom the perfect summer of 1911 had fallen far short of perfection.

Epilogue

I have been born at the end of the age of peace and can't
expect to feel anything but despair.

E. M. Forster

THE SUMMER WEATHER of 1911 had not lived up to the benign
early promise of the unruffled balmy weeks of May, although
they had been some of the warmest on record. The high temperatures had sent some people insane with discomfort, and the disastrous effect of the heat on the countryside had financially ruined
others. The country had been brought to a standstill during the
summer strikes, and the increasingly real threat of German aggression had rocked the nation's sense of tranquillity and security.

Despite this, much of the country was facing the autumn with
relief and optimism. A transition of monarchs had been smoothly
achieved when George V assumed the crown of the most powerful country in the world, and the Parliament Bill had passed into
law without requiring his extraordinary intervention. The debate
over Home Rule in Ireland looked set to continue rumbling, but
the antagonistic weight of the Conservative peers had been
diffused by the new Act. The National Insurance Bill would
become law by the end of the year despite protests from the
National Association of Domestic Servants, who wrote again to
Lloyd George saying it would do them 'serious injury.'

Though the dockers' anger and distress had been temporarily
appeased by the end of 1911, unresolved financial grievances

erupted again the following year and Ben Tillett, exasperated by his dealings with the Chairman of the London Port Authority, prayed 'Oh God, strike Lord Devonport dead!' An unsuccessful national miners' strike in the spring of 1912 contributed to the dockers', miners' and railwaymen's joint decision to form 'a triple alliance' that brought trade union membership to a powerful four million.

Mary Macarthur continued to fight passionately for women's rights as women workers continued to strike. During the next two years she raised money and support for, among others, the Somersetshire collar makers, the Bridport net curtain workers, the Kidderminster carpet girls, and the Kilbirnie thread workers. The suffragette movement, voluntarily dormant during the summer of 1911 out of respect for the Coronation ceremonies, renewed its activities at the end of the year with a terrible intensity when Asquith failed to keep his side of the bargain and address their demands. On 4 June 1913 Emily Davison, a militant suffragette, died for her cause after throwing herself beneath the hooves of the King's horse during the Derby.

F. E. Smith, one of the most outspoken Members of Parliament against Irish Nationalism during the Home Rule Crisis of 1912–14, was then appointed to the Government's Press Bureau and, paradoxically for a man so outspoken, was placed in charge of newspaper censorship during the First World War. He and Winston remained lifelong friends.

Eric Horne was horrified by the advent of the war, and by the capitalist *nouveaux riches* who 'filled their pockets while Tommy was fighting.' He did, however, publish two volumes of memoirs, calling the first *What the Butler Winked At*; the book went into four printings in the first month, so anxious were the 'Gentry' to discover what their servants really thought of them.

Diana Manners discovered Venice and loved Raymond Asquith 'hopelessly'. But Duff Cooper, a university acquaintance of her cousin (named, like her brother, John Manners) 'grew into my life as I grew into his', and wrote her love letters, 'sometimes three a day, in the lightest vein and gaiety.' It was not until after the war that Diana succumbed to Duff's wish to marry her; by then Raymond was dead, killed in the fighting.

In 1915 Rupert Brooke was in the Aegean on his way to Gallipoli when he died suddenly of blood poisoning at the age of 27, on Shakespeare's birthday, 23 April. In his obituary Winston Churchill declared that Rupert's 'War Sonnets' (published early in 1915) would be 'shared by many thousands of young men, moving resolutely, blithely forward in this the hardest, the cruellest and the least rewarded of all the wars that men have fought'.

No one who lived through that hot busy summer of 1911 – not Asquith, not Edward Grey, not even Winston Churchill, especially not George V – was fully aware of the dangerous shadow slowly approaching England from across the water. The crisis in Agadir had been settled to the Kaiser's apparent satisfaction when Germany was given land in the Congo in return for recognising Morocco as a French protectorate. The Kaiser was ignorant, however, of secret talks between England and France ending in an agreement that the British would safeguard the Channel and North Sea, ensuring French naval security in the Mediterranean. But the very real prospect of war had alarmed Sir Edward Grey, and over the next couple of years he was as conciliatory as possible towards Germany.

By August 1914 a dark cloud directly overhead had replaced the looming shadow. England concentrated no longer on what was happening at home, but fought on the Continent for its survival.

In 1914 Brian Calkin, former chorister and soloist with St Paul's Cathedral Choir, 'overstated' his age (he was 16) and joined the Queen's Royal West Surrey Regiment. On 6 June 1917, sixteen days short of the sixth anniversary of the Coronation at which he had sung for the King of England and the German Kaiser in Westminster Abbey, Brian was in France with his regiment. He wrote his family a letter and, on the front of the envelope, 'To be opened only in the event of my being killed in action'. Brian survived the next attack though he was severely

gassed, earning himself a precious few weeks at home to conva-
lesce before returning once again to the front line. While he was
in England, unknown to his family he gave the sealed envelope to
his father's office manager at Lloyd's Insurance brokers for safekeeping.

My dear Family,
I have just time to write you a short note, before going up to the
line to 'push', just to bid you all a fond farewell should it please
the Almighty to take me, in which case, only, will you receive this.

Our Brigade is to be in Reserve, not actually in the front line
to start with, but we are likely to be pushed up anywhere to
support the attacking parties.

We shall be in the thickest part of the Push, of which you will
doubtless have read ere, if ever, you read this.

Of course I have known of this for some weeks but for obvious
reasons have been unable and unwilling to mention it.

I am going up with HQ as assistant adjutant, though I should
as soon be with my platoon in the line. However I shall have
plenty to do.

It will comfort you to know that I am not in the least worried
or concerned about what may happen to me, but am perfectly
happy to leave the issue in the hands of God. My one concern is
for you all, should I be taken. Do not, I beg of you, be unhappy,
for I am, and you are, convinced that I shall be happier with Him.

Now I will refrain from soft talk etc: because it is not in my line,
but cheer up and keep smiling.

Good-bye all you dear ones. I could not have been blest with a
better family. May God bless and keep you all – and bring you all
in his good time to your loving

Brian

On 10 July 1918, only four months and a day before those catas-
trophic four years came to an end, and with Germany very close
to defeat, Mrs Calkin was given her son's letter to open. Brian was
twenty years old.

Dramatis Personae

Dowager Countess of Airlie (Mabell; 1866–1956): Confidante and Lady-in-Waiting to HM Queen Mary.

Herbert (Henry) Asquith (1852–1928): Liberal Prime Minister 1908–1916.

Margot Asquith (1864–1945): Wife of the Prime Minister and stepmother to Violet and Raymond Asquith.

Raymond Asquith (1878–1916): Scholar, son of the Prime Minister and leading light of a group of friends called The Corrupt Coterie. Killed in the First World War.

Violet Asquith (1887–1969): Only daughter of the Prime Minister, H.H. Asquith, and great friend of Winston Churchill.

Thomas Beecham (1879–1961): Distinguished English conductor, lover of Lady Cunard and grandson of cure-all pill inventor.

Max Beerbohm (1872–1956): Critic, essayist and caricaturist. Author of the novel *Zuleika Dobson*, published in 1911.

E. F. Benson (1867–1940): Novelist and famous creator of the characters Mapp and Lucia.

Annie Besant (1847–1933): Theosophist and feminist campaigner.

Rupert Brooke (1887–1915): Heart-throb poet and tenant of the Old Vicarage at Grantchester. He was writing his first volume of poems during 1911 and subsequently died of blood poisoning during the First World War.

T. W. Burgess: Cross-channel swimmer, successful on his sixteenth attempt.

Brian Calkin (1897–1918): Choirboy with St Paul's Cathedral Choir School.

Clemmie Churchill (1885–1977): Wife of Winston and mother of Diana and the newborn Randolph.

Winston Churchill (1874–1965): Liberal Party Home Secretary and future Prime Minister.

Albert, Duke of Clarence (1864–92): Brother of George V and first fiancé of HM Queen Mary. Prince Eddy, as he was known, died of influenza before their marriage.

Jennie Cornwallis-West (1854–1921): Winston Churchill's thrice-married American mother.

Lady Cunard (Emerald; 1872–1948): Famous hostess, wife of a ship-owner and the lover of conductor Thomas Beecham.

Lord Curzon (1859–1925): Ex-Viceroy of India, campaigner against the Parliament Bill and ambivalent lover of Elinor Glyn.

Sergei Diaghilev (1872–1929): Founder, producer and artistic director of the Ballets Russes, and lover of Nijinsky.

Roger Fry (1866–1934): Artist, critic and organiser of the Post-Impressionist exhibition in London in 1910.

HM King George V (1865–1936): Crowned King on 22 June 1911. Son of Edward VII, husband of Queen Mary, father of Edward VIII and George VI, first cousin of Kaiser Wilhelm of Germany, and grandson of Queen Victoria.

David Lloyd George (1863–1945): Liberal Party Chancellor of the Exchequer and future Prime Minister.

Elinor Glyn (1864–1943): Best-selling novelist and lovelorn romantic. Sister of Lucy Duff Gordon.

Lady (Lucy) Duff Gordon (1863–1935): Celebrated dress designer, owner of 'Madame Lucille's' salon and inventor of the catwalk model. Survivor of the *Titanic*. Elder sister of Elinor Glyn.

Duncan Grant (1885–1978): Artist, founder of the Camden Town Group, and part of the emerging Bloomsbury Group.

Sir Edward Grey (1862–1933): Foreign Secretary and widowed lodger at Winston and Clemmie Churchill's house in Eccleston Square.

Viscount Haldane (1856–1928): Liberal Party War Minister.

Eric Horne: Butler to the nobility and secret chronicler of activities both upstairs and downstairs. Eventual best-selling author.

Augustus John (1878–1961): Most famous English painter of his time, husband of Ida. By 1911 he was the father of seven children.

Tamara Karsavina (1885–1978): Fêted dancing partner of Nijinsky in the Ballets Russes.

Rudyard Kipling (1865–1936): Most famous and most wealthy writer in the world in 1911, and also an amateur farmer.

Philip de László (1869–1937): Leading society portrait painter.

Rosa Lewis (1867–1952): The 'Duchess of Duke Street'. Hotelier, the finest cook in London, caterer and party planner.

Mary Macarthur (1880–1921): Charismatic trade unionist and founder of the Women's Trade Union League.

Lady Diana Manners (1892–1986): The most beautiful young woman in England in 1911. An 18-year-old debutante and society celebrity, never out of the papers. The youngest daughter of the Duke and Duchess of Rutland. She married Duff Cooper in 1919.

HM Queen Mary (1867–1953): Wife of HM King George V and mother of six children (including the future Edward VIII and George VI).

Grand Duchess Augusta of Mecklenburg-Strelitz (1822–1916): Formidable great-aunt and confidante of HM Queen Mary.

Nellie Melba (1861–1931): Australian superstar soprano.

G. E. Moore (1873–1958): Philosopher and author of *Principia Ethica*.

Lady Ottoline Morrell (1873–1938): Wife of Philip Morrell MP, and Bloomsbury hostess.

Harold Nicolson (1882–1966): Diarist, diplomat and future husband of Vita Sackville-West.

Vaslav Nijinsky (1890–1950): Most brilliantly electrifying ballet dancer of all time.

Emmeline Pankhurst (1858–1928): Founding figurehead of the suffragette movement. The mother of suffragettes Christabel and Sylvia.

Alexander Paterson (1884–1947): Author of *Across the Bridges*, a study of the poverty-stricken area of south London where he lived.

Paul Poiret (1879–1944): French clothing designer who claimed to have invented the brassière. His more swiftly removable clothes were said to make seduction easier.

Marchioness of Ripon (Gladys; 1859–1917): Dazzling patroness of the ballet and the opera.

A. L. Rowse (1903–97): Cornish schoolboy who grew up to be a historian, a Shakespeare scholar and a biographer.

Vita Sackville-West (1892–1962): Poet, gardener, novelist and eventual wife of Harold Nicolson – as well as lover of Virginia Stephen (Woolf).

Siegfied Sassoon (1886–1967): Poet, fox-hunting man, cricket enthusiast.

Edith Sitwell (1887–1964): Sister of Osbert, and a distinguished poet.

Lady Ida Sitwell (1868–1937): Mother of Osbert, Edith (and Sacheverell).

Sir George Sitwell (1860–1943): Husband of Lady Ida, father of the above, and keen traveller and race-goer.

Osbert Sitwell (1892–1969): Writer and friend of everyone worth knowing in society.

F. E. Smith (1872–1930): Lawyer and Conservative MP. Winston Churchill's greatest friend.

Virginia Stephen (1882–1941): Novelist, Bloomsbury-ite and future wife of Leonard Woolf.

Lytton Strachey (1880–1932): Author, critic, aesthete and Bloomsbury-ite.

George Sturt (1863–1927): Wheelwright and recorder of the traditional ways of the countryside.

Duchess of Teck (1933–1897): Known as 'Fat Mary'. The mother of HM Queen Mary and a devotee of Rich Cream biscuits.

Ben Tillett (1860–1943): Founder and Secretary of the National Transport Workers' Federation, and champion of the dockworkers.

Leonard Woolf (1880–1969): Alumnus of The Apostles at Cambridge, political theorist, Civil Servant and future husband of Virginia Stephen.

Mrs Hwfa (pronounced Hoofa) Williams: Enthusiastic guest at all the best parties and married to the owner of the Sandown racecourse.

Bibliography

Newspapers and magazines

Daily Mail
Daily Telegraph
Daily Sketch
The Times
Country Life
Illustrated London News
The Lady
Punch
The Spectator
Tatler

Books

Airlie, Mabell, Countess of, *Thatched With Gold*, Hutchinson, 1962
Allison, Ronald, and Riddell, Sarah (eds), *The Royal Encyclopaedia*, Macmillan, 1991
Askwith, George R. A., *Industrial Problems and Disputes*, Ayer Company, 1920
Asquith, Margot, *An Autobiography: Part 2*, Butterworth, 1922
Baedeker, Karl, *Great Britain Handbook for Travellers*, T. Fisher Unwin, 1910
Baily, Leslie, *Scrapbook*, Frederick Muller, 1957
Baring, Maurice, *The Puppet Show of Memory*, Heinemann, 1932
Battiscombe, Georgina, *Queen Alexandra*, Constable, 1969
Bedells, Phyllis, *My Dancing Days*, Phoenix House, 1954
Bedford, John, Duke of, *A Silver-Plated Spoon*, Cassell, 1959

Beerbohm, Max, *Zuleika Dobson*, William Heinemann, 1911

Benson, E. F., *As We Were*, Longman, 1930

The Bioscope Annual and Trades Directory for 1912, Ganes Ltd

Birkenhead, Lord, *Lady Eleanor Smith*, Hutchinson, 1953

Birkenhead, Frederick, Second Earl of, *F.E. Smith: First Earl of Birkenhead*, Eyre & Spottiswoode, 1965

Birkin, Andrew, *J.M. Barrie and the Lost Boys*, Constable, 1979

Bone, James and Muirhead, *London Echoing*, Jonathan Cape, 1948

Bonham Carter, Violet, *Lantern Slides: The Diaries and Letters of Violet Bonham Carter 1904–1914*, Weidenfeld & Nicolson, 1996

—— *Winston Churchill As I Knew Him*, William Collins, 1965

Brendon, Vyvyen, *The Edwardian Age*, Hodder & Stoughton, 1996

de Broke, Willoughby, *The Passing Years*, Constable, 1924

Brooke, Rupert, *Poems*, Sidgwick & Jackson, 1911

Brown, Jane, *Lutyens and The Edwardians*, Viking, 1996

Buckle, Richard, *Nijinsky*, Weidenfeld & Nicolson, 1971

Campbell, John, *F.E. Smith: First Earl of Birkenhead*, Jonathan Cape, 1983

Chaney, Lisa, *A Life of J.M. Barrie*, Hutchinson, 2005

Churchill, Randolph S., *Winston Churchill*, Heinemann, 1967

Churchill, Winston, *Thoughts and Adventures*, Oldham, 1932

—— *My Early Life*, Collins, 1930

Clifford, Colin, *The Asquiths*, John Murray, 2002

Clunn, Harold, *Famous South Coast Pleasure Resorts Past and Present*, T. Whittingham, 1929

Collins, Michael, *The Likes of Us*, Granta, 2004

Cooper, Diana, *The Rainbow Comes and Goes*, Rupert Hart Davis, 1958

Coote, Colin R., *The Other Club*, Sidgwick & Jackson, 1971

de Courcy, Anne, *The Viceroy's Daughters*, Weidenfeld & Nicolson, 2000

—— *Circe*, Sinclair Stevenson, 1992

Dangerfield, George, Smith, Harrison, and Haas, Robert, *The Strange Death of Liberal England*, Smith & Haas, 1935

Edwards, Anne, *Matriarch: Queen Mary and The House of Windsor*, Hodder, 1984

Egremont, Max, *Siegfried Sassoon*, Picador, 2005

—— *Balfour*, Collins, 1980

Etherington-Smith, Meredith and Pilcher, Jeremy, *The It Girls*, Hamish Hamilton, 1986

Ewing, Elizabeth, *History of Twentieth-Century Fashion*, Batsford, 1974

Farmer, Alan, *Hampstead Heath*, Historical Publications, 1984

Fingall, Elizabeth, Countess of, *Seventy Years Young*, Collins, 1937

Forster, E. M., *Howards End*, Edward Arnold, 1910

Furbank, P. N., *E. M. Forster*, Secker & Warburg, 1977

Gardiner, Juliet, *The Edwardian Country House*, Channel 4 Books, 2002

Garnett, David, *The Golden Echo*, Chatto & Windus, 1953

Gilbert, Sir Martin, *Winston Churchill: A Life*, Heinemann, 1991

Gilbert, Sir Martin (ed.), *Churchill: Great Lives Observed*, Prentice Hall, 1968

Gilmour, David, *Curzon*, John Murray, 1994

Glendinning, Victoria, *Vita*, Weidenfeld & Nicolson, 1983

—— *Edith Sitwell: A Unicorn Amongst Lions*, Weidenfeld & Nicolson, 1981

Glyn, Anthony, *Elinor Glyn*, Hutchinson, 1955

Glyn, Elinor, *Romantic Adventure*, Dutton, 1937

—— *Three Weeks*, Duckworth, 1907

Grey, Sir Edward, *Twenty-Five Years: 1892–1916*, Hodder & Stoughton, 1925

Grigg, John, *Lloyd George: The People's Champion*, Eyre Methuen, 1978

Grigoriev, S. L., *The Diaghilev Ballet 1909–1929*, Constable, 1953

Hamilton, Mary Agnes, *Mary Macarthur*, Leonard Parsons, 1925

Harrison, Michael, *Rosa*, Peter Davies, 1962

Hassall, Christopher, *Rupert Brooke*, Longman, 1964

—— *Edward Marsh*, Longman, 1959

Hattersley, Roy, *The Edwardians*, Little, Brown, 2004

Hetherington, John, *Melba: A Biography*, Faber & Faber, 1967

Holroyd, Michael, *Augustus John*, William Heinemann, 1974

—— *Lytton Strachey*, Heinemann, 1968

Horn, Pamela, *Life Below Stairs in the 20th Century*, Sutton Publishing, 2001

—— *High Society 1880–1914*, Alan Sutton, 1992

Horne, Eric, *More Winks*, T. Werner Laurie, 1932

—— *What The Butler Winked At*, T. Werner Laurie, 1923

Hunt, Roger, *Rural Britain Then and Now*, Cassell, 2004

Jackson, Stanley, *The Savoy*, Frederick Muller, 1964

Jenkins, Roy, *Churchill*, Macmillan, 2001

—— *Asquith*, Collins, 1964

Jolliffe, John, *Raymond Asquith: Life and Letters*, Collins, 1980

Kemp, Sandra, Mitchell, Charlotte, and Trotter, David, *The Oxford Companion to Edwardian Fiction*, Oxford University Press, 2002

Keppel, Sonia, *Edwardian Daughter*, Hamish Hamilton, 1958

Keynes, Geoffrey (ed.), *The Letters of Rupert Brooke*, Faber & Faber, 1968

Kipling, Rudyard, *Something Of Myself*, Macmillan, 1937

Lambert, Angela, *Unquiet Souls*, Macmillan, 1984

Laver, James, *Taste and Fashion*, Harrap, 1937

Lee, Christopher, *This Sceptred Isle*, BBC Worldwide, 1999

Lee, Hermione, *Virginia Woolf*, Chatto & Windus, 1996

Lehman, John, *Rupert Brooke*, Weidenfeld & Nicolson, 1980

Leslie, Anita, *Edwardians in Love*, Hutchinson, 1972

—— *Jennie Churchill*, Hutchinson, 1959

Londonderry, Edith, *Retrospect*, Frederick Muller, 1938

Lycett, Andrew, *Rudyard Kipling*, Weidenfeld & Nicolson, 1999

Martin, Ralph G., *Lady Randolph Churchill: Volume 2*, Cassell, 1971

Masters, Brian, *Great Hostesses*, Constable, 1982

Melba, Nellie, *Melodies and Memories*, Liberty Weekly Inc., 1925

de Mendelssohn, Peter, *The Age of Churchill*, Thames & Hudson, 1961

Morrell, Lady Ottoline, *A Study in Friendship 1873–1915*, Faber, 1963

Mosley, Nicholas, *Julian Grenfell*, Weidenfeld & Nicolson, 1976

Nash, E.N., and Newth, A.M., *Britain in the Modern World: The Twentieth Century*, Penguin, 1967

Nicholson, Virginia, *Among The Bohemians*, Viking, 2002

Nicolson, Adam, *Bateman's*, The National Trust, 1996

Nicolson, Harold, *King George V*, Constable, 1952

—— *Small Talk*, Constable, 1937

—— *Curzon: The Last Phase*, Constable, 1934

Nijinsky, Vaslav, *The Diary of Vaslav Nijinsky*, Gollancz, 1937

Nowell-Smith, Simon, *Edwardian England*, Oxford University Press, 1964

Official Guide to the London & South Western Railway, Cassell, 1913

Official Guide to the South Eastern & Chatham Railway, Cassell, 1912

Oxford Companion to Edwardian Fiction, The, Oxford University Press, 1997

Paterson, Alexander, *Across the Bridges*, Edward Arnold, 1911

Pearsall, Ronald, *Edwardian Life and Leisure*, David & Charles, 1973

Pearson, John, *Stags And Serpents: A History of the Cavendish Family and the Dukes of Devonshire*, Macmillan, 1983

—— *Façades: Edith, Osbert and Sacheverell Sitwell*, Macmillan, 1978

Pember-Reeves, Maud, *Round About a Pound a Week*, G. Bell & Sons, 1913

A Pictorial and Descriptive Guide to the Isle of Wight, Ward, Lock and Co. Ltd, 1913

A Pictorial and Descriptive Guide to the Thames, Ward, Lock and Co. Ltd, 1909

Pimlott, J.A.R., *The Englishman's Holiday: A Social History*, Faber, 1947

Poiret, Paul, *My First 50 Years*, Gollancz, 1931

Pope-Hennessy, James, *A Lonely Business*, Weidenfeld & Nicolson, 1981

—— *Queen Mary*, Allen & Unwin, 1959

Priestley, J.B., *The Edwardians*, Heinemann, 1970

Read, Donald, *Edwardian England*, Harrap, 1972

Rose, Kenneth, *King George V*, Weidenfeld & Nicolson, 1983

Rowse, A.L., *A Cornish Childhood*, Jonathan Cape, 1942

Sackville-West, Vita, *The Edwardians*, Hogarth Press, 1930

Sambrook, Pamela A., *The Country House Servant*, Sutton Publishing, 1999

Sassoon, Siegfried, *The Weald of Youth*, Faber & Faber, 1942

Schneer, Jonathan, *Ben Tillett*, Croom Helm, 1982

Searle, G.R., *A New England?*, Oxford University Press, 2004

Seeling, Charlotte, *Fashion*, Konemann, 2000

Seymour, Miranda, *Ottoline Morrell*, Hodder & Stoughton, 1992

Shone, Richard, *The Art of Bloomsbury*, Trustees of the Tate Gallery, 1999

Sitwell, Osbert, *Great Morning*, Macmillan and Co., 1948

—— *The Scarlet Tree*, Macmillan, 1946

Smith, Eleanor, *Life's a Circus*, Longman, 1939

Soames, Mary (ed.), *Speaking for Themselves: The Personal Letters of Winston and Clementine Churchill*, Doubleday, 1998

—— *Clementine Churchill*, Cassell, 1979

Souhami, Diana, *Mrs Keppel and Her Daughter*, HarperCollins, 1996

Steele, Valerie, *The Corset: A Cultural History*, Yale University Press, 2001

Streatfeild, Noel (ed.), *The Day Before Yesterday*, Collins, 1956

Sturt, [Bourne – pseudonym] George, *Change in the Village*, Duckworth, 1912

Sykes, Christopher Simon, *The Big House*, HarperCollins, 2004

—— *Country House Camera*, Weidenfeld & Nicolson, 1980

Tillett, Ben, *Memories and Reflections*, John Long, 1931

Trussler, Simon, *British Theatre*, Cambridge University Press, 1994

Tuchman, Barbara, *The Proud Tower*, Hamish Hamilton, 1966

—— *August 1914*, Constable, 1962

Turner, E.S., *What The Butler Saw*, Michael Joseph, 1962

Williams, Mrs Hwfa, *It Was Such Fun*, Hutchinson, 1935

Wilson, Jean Moorcroft, *Siegfried Sassoon 1886–1918*, Duckworth, 1998

Windsor, Duke of, *A King's Story: Memoirs of the Duke of Windsor*, Putnam, 1947

Wollheim, Richard, *Germs*, Waywiser Press, 2004

Wood, Leslie, *The Romance of the Movies*, Heinemann, 1937

Woolf, Leonard, *Beginning Again*, Hogarth Press, 1964

Ziegler, Philip, *Britain Then and Now*, Weidenfeld & Nicolson, 1999

—— *Diana Cooper*, Hamish Hamilton, 1981

Index

Titles of rank are generally those applying at the time, but later titles and name changes are occasionally shown as an aid to identification.